Advance Pre

CW00919020

"The passionate description of bravery,
reader insight into the men who changed the armed services forever. I
found myself wanting to cheer for them, cry with them, and beamed with
pride in all they were able to accomplish."

— Pamela Gentry, Washington Bureau Chief, BET News

"This outstanding book stands as a shining example of what Americans
are capable of accomplishing. This elite outfit of paratroopers fought
both the Communists on the battlefield and racial prejudice and bigotry
from their own government. As a founding member of the Congressional
Black Caucus, I think this book will educate America's children, young
and old, about what others have sacrificed on their behalf."

— Congressman John Conyers, Jr., Michigan

"This book has it all: drama and daring, bravery and bigotry, combat and
courage. These remarkable men made the first airborne assault in Ranger
history on March 23, 1951 and ended their service with an outstanding
combat record that is now, finally, one for the history books."

— Tim and Daphne Reid, Producers, New Millennium Studios

"As a combat veteran of the Korean War, an author, actor, and "Above
the Call: Beyond the Duty" style US citizen of African American
descent, I found Edward Posey's *The US Army's First, Last, and Only
All-Black Rangers* an outstanding contribution to both our nation's
history, and the history of our country during wartime. I heartily
recommend this eye-opening and informative depiction of an incredibly
relevant page in American history."

— James McEachin, Silver Star, Purple Heart veteran, author,
actor, director, and producer

"There is a growing interest in the role of the African American soldier in our history, from the time of the Revolution to Iraq. *The US Army's First, Last, and Only All-Black Rangers* adds a fascinating personal note to this ongoing epic. Posey's story is important because it says so much about our history. It's destined to become an essential part of our understanding of the role black citizens have played in defending and defining our country."

— Charlie Maday, Senior Vice President, Military History Channel

"Formed as part of an army that clung to racial segregation, despite a presidential directive to the contrary, the Buffalo Rangers helped make racial integration a reality. This is their story."

— Bernard C. Nalty, author of *Strength for the Fight: History of Black Americans in the Military*

"Master Sergeant Ed Posey's story is a riveting account of the misuse of brave men, who made up the Army's first, last, and only all-black ranger company in what has come to be known as the Forgotten War, the US Army in Korea 1950-1953. While the local combatant commanders on the ground were clearly willing to use the 2nd Ranger Infantry Company (Airborne) in realistic tactical formations, senior officers at corps and higher were still guided by their own misguided prejudices grounded in WWI and WWII concepts about the black soldiers' inability to be competent leaders or fighting infantrymen—almost three years following President Truman's Executive Order 9981 to ensure equality of treatment and opportunity. Posey's firsthand experience, accompanied by the recollections of his peers, paints a vivid mosaic of life at the most basic level of the airborne grunt. It's a story that made me reflect on my experience as a small unit leader in the early stages of the Korean War."

— Julius W. Becton, Jr., Lieutenant General USA (Ret.), author of *Becton: Autobiography of a Soldier and Public Servant*

The US Army's First, Last, and Only All-Black Rangers

The 2d Ranger Infantry Company (Airborne)
in the Korean War, 1950-1951

Edward L. Posey

(Master Sergeant, Ret.)

SB

Savas Beatie
New York and California

Cataloging-in-Publication Data is available from the Library of Congress.

ISBN 13: 978-1-611210-77-4

05 04 03 02 01   5 4 3 2 1
First paperback edition, first printing

SB

Published by
Savas Beatie LLC
521 Fifth Avenue, Suite 3400
New York, NY 10175
Phone: 610-853-9131

Editorial Offices:

Savas Beatie LLC
P.O. Box 4527
El Dorado Hills, CA 95762
Phone: 916-941-6896
(E-mail) editorial@savasbeatie.com

Savas Beatie titles are available at special discounts for bulk purchases in the United States by corporations, institutions, and other organizations. For more details, please contact Special Sales, P.O. Box 4527, El Dorado Hills, CA 95762, or you may e-mail us at sales@savasbeatie.com, or visit our website at www.savasbeatie.com for additional information.

To all of the Buffalo Rangers
of the 2d Ranger Infantry Company (Airborne)
who served with us in Korea.

This book would not have been possible without the dedicated vision of Major James C. "Big Jim" Queen, Sergeant First Class William Weathersbee, and the collaborative efforts of the surviving members of the 2d Ranger Infantry Company (Airborne). The result of their decades-long journey is this wonderful book—their most important and final mission.

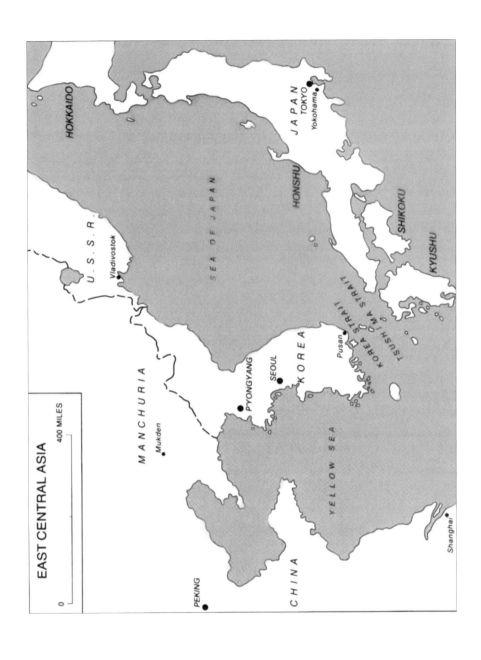

EAST CENTRAL ASIA

0   400 MILES

CHINA

PEKING

MANCHURIA

Mukden

U. S. S. R.

Vladivostok

SEA OF JAPAN

HOKKAIDO

JAPAN

HONSHU

TOKYO

Yokohama

SHIKOKU

KYUSHU

KOREA

PYONGYANG

SEOUL

Pusan

YELLOW SEA

KOREA STRAIT

TSUSHIMA STRAIT

Shanghai

Contents

Contents (continued)

Maps

Hand-drawn maps prepared by Major James Queen
for Munsan-Ni After-Action Report:

Photographs

A special photo gallery follows page 126

Foreword

This book covers the first eight months of the 2d Airborne Ranger Company's experiences during the Korean conflict. It complements the histories of the 3d and 4th Ranger Companies, which were both all-white, by telling the stories of an all-black unit.

There are marked similarities but some race-specific differences between the Ranger Companies, which makes this book significant to the history of African Americans in military service.

The US Army's First, Last, and Only All-Black Rangers: 2d Ranger Infantry Company (Airborne) in Korea 1950–1951 gives a general unit history of the 2d Airborne Ranger Company's combat experiences in Korea. It records an important chapter in the Korean War. It begins with the first year of the war and goes on to describe in great detail the test of American leadership, resources, training incompatibility, and inadequacies of the United States effort in Korea. It also examines the special problems posed to the fighting army during the months of stalemate in the summer of 1951. Like the stories of other Rangers who served in Korea, this book emphasizes the limitations imposed by terrain and weather on the fighting capabilities of the troops. For those in the profession of military history the operations of the 2d Ranger Company are described in careful detail, to provide a vivid description of the application of the principles of war.

This book is going to the printer more than fifty years after the end of the Korean War. It emphasizes the contributions of African Americans who served during the Korean era. It is important to study carefully such a recent and invaluable example of an American all-black Ranger company that performed superbly against many odds. I encourage military and civilian students and veterans alike to take advantage of this insightful journey into the lives of those African Americans who made great sacrifices when America was in need.

William E. Ward, General
Commander, United States Africa Command

Preface

The 2d Ranger Infantry Company (Airborne)—sometimes referred to in this book as 2d Ranger Company or 2d Ranger Infantry Company—has the distinction of being the first, last, and only all-black Ranger unit. First, because Ranger training had never before been offered to black soldiers. Last, because in late 1951, after several months of intense combat, 2d Ranger Company and all other airborne Ranger infantry companies were inactivated. Only, because that was how it happened. One group of elite soldiers trained, fought, and was disbanded—but not before leaving behind a legacy of heroism and honor. Prior to the Korean War it was commonly thought that blacks would not fight if placed in combat situations, and white soldiers would not follow the orders of black officers. Only through the exemplary performance of soldiers such as the Buffaloes of the 92d Infantry Division in Italy in World War II did we begin to dispel these myths.

After Executive Order 9981, which was signed into law on 26 July 1948 by President Harry S. Truman to desegregate the American military, the Army was the last of our services to comply. In 1950, during the 2d Ranger Company's training at Fort Benning and in 1951 while in Korea, the black soldiers of the 2d Ranger Company were very much living two lives: one as highly trained, respected members of the elite Ranger forces, and another as black servicemen subject to the laws of segregation. In combat, all soldiers were colorblind—hospitals and aid stations treated everyone together, and the rules of segregation that dominated civilian situations at home did not exist. Stateside, these were years of uncertainty, racial tension, and a sense of inevitable, lasting changes to come. But unless you were overseas, under fire, and in close combat, the concepts of respect, racial equality, and civil rights often did not apply. Nonetheless, segregation was costly and inefficient for the military, particularly during a time when armed forces manpower was needed. When Rangers from 2d Ranger Company boarded a plane for their historic combat jump at Munsan-ni, one Ranger made the comment that "it took the Chinese to integrate the American Army," and he was right. Chinese intervention in Korea was a wake-up call for Army integration: there was a realization that if we did not use black troops, we could lose this war.

The changes necessitated by desegregation did not come easily and were accompanied by many awkward moments. Even over fifty years after the inactivation of the Ranger companies, the authors and those Rangers who aided them in the completion of this book found desegregation difficult to discuss. Nonetheless, the events that shaped America's first, last, and only all-black Ranger unit are described from its activation in 1950 to inactivation in August 1951, as compiled by the unit's Executive Officer and two sergeants, with help from many 2d Airborne Rangers who served alongside the authors. In the military the old World War II policy that no black officer would command white personnel, maintained by the 92d Infantry Division, contributed to racial tension.

But there also were other times when white soldiers turned against bigotry and stood with blacks to demand equality. For example, Lieutenant Richard E. Robinson, the only black in the 187th Airborne Regimental Combat Team (RCT), got there because the white officer paratroopers of his Officer Candidate Class who were singled out to join the 187th Airborne RCT said they would not go without him. Major Joe Jenkins, S-1 of the 187th, offered the opportunity to all of the officers—except Robinson, because "no colored soldiers" were in the 11th Airborne Division. But because the rest refused to go without Robinson, on 20 October 1950, when the 187th RCT jumped at Sukch'on, Korea, Robinson became the first black paratrooper in the history of the U.S. Army to make a combat jump.

Yet, nearly a decade after black mess attendant Dorie Miller, U.S. Navy, valiantly fired from the deck of the USS *West Virginia* while the ship was under attack in Pearl Harbor, using a machine gun he could not have trained officially to use, white soldiers and prominent military figures continued to question whether blacks had the courage and desire to perform ground combat duty, to fight for their country. Members of the 2d Ranger Company did, and this book has been written to record those events and commemorate their place in history.

The Korean War has been called "the Forgotten War," and in many ways it would be comforting to forget segregation and the efforts that were required to desegregate the military as well. But segregation was not just a dream—it is a part of American history and should neither be forgotten nor overemphasized. Unless we show our descendants how to see beyond the past, racism will remain; and true equality, in which all individuals are treated without preference or prejudice, will never be achieved.

After the Korean War, many of the 2d Airborne Rangers decided that they had "found a home" in the Army. Some took their Ranger expertise to a different branch of service (such as James Taylor, Navy SEAL, or James Allen, Roland Hodge, and William Rhodes, U.S. Air Force), but in addition to those few, 64 of 140 Rangers who served in the 2d Ranger Company from 1950 to 1951 retired from the military after twenty years of service. Approximately fifteen Rangers later became officers. This was an exceptional company of men. For many, their Korean War experiences left a lasting impression that would shape their lives. Likewise, their experience in the first, last, and only all-black Ranger unit left a lasting impression on the military.

Master Sergeant Edward L. Posey
(U.S. Army, Retired)

Acknowledgments

Special thanks are due Colonel (Retired) Robert Black of the 8th Rangers for inspiring us, for encouraging all infantry companies (airborne) to publish a unit history book, and for providing the initial morning reports (M/Rs). We also give special thanks to retired Colonel Robert "Bob" Channon, 3d Ranger Infantry Company (Airborne), author of *The Cold Steel Third* about the Third Airborne Ranger Company—Korean War, 1950-1951 (Franklin, North Carolina: Genealogy Publishing Service, 1993) for his editorial assistance and encouragement.

We are also grateful to Joe Watts, author of *Korean Nights* about the 4th Ranger Infantry Company (Airborne), 1950, 1951 (St. Petersburg, Florida: Southern Heritage Press, 1997) for reminding us of incidents we had forgotten and for providing the copies of early morning reports about our experiences with the 4th Company (T/A). We are deeply indebted to Constance A. Burns, U.S. Army Center of Military History, Fort McNair, D.C., for her willingness to serve as coordinator, manager, and researcher for the 2d Ranger Company's history. Constance spent many hours in the final editing, preparation, and organization of this manuscript, and worked closely with our publisher, Savas

Beatie, managing director Theodore P. Savas, and marketing director Sarah Keeney. Although most of our research was conducted before the manuscript was completed, it proved of great benefit to have Thomas Faith to retrieve additional documents for our review. We express our appreciation to Cathy Frye for her editorial comments and reviews.

Without the extraordinary efforts of the members of the 2d Ranger Company this book would have been impossible to write. I owe a debt of gratitude to all members of the 2d Ranger Company; when we first consulted about this book, we determined to make it a collective effort to make our accomplishments known.

I also wish to acknowledge my grateful appreciation to Major James Queen and SFC William Weathersbee for their hard work and effort in compiling information and researching this book. Without their contributions this story would not be told. Major Queen and SFC Weathersbee were the force—with the support of many other members of the 2d Ranger Company—to make sure that as much information as possible was collected. Major Queen and SFC Weathersbee died before this book was completed. I would like to express my gratitude for their honorable service and loyal dedication to the Ranger spirit.

I also wish to thank Herculano Dias and Lawrence Estell for their invaluable help in compiling material. These men and I also owe special thanks to the wives, Linda Dias, Linda Estell, Phyllis Queen, Alberta Weathersbee and Mary A. Posey, for assuming the family duties while we roamed the world attending veterans' activities. They not only had the children, but also played a major role in their upbringing. Last but not least, I would like to thank my nephew, Michael Evans, for doing a lot to help me gather my thoughts and describe actual events.

Introduction

At the end of World War II, Korea was divided into two parts along the 38th Parallel as a temporary solution until a unified Korea could govern itself. By 1948, Communist North Korea and Democratic South Korea had each established independent governments. The Korean War erupted on June 25, 1950, when North Korean combat troops of the Korean People's Army (KPA) crossed the 38th Parallel on the peninsula in eastern Asia. After the North Korean attack, President Harry S. Truman immediately committed U.S. forces to face the North Korean challenge. And so it was that just five years after World War II ended, the United States again found itself involved in a war halfway around the world with "a people they had never met."

When the Armed Forces of the United States joined the Republic of Korea and twenty-one other countries to fight together under the United Nations banner against Communist North Korea and, later, China, it was in the wake of a rapid military draw-down of American forces after World War II. Unprepared to meet any new or emerging national security threats, American forces were plagued with deficiencies in personnel, equipment, training, and technology. Furthermore, World War II veterans and their families were ready for the peace and tranquility of civilian life. The GI Bill and the postwar economic boom offered many white veterans opportunities in civilian life they never before had imagined. Black veterans also were able to take advantage of education and home ownership. Reenlisting to fight another war in a faraway land held little appeal for most American veterans. Blacks in the agrarian South, however, were left with an uncertain financial future when the country's new economic prosperity caused farm opportunities to decrease. For many blacks who previously had known only a rural life, the Army was their ticket out—faced with limited economic opportunities, they viewed the Army as a way to receive training, gain experience, and travel. These men and women were an ideal new resource for the country's defense.

Many blacks saw America's campaign against Communism in Korea as an opportunity to challenge segregation in the military. Under pressure from civil rights political leaders and Senator Hubert Humphrey, President Truman signed Executive Order 9981 in July 1948, which called for "equality of treatment and opportunity for all persons in the armed forces without regard to race, color, religion, or national origins." The order was to be implemented "as rapidly as possible, having due regard to the time required to effectuate any necessary changes without impairing efficiency or morale." Although the word *desegregation* did not appear in the Executive Order, and the means by which each military service should accomplish racial equality in the armed forces was not specified, this document served as the basis for racial integration in America's armed forces.

It is important to place segregation in the context of the times. When World War II began, blacks in the Army and Navy held only menial positions. There were no blacks in the Air Corps—what later became our Air Force—and no blacks in the Marine Corps. Throughout the 1940s racial discrimination, prejudice, and bigotry were common and, sadly, often accepted in our nation and our military. Desegregation was the first step toward racial equality. For our armed forces, this important step was taken during the Korean War.

Unfortunately, since Executive Order 9981 neither specified a means to accomplish integration nor a timetable for full desegregation, black servicemen often trained, worked, and lived in segregated settings during the Korean War. Although the Air Force led the way with a plan for racial integration in January 1949 and in 1950 adhered to a racial integration policy that placed each person in a position solely on the basis of aptitude, desegregation was a slow, multi-year process throughout all of the other branches of American military service.

Both the Army and the Marine Corps entered the Korean War with racially segregated forces. By October 1951, the Army had begun the work of integrating its units, which would take three years to complete. Not until October 31, 1954, would the Army report that no segregated units remained in its ranks. Although some, like the members of the 2d Ranger Company (Airborne), were allowed to train for equal opportunities, they were still treated differently and remained segregated in an all-black unit.

Of the United States' nine major wars, the Korean War is the least remembered. Known as a brutal test of survival in a hostile land filled with hardships caused by its hilly terrain and harsh weather conditions, the Korean War was America's first real experience with guerilla tactics. Six million American men and women served in Korea as soldiers, nurses, clerks, chaplains, rangers, and combat and support staff. Blacks comprised about eight percent of total U.S. military manpower and were represented in all combat and combat service elements. Total black casualties in Korea were heavy, with estimates of more than 5,000 killed in combat, of which thirteen were members of the 2d Ranger Infantry Company. Numerous blacks were awarded medals, including the Distinguished Service Cross, Silver Star, and Bronze Star. Four members of the 2d Ranger Company—Captain Warren Allen (1996), Major James C. Queen (1994), Master Sergeant Edward Posey (2002), and CW4 Cleveland Valery (2005)—were inducted into the U.S. Army Ranger Hall of Fame for heroic actions during combat. The 2d Ranger Company was awarded the Combat Infantry Streamer, a commendation awarded to units receiving more than sixty-five percent of casualties in a particular engagement with the enemy. For their courage and valor, members of the 2d Ranger Company also received the Combat Infantry Badge or Combat Medical Badge; others earned the Purple Heart, the Bronze Star, and Silver Star.

This book has provided the 2d Ranger Company's unit history by sharing its wartime experiences, as seen largely through the eyes of Major James C. Queen, an officer, and Sergeant First Class William Weathersbee and Master Sergeant Edward L. Posey, both enlisted men. Their stories of valor (and many more by several other Rangers) are punctuated by the inequalities routinely encountered by black soldiers in the years leading up to the civil rights movement. Their experiences are important. They demonstrated with great force and clarity that black soldiers could and would fight for their country with as much courage and ability as white soldiers. They also served as a snapshot in time of our nation and culture during a turning point in American civil rights.

Constance A. Burns, B.S., M.A.
Specialist in Minorities in Military History
Department of the Army
U.S. Army Center of Military History
Fort Lesley J. McNair
Washington, D.C.

Part I

The soldiers of the all-black 2d Ranger Infantry Company (Airborne), like other black units, were nicknamed the "Buffalo Soldiers." There is more than one explanation of how the nickname came to be, but a commonly accepted account is that sometime around 1870, the 10th Cavalry Regiment was given this nickname by the Cheyenne Indians who "saw a similarity between the curly hair and dark skin of the soldiers and the buffalo."[1] The nickname gradually came into usage whenever referring to any black soldier fighting the Plains Indians, and was "so popular among the members of the 10th Cavalry that they adopted the figure of a buffalo as a prominent feature of their Regimental Crest."

During World War I, the soldiers of the 92d Division adopted the nickname, and the unit was called the Buffalo Division. Each member wore a shoulder patch on his uniform adorned with the solitary figure of a black buffalo. In 1942, the 92d Division "kept the nickname and apparently acquired a live young buffalo as a mascot."[2]

In 1950, throughout their training days at Fort Benning, Georgia, and before the Buffalo Rangers who were to fight in Korea went overseas, "Buffalo" was a term of respect. In it there was solidarity. We are Rangers AND we carry the traditions of earlier Buffalo soldiers—we are strong, we are resilient, and we are united to destroy the enemy.

Chapter 1

Training at Benning

"…[T]raining of Ranger-type units was to begin at Fort Benning, at the earliest possible date. The target date was set for October 1, 1950, with a tentative training period of six weeks. The implementing orders called for formation of a headquarters detachment and four Ranger infantry companies (airborne). Requests went out for volunteers who were willing to accept extremely hazardous duty in the combat zone in the Far East."

— www.ranger.org/html/korea_history.html[1]

Sometime around the 25th of September 1950, rumors started circulating around Fort Bragg, North Carolina, that a Ranger recruiting team was on base looking for a few good triple volunteers: soldiers who had volunteered for the Army, the Airborne, and to see combat as a Ranger. Triple volunteers committed to: (1) a minimum of three years of service, because there was no draft in operation at the time; (2) parachute and glider school that produced two sets of wings when satisfactorily completed; and (3) combat in Korea, which is where all Ranger volunteers were headed. Fort Bragg was the home of the 82d Airborne Division, a major portion of the United States strategic forces.

The 82d Airborne Division was the only combat-ready unit still stateside when the call for Ranger volunteers went out. The 11th ABN was just getting reorganized after returning from Japan and was stripped of personnel to bring the 187th Airborne Regimental Combat Team (ARCT) up to strength in time for the Sukch'on and Sunch'on jump in October 1950. The main post at Fort Bragg could not hold all of the units assigned to it. The majority of the 82d was located in the main post area, but upon the reactivation of the 325th Glider Unit, the 325th was moved into the old Recruit Training Center (RTC) located across Highway 24, where non-airborne engineer units and the reception center for personnel newly assigned to Fort Bragg also were housed.

The black troops were located in the Spring Lake cantonment area on the south side of Highway 24, near the small town of Spring Lake. Murchison Road, the other main road leading into Fayetteville, North Carolina, is adjacent to this area and ran through the main black area of the city. It usually took about a day for the "official" information to come from the main post to the Spring Lake area, and two days for information to reach the RTC area. The rumors were usually passed at the Division schools because the housing and recreation area on post and in the community were "separate but equal." Some of the black troops had regular duty assignments on the main post, and this was another way in which word of the recruitment of blacks for Ranger training was disseminated. The main black units in the Spring Lake area were the 3d Battalion, 505th Infantry Regiment; the 80th Anti-Aircraft Artillery Battalion (AAAB); and the 758th Tank Battalion (Airborne). The 758th was kept on "jump status" and was to provide tank support to the 82d Airborne Division in case of war. Throughout September 1950, it grew obvious that we were going to be sent overseas, because we were the only unit in the 82d Airborne that was over-strength.

Corporal James Fields, who was recruited from the 80th AAAB, describes a typical Fort Bragg recruitment session as follows:

> A white officer on a physical training (PT) stand started to speak as soon as we were assembled. 'We are forming the toughest, meanest outfit in the United States Army. I don't know if you will go in by submarine, parachute or what, but you will be fighting. The unit will be called Rangers. We want volunteers. The line forms to the right.' I had to be in the outfit. I knew what Rangers had been in World War II. I had done research on Darby's Rangers, and the Post library had information and pictures of the men in the Rangers Battalion. I knew about British Commandos—missions carefully planned, split-second timing, hit and run. I gave the interviewing officer such a persuasive spiel that I could not be turned down. I was in.

Like Fields, many were apprehensive and excited—but subdued. Orders from division headquarters usually arrived so late to the company at the Spring Lake cantonment that the normal procedure was "Hurry up and give me your decision, *now!*"

That decision sent men from Fort Bragg to Fort Benning in Georgia, where six weeks of Ranger training began. At that time, the Rangers training at Benning either belonged to the all-white 2d Ranger Company or the all-black 4th Ranger Company. At Benning's Harmony Church cantonment area, both units trained together but lived separately. The 2d and 4th would exchange unit designations on 13 November 1950. From that date until its inactivation on 1 August 1951, the all-black unit was known as the 2d Ranger Company.

The Harmony Church cantonment area was a small living and training area, for Rangers only, at the far southeast corner of the post about ten miles from the jump towers. It was near the town of Buena Vista. Toward the end of World War II, Harmony Church had been the housing area for the Officer Candidate School (OCS) and the compass course areas. The 25th Infantry Regiment was located in "Sand Hills" and the Small Arms Ranges and Jump School were in the South Post area. The black troops' area consisted of the last quadrangle, a small PX, a movie theater, and a barber shop.

The bus could go directly to town from Harmony Church or come up to a variety of locations on the main post. The local custom of blacks riding at the rear of the bus prevailed. The only time the Rangers needed to come on post was for range firing and parachute training. The 3d Infantry Division was trained there before deployment to Korea. The 11th RCT acted as school troops.

Physical Conditioning and Training

The training at Fort Benning was rigorous. The day usually started with a three- to five-mile run before breakfast nicknamed "The Airborne Shuffle." Even before entering the mess hall, there was physical training (PT): a pull-bar was posted over the door to the mess, and only after doing five or more pull-ups were you allowed to enter the mess hall. Marching to the training sites with all equipment was routine. The trick of going without a lot of water was learned very early. You put a small pebble under your tongue to stimulate the saliva glands, causing the mouth to stay wet and lessening the need for water. These were skills we would later rely upon on the battlefield.

All men assigned to Ranger Training Command were already qualified paratroopers and had passed the standard PT test with a score of at least three hundred points. The standard test consisted of five hundred points. The average trooper could easily make the three hundred points required to pass.

The pull-ups were usually the most difficult part of the test. The physical run was no problem—except with a hangover. Very few fell on the runs. Usually, the Airborne "Jodie" cadence was modified from "Airborne—all the way!" with the word "Ranger," as follows:

Platoon Sergeant:"AIRBORNE!"
Platoon Reply:"RANGER!"
Platoon Sergeant:"ALL THE WAY!"
Platoon Reply:"RANGER!"

Those of us who had come from Fort Bragg were in good physical condition. Back at Bragg, the troopers of the 3d Battalion frequently ran about five miles down to Pope Field from the Spring Lake area.

From October through November, the Rangers conducted familiarization firing of most of the weapons (.45-caliber pistol, carbine, M-1 rifle, Browning automatic rifle, or BAR, and .45-caliber submachine gun), including a few Russian and Chinese weapons such as the Chinese grenade (which used a pull string). The Rangers moved on to tactical training, starting at the squad and platoon levels. Ranger recruits learned map reading, which included U.S. military maps, foreign maps, and maps of Korea printed by the Japanese when they had occupied the peninsula. Rangers also learned land navigation, night patrol/day patrol methods, interdiction operations, phone and electric power line sabotage, assassination methods, improvised killing, martial arts, hand-to-hand combat and raid procedures, and completed demolition training, water training, and small boat and rubber boat (RB-15) training.

The training day was usually twelve and sometimes as long as fifteen hours. Soldiers got used to walking in their sleep during the long road marches. Sometimes the column would turn but a sleepwalking Ranger would continue walking until he hit a tree or walked into the wood line. Rangers tried to drink enough coffee before a march to stay awake, but not so much that they would need to stop, at the risk of being left behind or becoming a skunk attraction.

The roughest training problem was a company raid to blow up a big bridge deep in enemy territory. This exercise was held near the town of Buena Vista on the far side of Fort Benning. We must have walked twenty miles that night (there was a real sleepwalker problem that evening). The action started when Lieutenant James Queen hit a Bouncing Betty style of trip flare on the bridge just as the charges were set, which gave the alarm. This helped to clear the bridge in record time. We took off down the railroad tracks on the escape route and successfully passed the training exercise.

During one of the exhausting, 24-hour, platoon-size patrols, the First Platoon commander fell asleep and failed to post adequate security. It just so happened that Colonel John Gibson Van Houten, the Ranger Brigade Training Commander, came out to check on this training problem in person. He walked through the majority of the platoon area without being challenged. If a mistake like this had happened in combat, the entire platoon could have been killed. So the platoon failed and had to repeat the grueling patrol. When the unit got back to the barracks, Colonel Van Houten called in all of the company officers for a critique. Needless to say, everyone was extremely embarrassed. He ended his critique with an often-heard racial slur, "You people won't fight when you get to Korea!" This caused immediate anger among the company officers. All of the previous racism they had experienced seemed to be summed up in this one, biting criticism. The innuendo behind the words "you people" always provoked images and emotions of racism. The officers bit their tongues and offered no excuses, but resolved never to be in such a shameful position again. And it never did happen again. Still, that one mistake left a sting still not forgotten. The colonel's remarks were never passed on to the men because it was the officers' leadership failure that had allowed this situation to occur. But copies of the first award orders from combat were later sent to Colonel Van Houten as proof that his assessment of the unit's probable conduct during combat had not been accurate.

During Ranger training the word was that the North Koreans were on the run and the action in Korea was just about over: all of the men would be home for Christmas, and the trainees at Benning would never see combat overseas. Many of us were disappointed. But on 3 November 1950, the Chinese entered the war and the UN Army was in full retreat. It was now inevitable that the Rangers of 2d Company would see combat in Korea. Corporal James Fields attests that "2d Company pushed itself to the limits, training day and night to reach top combat efficiency. Under the command of First Lieutenant Warren E. Allen, his career officers and top-notch NCOs molded us into a cohesive fighting force in a very short time. Our training never let up."

Allen, one of the most well-respected officers to emerge from the 555th Parachute Infantry Battalion, was all business. The Rangers under his command often felt that it was because of his leadership that they were successful. Many believed the 2d Ranger Company was designed for Allen's leadership. Typically,

Allen would hold the men in the bayonet "long thrust" position until their arms quivered. Whenever there was time for refresher PT, it always included bayonet drill practice to instill a spirit of confidence and aggressive behavior until it became an automatic response. He despised common barracks profanity. If one of his men made a mistake and used such words in his presence, he would get an angry stare from Allen, followed by a quick rebuke. If you were an enlisted man (EM) and used profanity in the presence of a woman, you were sure to end up on KP or digging a 6' x 6' garbage dump. If you were an officer, you got the next miserable detail that came up. Corporal Samuel "Shorty" Payne remembers Allen as a "no-nonsense leader who gained respect from the men and non-commissioned officers under him. He had a cadre of men that rallied and supported him. Allen would push, push, and push some more so that the men in the first black Ranger company would be the best that the Army could offer."

On 13 November 1950, all members of 2d Ranger Company were given a small Ranger tab to display on their uniforms. This tab was new and held no meaning for the Rangers, some of whom were insulted by the award. A group of Rangers went into town to the local Army-Navy Store and bought surplus World War II Ranger Battalion scrolls, had them modified to change "Battalion" to "Company," and wore these custom-made insignia with pride.

During November, the Rangers conducted several increasingly difficult company-sized training missions. One exercise involved traveling through swamps and making a dawn raid on a fixed-wing light aircraft field. The swamp was negotiated with a compass heading. The company traveled in single file, and the swamp area was so dense and the night so dark that the Rangers could use a flashlight and not be seen from more than fifty feet away. It took the Rangers four to five hours to travel less than three miles. They were extremely lucky that they did not lose anyone. The Rangers came out directly on the airfield at the break of dawn and hit it before the force tasked to hold the position arrived to defend the airfield. Another milestone was achieved.

Another of the company-sized training missions was crossing Victory Pond and making an assault landing on the opposite side. The November wind was offshore and the weather was cold. The training film shown the night before made the exercise look straightforward: cross two rifles and secure them, then take two shelter halves to make a raft. Each Ranger was ordered to put his equipment on the raft and push it in front as he swam. With the rafts, the men had to paddle upstream, reach a certain landing point, scale the cliffs while carrying combat gear, and continue on with the assault mission.

The actual exercise did not unfold as it did in the training film. The Rangers looked bad in planning, coordination, and execution. The company failed to get to shore in a satisfactory manner. We ran into the following unanticipated problems:

— Very few of the men were good swimmers, and many of the men did not have even the basic ability to swim unassisted for a distance of fifty feet, which caused some anxiety in the ranks;

— Very few of the troopers had previously received boat or raft training. Even those who had gone to Combine II in Florida or the R&R Camp at Myrtle Beach, South Carolina, lacked this type of training;

— We used small 4-to-5-man rafts, with small wooden paddles;

— The rafts were not loaded according to the troopers' swimming and climbing ability, such that each raft had both experienced and inexperienced swimmers;

— We had to scale a ten-foot cliff of red Georgia clay. The walls of the cliff became extremely slippery, making it almost impossible to scale without a team effort.

In combat, these types of mistakes could prove fatal. Lieutenant Allen, commanding 2d Ranger Company, was rightfully aggravated. He had the company rescheduled for weekend training until the lake crossing was mastered. We repeated the drill on Saturday morning. Troopers, including Bruce Johnson, McBert Higginbotham, and Samuel "Shorty" Payne, led assault rafts, with others—including Jim Queen, Jack Murphy, Richard Glover, and Edward Posey—leading the way and organizing climbing parties. The idea was to use the big, physical troopers to boost the smaller troopers up the cliff. These smaller men, in turn, would help by reaching down with modified jump ropes to pull up the larger troopers. Through the use of this type of human relay, the Rangers got over the cliffs rather easily and assembled, assaulted, and captured the hill. The company completed the mission by 1300 hours with "flying colors." A nearly audible sigh of relief was heard throughout the ranks.

This type of teamwork was typical of the 2d Ranger Company at its best. Several factors contributed to the close-knit nature of the entire unit. First, this group of officers had at one time or another served in all of the companies. All of the officers had performed guard duty or courtesy patrol with men from each of the companies. The company was close because of its isolated location at Harmony Church Cantonment Area, and because of its racial composition. The informal fraternization between the officers and ranks was probably akin to the climate of a state National Guard unit, in which the vast majority of a unit came from one small town. Except for Lieutenant Albert D. Cliette, the officers had been commissioned through OCS and had spent a long time as non-commissioned officers (NCOs). Also, the social climate on post almost mirrored the social climate outside in Fayetteville, North Carolina, where a colonial-era market house was situated at the demarcation line between the black and white commercial areas; it was, in some cases, us versus them.

As the troopers got into better physical condition, rumors of the ability of the Rangers to "whip" Legs (soldiers or officers who were not qualified for parachute jumps) increased. This was like a fish story in which the fish that was caught keeps getting bigger each time the story is told. At first, the estimate was that each Ranger could take on six to eight Legs. But by the time we completed hand-to-hand combat training this number had grown to ten and our reputation grew with it. We were in top physical condition and everyone knew it. You didn't mess with a Ranger unless you were looking for trouble.

Weapons and Demolition Familiarization Experiences

The normal small arms weapons training (assembly, disassembly, and range firing) started with the .45-caliber pistol. All of this was done in a satisfactory manner because the range procedures were well known. The men from Company M were the best in heavy weapons, such as the 75 mm recoilless rifle, the .30-caliber machine gun, and the 81 mm mortar. Several new weapons were demonstrated: Rocket launcher, 3.5-inch (to counteract the Russian T–34 tank with which the North Koreans were outfitted), and the Swedish armor-piercing anti-tank rifled grenade.

Demolitions training was not too difficult because the Rangers had some "3d Battalion" Ammunition and Pioneer (A&P) Platoon troopers, such as Lawrence "Larry" Estell, among the company membership. Men selected for this platoon had the skills of a handyman, and handled the ammo for the battalion. Rangers learned how to make "shaped charges" and "bangalore torpedoes" for the destruction of pillbox emplacements. However, the 2d Ranger Company did not end up using any demolitions in combat because neither the Koreans nor the Americans went into reinforced fortifications until July 1951.

Jump Exercises

The Company conducted one nighttime jump without any casualties on an all-dirt light aircraft field. It was rumored that one of the companies—not the 2d—had a man killed. He landed in a tree and was knocked unconscious. His camouflaged parachute hid him so well that he could not be located from the ground nor spotted by helicopter from the air. His dead body was found when buzzards began circling the tree in which he had landed. This was a shock because we never thought we would not be spotted easily from the air. We had forgotten about the smoke jumpers who died similar deaths in the dense forests of the Pacific Northwest in 1945.

Nitty-Gritty Pep Talk

Those men who were injured or hospitalized for more than three days during training were shipped back to Fort Bragg. The same was true of men who showed a training deficiency. Troops were weeded out in preparation for combat duty. On Friday the 13th in October 1950, the 1st, 2d, and 4th Companies were assembled in the Harmony Church Theater for a realistic pep talk by the Ranger Center Staff. Colonel Van Houten, commander, painted a bleak picture of what the future six months would bring. He said that half of us Rangers would be casualties, so if anyone wanted to drop out, now would be the time to do so, without any fear of repercussions. No one left. And he was not wrong. We entered Korea with 110 men and lost about 65 in the first fourteen days of combat due to a variety of reasons: killed in action (KIA), wounded in action (WIA), frostbite, and other injuries.

In mid-November of 1950, the 1st Ranger Company finished its training and shipped out without any pre-embarkation furloughs. It joined the 2d Infantry Division in Korea after a brief stop in Japan. Back at Benning, this was a clear sign that we were next; it would not be long before we went overseas. Another unmistakable sign: replacements who would go to Korea in March

1951 began their training at Benning and were stationed at the main post. On Thanksgiving, the Rangers in 2d Ranger Company had a feast, for which the unit cooks helped the cadre cooks. Lieutenant Allen and his fiancée Mary were married that day. While the Rangers of 2d Ranger Company were still stateside, wives such as Phyllis Queen and other family members took the opportunity to spend time with their loved ones during the Thanksgiving feast.

Within 72 hours, 2d Ranger Company was on its way to Korea.

Chapter 2

The Officers' Advance Party

"All Rangers are to be subject to the rules and articles of war to appear at roll-call every evening on their own parade, equipped each with a firelock, sixty rounds of powder and ball, and a hatchet . . ."

— Journals of Major Robert Rogers[2]

The 2d and 4th Companies finished their training cycle about the last week in November and immediately began to prepare for the trip to Korea. The Morning Reports of 1 and 2 December show some last-minute losses. In anticipation of the unit's departure, some men were dropped from the rolls and a final roster was submitted with the Morning Report.

On 1 December 1950, the Executive Officers of the 2d and 4th Companies, Lieutenant James C. "Big Jim" Queen and First Lieutenant John "Jack" Warren, respectively, were dispatched from Columbus, Georgia, to travel together by commercial air to San Francisco, California. Each officer— Queen for the all-black 2d and Warren for the all-white 4th—acted as a one-man advance party for his unit.

Jack Warren of 4th Company was a short, cool, and sophisticated New Yorker. He had an aristocratic flair and the poise of a New Englander. Jack carried his cigarettes in a case in the inner breast pocket of his Eisenhower jacket. Whenever he withdrew one, he would tap the end on the case and use a lighter. His wife was a New York City telephone operator, and each evening he would call so they could chat.

Preparations at the POE

Queen, who was very tall, and Warren, who was very short, were the "Mutt and Jeff" advance party team. They would discuss and rehearse their lines ahead of time before going to see any of the point of embarkation (POE) officials—

whether in Finance, Transportation, or Ordnance. Although 1st Ranger Company had passed through a month before, 2d and 4th Companies had not gotten any special briefings. No one had a copy of 2d or 4th Company's TO&E (Table of Organization and Equipment, the official document showing the exact personnel and equipment that belonged to a unit), nor did anyone have a copy to show orders with authorized allowances. The technical department personnel did not have any experience with airborne or Ranger units. So Queen and Warren greeted them with patriotism and gusto: they were volunteers going to combat, because things had turned for the worse in Korea after the entry of the Chinese; they were Rangers and paratroopers, triple volunteers who had signed up for the military, signed up for special training, and signed up to jump out of airplanes behind enemy lines. They were very convincing, and their routine helped get the extra supplies both companies would rely on in Korea.

When they got up to the Ordnance Depot, Queen and Warren met a very pretty black lady who was the chief clerk. With a straight face and all sincerity, they told her that:

— All paratroopers carried a .45-caliber pistol as a standard second weapon in a shoulder holster. (The submachine gun .45 was what was supposed to be carried by Rangers, so they got those, too.)

— All paratroopers carried "jump knives" as a standard item for use in cutting themselves out of their parachutes in case they landed in a tree or in the water. (These were switchblade knives; only the 2d and 4th Companies carried knives at all.)

— All paratroopers received eighteen Browning Automatic Rifles (BARs) per company and three .30-caliber Light Machine Guns (LMGs) per company, one for each platoon, and didn't need any heavy machine guns at all because there weren't enough men to physically handle them, and even if there were, the cold weather in Korea would freeze up the guns' water jackets. But the additional LMGs were needed because paratroopers jumped with their LMGs in an individual weapons container that attached to the jumper parachute harness with a pongee cord (a 30-foot, rubberized, stretch rope), and these weapons frequently broke loose from the harness and were lost.

After this masterful, dramatic performance, they convincingly and politely asked for three M1–C Sniper Rifles, each with a six-power scope, for each company. One of those M1–Cs would become Queen's primary weapon just a few weeks later after the early morning firefight at Tanyang Pass on 14 January 1951.

While in California, Mutt and Jeff put in requisitions for everything except ammo, and hoped that the requisitions would be filled and all of the items would be in Japan when the units arrived there before reaching Korea. Some weapons would be used to train raw recruits on board the Navy ship that would transport the men of the 2d and 4th to Japan for the longest leg of their travel to Korea.

Both XOs got their men three-pouch hand grenade carriers they had not seen before. The problem with this carrier was that it fit on the pistol belt and not up high, the way General Matthew B. Ridgway was famous for carrying his grenades. Like the .45-caliber holster, it hit against the leg or hip when you walked. Throughout the war Jim Queen never carried more than two grenades in it (one fragmentation and one white or color smoke phosphorus grenade). The color smoke grenades were carried by the officers and the radio operators, in case they were needed for identification from the air or to mark the front lines. In general, each trooper carried the grenade he wanted. Some liked white phosphorus grenades to burn down buildings or set fires in foxholes. For special missions, the Rangers were taught to use thermite grenades to produce extreme heat.

The last requisitioned items, air/color panels, were worn on the back of the SCR–300 radios or on the light pack while on the move, if the Rangers needed to call in an air strike. At a minimum, every Ranger in Korea from 2d Company had a pistol, knife, rope, and medical kit with morphine, as well as any specialized materials needed for his assignment (for example, radio operators carried SCR–300 radios).

In addition to requisitioning supplies for their units, both XOs spent time at the Finance Office getting travel pay for the permanent change of station (PCS) move for spouse/family home from last registered address and making out final allotments. Queen allotted all of his pay to his wife—except for ten dollars, which he thought he might need for PX supplies while in combat.

The cool nighttime weather in the San Francisco Bay area meant that winter uniforms were worn on a year-round basis. There was no snow, but the town was very hilly and at night the cool ocean breezes came on shore.

When business was done, there was time to socialize. Both XOs went to town together once, and after that went separately. They didn't encounter any blatant prejudice; each wanted to explore different sections of the city.

Jim Queen went into town about three times during the week he was in San Francisco. He loved the old trolley cars, which were similar to the ones in his hometown of Washington, D.C. He went into a friendly little bar twice and had to show them how to make the "Paratroopers/Airborne Cocktail" (cheap champagne with milk). The next drinks were purchased by a friendly crowd of black locals who had never seen a black Ranger officer and were sympathetic to our fighting men in Korea. With the Chinese now in the war, things didn't look too rosy from this side of the Pacific—particularly considering San Francisco's very large Chinese population.

The XO's State of Readiness and Foresight

The 2d Ranger Company's XO took time throughout the week in San Francisco to prepare himself for combat in Korea. Few realized how cold and inhospitable Korea could be. The terrain was hilly, which would not only make it difficult underfoot but would add wind chill to temperatures that froze water in canteens, cut the battery life of both radios and vehicles in half, and made frostbite a constant reality. The weather would quickly dip to sub-zero temperatures, and blinding snow coupled with the cold would cause weapons such as carbines and BARs to freeze up, mortar tubes to crack, and blood plasma and rations to freeze. It was a heck of a place to fight a war.

Queen, however, had done a two-year tour in the Aleutian Islands and Alaska before going to the 82d Airborne Division, so he knew how to prepare his clothing and equipment for fighting during the winter in Korea. He prepared as best as he could. He bought a pair of finger gloves to wear inside his mittens for added warmth, and purchased a good sewing kit and sewed the pile liner from his old Alaska jacket into the hood of the field jacket he would wear for the next eight months in Korea. He also bought a pair of hunter's gloves (mittens) at a local Sears & Roebuck (mittens were warmer than gloves and could be worn over gloves). The hunting mitten had a slit cut in the palm of the right hand that would allow a hunter to reach through with his finger and pull the trigger of a weapon. Queen cut a slit in the palm of the left glove and sewed up the edges in a similar manner to match the right-hand mitten to allow him to load a magazine or clip with either hand, as needed. He sewed a half-inch-wide, one-foot-long, elastic tape to each mitten, then fixed a loop to it so that it could be attached to the sleeve/cuff button of the field jacket. That way, if he dropped a mitten or took it off, it would not be irretrievably lost in the deep snow. School kids would call these "idiot mittens," but in the field they could save his fingers from frostbite.

Queen also picked up extra white, civilian, woolen socks and placed one pair in his pack and another in the side pockets of his "jump pants." Damp socks in cold weather also meant frostbite, and dry socks were more essential than rations. He padded the knees and seat of his jump pants and the elbows of his field jacket. With his sewing kit and extra large needles, he sewed extra pockets onto his pants and field jacket. He added an extra six inches to the bottom of his pants because regulation pants were too short to cover his long legs. As he made these alterations, Queen thought of how often he had been in trouble with his old battalion commander for modifying his field uniform and equipment. For example:

— Queen preferred to wear buckled combat boots instead of jump boots in the field, because jump boots would get wet if you walked in grass heavy with dew. Combat boots had a better chance of keeping feet dry and of fitting his size 14E feet. The largest size Corcoran jump boot from the PX was a 12E or a 13E—if you sent away for it. Any infantryman and any Ranger will attest to how important it is for boots to fit.

— Queen got an M2 compass, instead of the basic lensatic compass, for indirect fire with the 75 mm Recoilless Rifles.

— He purchased a rucksack instead of a musette bag or a full field pack because the rucksack could carry more and be packed more quickly.

As he made these preparations he still wore his insignia, in spite of warnings about snipers seeking to kill officers who wore outside insignia. However, he knew Koreans and Chinese did not shoot as precisely as Germans. Queen had that stereotypical view of all Asians wearing glasses—his own prejudice, perhaps. He still had a Red Cross knit scarf from his enlisted man days in World War II, and a wool knit sweater on which he reinforced the buttonholes so that things would not come open too easily during rigorous movements. He would wear these same clothes for the whole eight months he would spend in Korea, washing his clothing and waiting for it to dry whenever he reached a shower point because he seldom found his sizes in the available Quarter Master (QM) clothing table at the end of the shower line. He wouldn't see his "B bag"—a duffle bag with extra clothing not needed in combat—until he returned to Japan with the 187th ARCT in August 1951—after the 2d Ranger Company was inactivated and the Rangers were reassigned as needed. He would later learn that the 7th Infantry Division had kept this gear some place in Taegu, at Division Rear, for the whole time he was in Korea.

Queen cut a slit in his long johns and two pairs of boxer shorts, so his butt would not freeze when heeding nature's call; nor would he ever be caught with his pants completely down and unable to haul out in a hurry. He took a pair of pack suspenders and hooked them up to an M1 pistol belt so he would be able to drop his pack quickly and still have a rifle–pistol belt carrying a .45 (with two extra magazines), compass, grenade pouch (with two grenades), bayonet and scabbard, canteen, binoculars, first aid kit, and poncho. He also would sling an extra bandoleer of six clips of eight rounds each across his chest so he would have more ammunition for combat.

Travel to Japan and Preparation at Camp Zama

As the troops of the 2d and 4th Ranger Companies were arriving at Camp Stoneman, California, their advance party headed for Camp Zama, Japan. After their week of preparations in San Francisco, both officers believed they had done a good job getting equipment for their units. Queen and Warren boarded a Trans World Airlines plane at Travis Air Force Base bound for Japan. The XOs flew on a civilian aircraft similar to the C-54 (four props, non-jet) with female hostesses.

The first stop was at Honolulu Airport, Hawaii, for refueling, where they landed in daylight and stayed on the ground about an hour. The weather was delightful, with a slight breeze, but no young ladies in hula skirts met them with leis. During the long flight from Hawaii to Wake Island, they got up and walked around the plane. Both XOs kept thinking about what would happen if the plane went down. They were flying in a prop-driven aircraft because in 1950 commercial jets were not yet flying that route. This was a regular flight with a civilian crew, a few Marines, and some Red Cross workers. There was emergency equipment (rubber life rafts, buoys, radios) stowed on the floor in the rear. Both XOs lay down on the pile of emergency gear, which made a better bed than folded-out web aircraft seats along the inside of the fuselage.

After several hours of sleep they landed at night on Wake Island, part of the Marshall Island group in the northern Pacific. This American territory had a combination military/civilian airport and was used mainly as a refueling stop and weather station. After leaving Wake they headed to Tokyo, Japan, without stopping at Okinawa or Formosa, and landed at Okida Airport in the morning. Although crossing the International Date Line was an unusual event in 1950, there were no special ceremonies, although both XOs made sure to reset their watches.

As they circled Tokyo in preparation to land, they could see Yokohama Harbor and Mt. Fuji. Queen thought about how far away they were from Fort Benning. After landing, both XOs were taken to Camp Zama because billets in Yokohama or Tokyo were very unusual without special circumstances or VIP status. Camp Zama was a small Army base near Yokohama used for the staging of units and replacements.

At that time Camp Zama held a group of former POWs from the 1st Cavalry Division. These soldiers had been captured by Chinese forces when the Chinese entered the war and overran the 8th Cavalry Regiment. Some had been released by the Chinese without being taken to POW camps; some had escaped in the confusion of the battle. This group was being debriefed by the Military Intelligence personnel at Camp Zama and processed for return to the States, because under the Geneva Rules of Land Warfare those prisoners released voluntarily could not be returned to combat against the same enemy in the same theater of operations.

In talking to several of the officers, both XOs soon realized the magnitude of the equipment that had been lost, destroyed, or abandoned in the fighting. The officers told of huge waves of Chinese attacking with bugles and whistles blowing. They talked of the very cold weather and the lack of proper winter clothing; some had frostbite. They told of atrocities committed by both the Chinese and Koreans. (Very much later, several boards of inquiry would conduct postwar investigations, though without detailed findings.) None of the officers had been taken to any of the rear POW camps, and they considered themselves to be very lucky and were glad to be leaving. None of them seemed to have been tortured or had any real horror stories to relate. Both the 2d and 4th Ranger Companies would later attend escape and evasion (E&E) orientations held by the cadre at Zama. The release of these prisoners was seen as a propaganda ploy, because later captives were not released until 1953, after the Armistice.

The day after both XOs arrived at Zama they took a short trip to the depot near Yokohama to check on their equipment requisitions. They found everyone to be cordial, but Jim Queen was a little afraid of Japan and its people. He had read about earthquakes in Japan, and the ground didn't seem too solid to him when he got off the airplane. The myth of the invincibility of the Japanese soldier was lingering in Queen's mind, which was filled with images of the bloody battles on Iwo Jima and Okinawa as he headed back to camp. On his way, a young Japanese man stopped him to ask if he wanted a silk screen painting. The offer was not what he had expected, and the eager young artist was also far from what Queen had expected. The sample the artist showed him looked very nice, and Queen had some Japanese money, which he had not learned to count too well. So Queen took a photo of his wife, Phyllis, out of his wallet and gave it to the young man, with the money that he counted from the handful that Queen showed him. Queen gave the artist his wife's name and their address in Raleigh, North Carolina. The artist didn't give him a receipt, and Queen soon forgot all about it. Later, Queen thought that he had just gotten ripped off, but true to his promise the artist made an excellent painting and sent it to Queen's wife, Phyllis. Queen didn't see it until over two years later, when he rotated back to the States in March 1952.

Chapter 3

The Company's Trip to Korea

"It is hereby declared to be the policy of the President that there shall be equality of treatment and opportunity for all persons in the armed services without regard to race, color, religion or national origin. This policy shall be put into effect as rapidly as possible, having due regard to the time required to effectuate any necessary changes without impairing efficiency or morale."

— Executive Order 9981[3]

[2 Dec 1950] RECORDS OF EVENTS SECTION

Reld fr asgmt 3d Army to 6th Army with station at Camp Stoneman, Calif, per Inf Cen Ltr dtd 15 Nov 50 departing 3 Dec 50 permanent change of station Ft Benning Ga 5 Off EM 117.

On Sunday, 2 December 1950, the Buffalo Rangers prepared to leave Fort Benning for the 29-day journey to Korea. The trip would take them by bus to the train station in Columbus, Georgia, and then across the country to Camp Stoneman, California, from which they would board the *USS General H.W. Butner* to Yokohama, Japan, with a stop in Pearl Harbor, Hawaii, and then, finally, proceed by air from Japan to K-2 Airfield in Taegu, Korea. Once in Korea, the 7th Infantry Division (ID) would send deuce-and-a-half trucks to pick up the Rangers at K-2 to shuttle them to the division assembly area by truck convoy.

From Benning to Stoneman

On this particular day at Benning, as the 2d Platoon fell out for reveille, SFC James "Dude" Walker noticed that Corporal William F. Washington was absent without leave (AWOL). Apparently he had slipped off to Columbus and not returned. Someone in the rear ranks told Platoon Sergeant Walker that

Washington had been arrested several times during the night but had escaped from the Columbus police and the MPs each time. It was well known that the local police gave blacks a hard time because a civilian fine would be levied in addition to any military punishment. The Rangers of 2d Company fully believed that the Columbus police had the power, from the state of Georgia, to take your life if they desired to do so. During the previous week a man from 2d Ranger Company had been jailed in Columbus. When Lieutenant Warren Allen, the Company Commander, went to the jail to arrange for the man's release, Allen was jailed as well. The post commander—who was white—and Colonel Van Houten both had to go to Columbus to arrange for their release from jail. Usually, if the CO signed, a soldier was released and both would appear later at trial, or the civilians might let the military handle the whole problem. So the idea that a black Ranger was dodging the local police all night came as a shock to no one, considering that the domineering attitude of the Columbus police was well known.

At the time of reveille it was still dark, and the Ranger who spoke assured Sergeant Walker that Washington would make shipment. In the vacant spot where Washington should have been was all of his equipment, which had been brought to the formation by his fellow squad members. Behind Washington's equipment and the rest of the first squad was Ranger William Weathersbee, a member of second squad. Sergeant Walker solved the immediate problem with a concise order: "Weathersbee, pick up his mother fucking shit and you'll be responsible for it." The post band was playing across the field. It was dark as hell and Weathersbee had a feeling that the members of the band would all rather be in bed sleeping. Walker had just doubled Weathersbee's load, and had given his order to a Ranger who was not even in first squad. Although Weathersbee was furious that first squad was not going to take care of its own member's equipment, he did what a Ranger is supposed to do and carried out the order without saying a word. He had just been in the wrong place at the wrong time. Hopefully, that would not be the case in combat.

Brand new city buses lined up on the parade field to take the troopers to the train station in Columbus. Corporal Fields remembers getting on the buses and being faced with the signs that said "COLORED," placed where blacks were to be seated—from the rear forward. As a farewell statement, the Rangers took the signs with them. The bus ride to Columbus was uneventful, but boarding the train brought another racial indignity. The white troops of 4th Company had no problem—they could walk through the main train station—but the Station

Master didn't want the black troops of 2d Ranger Company to do likewise. To make matters worse, the white train porters led the members of the 2d Ranger Company into the station when they knew the Station Manager would have the black troops go back outside and come into the station from the side entrance. Even though the 2d and 4th had trained together, had equal skills and expectations, and would bleed the same red blood in combat, they had to proceed through the Columbus, Georgia, train station via different paths toward combat in Korea. At the time, it was simply how segregation laws worked. Looking back, it was absurd, but local laws governed the situation.

The train was delayed approximately ten minutes, just long enough for Ranger Washington, followed closely by several police cars with their red lights flashing, to appear at the station and catch up with his platoon. As the train started moving, Washington was running down the railroad tracks alongside the train, with Sergeant Walker yelling for the 2d Company Rangers to "get up and help him!" The Rangers opened the train door so Washington could leap on board.

In the safety of the train, he leaned from the still-open door and gave his pursuers a farewell salute before slumping down in the seat in front of Weathersbee. Exhausted, Washington put his head on the armrest and fell into a deep sleep. Sergeant Walker looked down at Washington and smiled, because Washington had gotten away and made the shipment; after all, Rangers were supposed to be the best at infiltrating and escaping. It had been the right call to bring his equipment along, and the men had been right to think that Washington would show up. From that day forward he was nicknamed "the Ghost" because of his ability to get in and out of tight situations. Later, after 2d Ranger Company left Korea and was sent to Japan to the 187th ARCT, Washington was assigned to Battalion Headquarters. In a few short months, while working with Japanese civilians at the camp, Sergeant Washington became fluent in Japanese.

[3 Dec 1950] RECORDS OF EVENTS SECTION

Departed Ft Benning, GA. Company en route to Camp Stoneman, Calif 0630 arr New Orleans, LA 2400 distance travel 434 miles per Hq Trp Inf Cen Ltr dtd 16 Nov 5 Company Strength: 5 off and 117 EM

3 Dec left Ft Benning Ga enroute to Camp Stoneman Calif 0530 arr New Orleans 2[4]00 distance travel 434 miles—The In Cen Ltr dtd 14 Nov 50

It took five days to get to Pittsburg, California, and Camp Stoneman. The train had Pullman railcars and porters. The men rode in double seats with their packs in the overhead racks. In the evening the porters changed the seats into double bunks. The 4th Company rode at the front of the train, followed by the kitchen cars, and then 2d Ranger Company. Once again we were seated from the rear to the front. On the long ride many Rangers wrote letters, played cards, or just looked out the windows when not napping. There were the usual high jinks— practical jokes, gambling, drinking, arguments on things like seating and bunk selection—that accompanied any long train ride for young soldiers with little to do to pass the time until the combat duty that lay ahead of them. Whenever the train stopped for servicing or to let civilian trains pass by, the Rangers had PT to ensure that they arrived at the battlefield in top condition.

In Texas, at one of the short watering and refueling stops, some local Indians put on a tribal dance for the Rangers. During another stop Ranger Weathersbee gave $20 to a porter to buy items for sandwiches at a store that would not serve blacks. The porter liked Weathersbee's idea so much that he returned his $20 and decided to use the sandwich makings he had bought to make and sell sandwiches to the Rangers at rip-off prices back on board the train. Incidents like this were yet another reality of Jim Crow days.

During the trip, Walter "Iron Head" Gray saw a huge cow standing in a corral. Iron Head called out loudly, "Look at that big cow!" Someone called to him, "That's a *buffalo*, Iron Head!" This added more lore to the Buffalo nickname, and was talked about by both 2d and 4th Companies.

After disembarking from the long train trip west, the 2d and 4th Companies spent about two and a half days at Stoneman, which was forty miles northeast of San Francisco. The site was used as a staging area and rifle range for basic troop training by the Army. Camp Stoneman was the principal jumping-off point for more than one million American soldiers destined for military operations in the Second World War's Pacific Theater, and continued to serve this purpose during the Korean War. As the San Francisco port of embarkation's primary troop staging center, the function of the post was to receive and process troops for overseas service by completing paperwork and updating records, arranging for last-minute training, providing medical and dental care, and issuing and servicing equipment.[4]

Passes were issued once we arrived at Stoneman. Corporal Samuel Payne, Jr., remembers that 2d Ranger Company received shots, had an orientation about Korea's cold weather, and participated in several fights. Lieutenant

Vincent Wilburn, who was Officer of the Day (OD) when the fistfight started, asked, "Why me?" Sergeant James Monte recalls that after the fight the men were restricted to camp, but "Lieutenant Wilburn told us where to find the hole in the fence." Oakley and Payne took their passes and went into nearby Richmond, only to turn a corner and walk into Lieutenant Allen, who had family in the Richmond area. "Aren't you guys on restriction?" he demanded. "I am taking you back to post." Oakley and Payne managed to avoid going back to Stoneman with him (again, the Rangers were trained to evade). They met some girls, and later returned to camp the way they had gotten out—through the fence. Several others went to Sergeant Cleveland Valery's house in Oakland.

Aboard the *Butner* and at Camp Zama

On 9 December 2d Ranger Company was relieved from assignment to Camp Stoneman. Rangers from the 2d and 4th Companies boarded a ferry from Stoneman to cross San Francisco Bay and then boarded the *USS General H.W. Butner*. Many, like Corporal Fields, had images of walking up a gangplank to board the ship, and were surprised to find that enormous metal doors in the side of the ship slid back so the troops could enter at dockside. Some family members, such as Sergeant Sherman Daniels' mother and sister, were waiting to see them off when they boarded the *Butner*. "It had been a wild time in that old San Francisco," remembered one Ranger, but that was behind them now. On board the *Butner* the men of the 2d and 4th Companies found themselves under the authority of the Navy, where "they take especial pleasure, it seems, in stuffing soldiers and Marines into the smallest of places."[5]

"We were on our way to Korea in December 1950 on the *Butner*," remembers Sergeant Herculano Dias, "with our brother company, the 4th Ranger Company, which was an all-white company. After we left San Francisco and got out to sea almost everyone got a Mohawk haircut from our comrades who professed to be barbers." The Ranger Mohawk haircuts served to strengthen the bond between the companies, as well as the use of the call sign "BUFFALO." Private First Class Gerald Germain missed getting a haircut because he was on guard duty.

Allen wrote to his wife Mary nearly every day. One of his letters included: "Four days out from Frisco, should arrive Pearl Harbor tomorrow. Weather on ocean has been good. No liquor or gambling allowed on board. Number of service wives and children on board. (None colored.)"[6]

At Pearl Harbor, passes were given because the ship remained overnight. Ranger Fields remembers being surprised by the stop. "There had been no indication that we would be stopping in Pearl Harbor, let alone get shore leave. I was able to see downtown Honolulu and have a good meal at a Chinese restaurant. It was hotter than blue blazes and all we had were winter uniforms."

"When we stopped in Hawaii," Ranger Dias recalled, "we were told that we could leave the ship around 10:00 a.m. and return by 7:00 a.m. the next morning." Herc continues with his recollection:

> About a dozen of us traveled together into Honolulu. We traveled together because half of us were broke and the others had money, some made by gambling aboard ship. First, we tried to rent some cars but were flatly refused. Next, we went in pursuit of something to drink. I had heard about prejudice in Hawaii from older soldiers when I was in Fort Bragg, so I discouraged the guys from trying to get into the better and more expensive bars.
>
> Here we go into town and found some bars to drink in. We (both black and white Rangers) even went to the barber shop and had the sides of our heads shaved to have a better-looking Mohawk haircut. No [racial] problems so far. Later that night, after having a good time, some of our white comrades said for us to go to a "dime-a-dance hall" that we came across. The woman at the window said, "You soldiers can go in," meaning the whites, "but you soldiers," meaning the blacks, "cannot."
>
> Of course, we all protested to no avail. Our white brothers said that if the 2d Ranger Company couldn't go in, they wouldn't go in either. I protested so bitterly about the rule that before you knew it a policeman, the same color as me, but obviously a native islander, told me to take a hike. I cursed and told him about our volunteering to go to war, but that meant nothing to him. He actually raised his billy club to hit me but was stopped by all of the Rangers. We moved on.
>
> I was still upset the next morning. As we returned to the ship I remember telling Lieutenant Allen, our CO, who was waiting at the *Butner* for us, what happened. I will never forget the feelings of anger and humiliation that were still with me that morning as I returned to the ship to sail to the

war in Korea. How could something like that happen to men who volunteered for the U.S. Army, the Paratroops, and the Airborne Rangers to go to fight in Korea? All for a lousy dime-a-dance joint.

Allen sent sets of oriental pajamas to Mary and her mother with a letter saying, "Yesterday was spent in Honolulu. Entertainers got on board . . . MC, Hawaiian band, girl vocalist, and dancer. Losing a day tomorrow. Crossing the 180th meridian sometime tonight. Will go to bed tonight on Sunday and get up tomorrow on Tuesday."

Back on board the *Butner* the Rangers had PT every day, and they gave weapons training to the other soldiers going to Korea as replacements. Corporal Fields watched 2d Ranger Company fall out for PT on the deck of the *Butner* from his vantage point above the fantail where he was on guard duty, and saw the men of 2d Ranger Company with their Mohawk haircuts doing calisthenics with the precision of a well-practiced dance team.

During the Korean War almost 600 military nurses, some black, served in military hospitals established in the Korean theater. The *Butner* carried the Rangers toward Korea and also carried members of the Women's Army Corps (WACs) headed to hospitals that would be integrated when they got to Korea, or to hospitals in Japan in direct support of the war.[7] According to Corporal Lorraine West (retired), on board the *Butner*, "The presence of the Rangers was something to behold. Amazement! They were unique. First, their uniforms—the Ike jackets—were tailored to fit. The trousers were tucked inside shined combat boots. They had athletic bodies, shiny eyes, smooth skin, young soldiers wearing the Mohawk haircut. They exuded confident self-assurance—even their stance was different. But most admirable was the camaraderie."[8] Ranger Wilburn enjoyed a dinner with Arline Haywood Wall, another WAC aboard the *Butner*, who noticed the Rangers' professionalism and patriotism.[9]

[18 Dec 50] Crossed International dateline, 9th day at sea distance traveled 475 miles.

There was always a confrontation between the Rangers and the Marine guards on board. The Marine guard detachment is usually responsible for the security on the upper decks of a troopship that might be carrying families, women, or high-ranking State Department civilians. Usually this area is "off limits" to the troops. On ship the WACs were berthed with the officers and

Department of Army Civilians (DAC), while the enlisted men were berthed on the lower deck. The Rangers were located at the fantail of the ship. "We all got together in Hawaii," remembers Corporal West, noting that the weather from San Francisco to Hawaii had been idyllic. "These particular Rangers became my friends. Our conversations were light, filled with laughter. There wasn't much talk about Korea. In fact, the scuttlebutt had it that the conflict was winding down. As we neared Japan, not only did the weather become cold and gray, but the rumors were disquieting: hordes of Chinese with horns and bugles were massing on the border separating Communist North Korea from Democratic South Korea, to join forces with the North Koreans."[10]

[24 Dec 50] 14th day at sea distance traveled 475 miles Auth par 67 SO 342 Hqs Camp Stoneman Calif. Docked Port of Yokohama Japan. Billeted Camp Zama Japan Reld from shpnt No 5458-A

"Landed in Yokohama on Christmas Eve," Lieutenant Allen wrote to his wife. "Some of the men have seen Major Gott and others from Bragg." He also told her not to worry when she received his footlocker, as he was sending home things he wouldn't need and, again, not to worry if it was some time before she got any more mail. In return, Mary Allen sent her husband a prayer book to carry with him in combat, quoting Psalm 121, her favorite, "I will lift mine eyes to the hills."

When the *Butner* arrived at Yokohama, Japan, the Rangers were entertained at dockside before the trip, via trucks, to Camp Zama. Lieutenant Queen met the ship once it docked and the Japanese tried to beg cigarettes as the trucks were driven through the narrow streets to Camp Zama.

Last-Minute Preparations

Camp Zama, Japan, had been the home base of one battalion of the 1st Cavalry Division. Before World War II, Camp Zama was the Japanese equivalent of West Point. During the Korean War, it was used as a staging area for troops sent to Korea and returning former prisoners of war (POWs). It was located about forty miles from Tokyo and was used by the American Occupation Forces as a housing area for the service personnel working in Tokyo and Yokohama and their families. The military commander of the camp was responsible for the logistical support and maintenance of Army war reserves and stocks for contingencies. In peacetime, American forces in Japan had a full range of housing, schools, and recreation services. The 4th Replacement Depot operated the transit barracks and quarters.

After the Rangers had stored their equipment they were given passes. Sergeant David "Tank" Clarke remembers, "Most of us were rather carefree and happy as we looked for women and drink. After all, we had just gotten off the boat after two weeks at sea. We made the best of almost three whole days of liberty and a rather carefree existence." Commenting more than fifty years later he admits, "The men of 2d Ranger Company had no idea what we were getting into."

The Company spent five days at Zama performing final preparations, such as drawing more cold-weather gear and test-firing and zeroing individual weapons. Orientation held in the post theater covered cold-weather survival, the enemy, the terrain, and escape and evasion (E&E) as a POW. At Zama the jump knives requisitioned by XOs Queen and Warren nearly a month earlier were distributed to the men, as were the .45-caliber pistols with shoulder holsters for most and a hip holster for Lieutenant Queen. Weapons such as BARs and LMGs were still in cosmoline, a heavy grease used to prevent rust on weapons when they are in storage. These had to be cleaned and test fired.

Zama's barracks were of the World War II type, so old that the fire warning sign read "BURNING TIME 6 MINUTES"; the latrines were in an outside building. Fourth Company was billeted on the second floor while 2d Ranger Company was on the first floor of the same barracks. Space was very limited at this small post. While in the barracks one of the 2d Company Rangers thought he had unloaded his .45, but was wrong. He accidentally fired through the ceiling above into the 4th Company area. Luckily, no one was hit. The incident was a sobering reminder of the danger of issuing pistols to everyone, because many were not used to handling them. The near-fatal fiasco stopped any more horseplay, and playing cowboy while quick-drawing on each other ceased.

"Received word today," Lieutenant Allen wrote to Mary, that they would fly to Korea the next day. "Company morale is high," he wrote, explaining that he felt his men would give a good account of themselves no matter how they were committed to battle.

[28 Dec 50] Reld fr atchmt JLC & Yokohama Command — moved to Taegu Korea, Shpmt # 40004 auth par 1 MO 229 Hq JLC & Office of CG APO 343 dtd 28 Dec 50.

Although the orders in the Morning Report were dated 28 December, the 2d Ranger Company stayed at Camp Zama until 30 December. On 30 December, about 1800 hours, 2d and 4th Companies departed Camp Zama via truck for Tachikawa Air Base. The Rangers took on full field packs; individual weapons, including pistols and knives; and LMGs. Left behind were the B-Bags, including the company desk.

Before loading onto the airplane to leave Tachikawa for Taegu, Major Richard W. "Black Daddy" Williams, who had commanded the 555th Parachute Infantry Battalion (PIB), came in from Korea and reviewed the company formation. He trooped the line and talked to the Rangers. Sergeant Estell noticed that Black Daddy was wearing the Combat Infantryman's Badge (CIB) and the ribbon indicating he had been awarded the Silver Star. Corporal James Oakley said to Estell, "Did you see Black Daddy's CIB? I'm going to get me one of those."

After Black Daddy's review, the Rangers were loaded onto planes for the last leg of their long journey to combat in Korea. Each airplane left and landed individually at K-2 airfield, Taegu. Split among a variety of aircraft, the Rangers reached their destination in piecemeal fashion. Corporal Craig Paulding remembers being on a C-54 aircraft whose pilot let Rangers come up into the cockpit and fool around with the controls. "It's a wonder that SOB didn't fall out of the sky," exclaimed Corporal Payne. On another plane, Tank Clarke recalls being given "Mae West" floatation gear and parachutes for an emergency exit in case of aircraft failure. "The chutes were manually operated—i.e., rip-chord type—which none of us were familiar with; even though we had made many practice parachute jumps, all were with static-line type chutes." With a static-line jump, the line is attached to a cable in the airplane and it opens the chute as the paratrooper jumps from the plane.

Rangers from 2d Company landed at Taegu, were placed on trucks at the airfield, and moved to the 7th Division Replacement Company. Some, like Ranger Weathersbee, traveled as part of the advance party on the lead aircraft to Korea, a C-54 on which SFC James Freeman was the senior person in rank. Corporal William Tucker recalls, "We landed about midnight but didn't get to Replacement Company until about 0300" because the truck carrying members of the advance party broke down. While waiting for a replacement truck, the Rangers used a steel entrenching tool to cut down a tree and poured gasoline on it to make a fire, but it didn't burn. They used about 55 gallons of gasoline trying to keep warm. According to Sergeant James Monte, "We were wondering why that tree wouldn't burn." When one of the Rangers spotted a Korean house with a pile of wood, he paid the South Korean owner for it. With a fire for warmth, they crawled into their sleeping bags and went to sleep. A replacement truck arrived before daybreak. When the men emerged from the sleeping bags, they found the weather "cold as hell."

"Upon arrival at Taegu," says James Fields of the main body of troops, "our gear was thrown from the aircraft to the tarmac. It was not quite dark, so we were able to find our individual equipment." The truck that was to transport Fields and others to Replacement Camp was the last in a convoy carrying Rangers. Not far into the journey north, it too suffered from mechanical failure and, according to Fields, "We could see the black-out lights of the truck we were following fade into the distance. It was extremely cold and it was some time before they came back for us. I remember thinking, *this is the way it is going to be*. Later, while heading north again we met up with some troops that had been traveling by rail on a train with the windows shot out and no heat." As the troopers were now experiencing, winter in the Korean hills was extremely cold and unforgiving.

The Replacement Company housed the 2d Ranger Company in some walled, squad-sized tents with straw on the ground. The Rangers slept in the winter sleeping bags each carried attached to his pack. The Replacement Company was located close to Division Headquarters because the division had only been out of the Hamhung evacuation about ten days and it was hurting for everything. The division band was nearby. At a 0600 formation, all were present in Korea except the four men accompanying the vehicles, orderly room, kitchen, and supply gear; they came over by ferryboat with the Company train and caught up with the Company about seven days later. The Company trains (Supply and Mess) were under the command of Supply Sergeant, Sergeant First Class Orrie Tucker and Mess Sergeant, SFC Nathan Parks. They remained at Camp Zama to bring over the materiel not carried by the troops on board the aircraft that flew them to Korea.

SFC Orrie Tucker joined the 2d Ranger Company from Company L, 3d Battalion, an all-black unit except for the COs and XOs, which was then under the command of Captain "Warm Body" Clarke. Sergeant Tucker had a rather distinct Boston accent and had moved up rapidly in the supply field. The 2d Rangers were glad to get him. He was one of a few Rangers who did not advance in rank within the Company because he was already at the top NCO rank when he left Company L. He certainly must have left a big hole in Captain Clarke's company.

Supply Sergeant Nathan Parks was unique. Sergeant Parks and Sergeant John Ford, Jr., were "golfing partners" at Bragg in the late 1940s. This was extremely unusual because it was rare for blacks to play golf, since access to courses was very limited for blacks—even in the nation's capital—during these years. Parks and Ford, in civilian attire, frequently "suckered" officers into playing against them. Both would pretend they were novice golfers. In the days long before Tiger Woods, when golf was clearly a white man's game, this was a very believable act. They would play for a dollar per hole. Since many divisional staff officers thought that they were superior in everything, they would fall for the bet and end up losing $20 to $25 on nine to eighteen holes. This was equivalent to half a month's EM jump pay at that time. (Using the U.S. Department of Labor Consumer Price Index, $20–$25 in 1949 dollars is equivalent to $150–$200 in 2003 dollars.[11])

The company trains' personnel (Supply and Mess) rode with their vehicles on the Japanese troop train to the Port of Sasebo, Japan, from Zama. They were loaded onto a Japanese ferryboat and took an overnight trip to the Port of Pusan, Korea. It was rumored they started out with fairly new trucks, but the trucks were switched on them while they were on the ferry. After landing they joined a Quartermaster Supply convoy up the X Corps main supply route (MSR) from Pusan to Taegu to Yongchon to Andong to Tanyang Pass. They caught up with the Company at Changnim-ri on about 6 January (although the Morning Report erroneously does not show their arrival until about 20 January).

The first order of business on 31 December was to get chow and ammunition. The Rangers of 2d Company ate in Replacement Company, which also fed the Division Band. They soon found out that ammo was in very short supply. The divisions coming in from the Hamhung evacuation had lost a lot of equipment and supplies. Whatever could not be carried out in one trip was burned or blown up so the enemy could not make use of it. The 2d Ranger Company scrounged up some ammo from the band—about enough to give each person one hundred rounds for small arms. They also received one case of twenty-four fragmentation grenades for the entire company.

The Rangers were impressed by the very cold weather. The bare landscape also drew their immediate attention: the hills were without vegetation and there was a noticeable lack of trees. The roads were so narrow that two vehicles could hardly pass each other. Beside the roads were deep drainage ditches, and bare rice paddies extended out beyond the ditches.

"Arrived early yesterday morning," Lieutenant Allen wrote to Mary. "Assigned to the 7th Division. At present quite a ways from the fighting. Expect to be in or near the front in the next couple of days. . . . Weather is cold but we have clothes to withstand it. The terrain here is pretty mountainous and barren. You can travel for miles without seeing a soul, then you will hit a village. It seems as if the whole population is thrown together in small settlements. I was told that we are the only Negroes in this whole Division. I don't know whether that is good or bad. So far we have been treated very nice."

The company had been told in Japan that it would be assigned to the 25th Infantry Division (ID). First Lieutenant Bernard Pryor had been sent on from Japan as an advance party of one to the 25th ID and 24th Infantry Regiment on 27 December 1950. The assignment orders to the 7th ID were changed after Pryor left, and he would not catch up with 2d Ranger Company until about 6 January 1951. The next morning, when these orders were cancelled, 2d Ranger Company prepared to move north with the 7th Division, still part of the X Corps.

Hitching a Ride into Combat

[4 Jan 51] RECORD OF EVENTS SECTION
Departed Yonchon Korea 0730 hrs by Mtr Trans arrived Andong
Korea 1700 hrs distance traveled approx 90 miles {DS...4-EM/Train}

The Rangers of 2d Company were attached to the 17th Regimental Combat Team (RCT) under the command of Colonel Herbert B. Powell, one of Colonel Van Houten's friends. On 4 January 1951, about 0700 hours, the company, with the exception of Sergeants Tucker and Parks, climbed aboard uncovered deuce-and-a-half trucks for the trip north. The division was divided into RCTs and the order of march was 17th RCT, 32d RCT, Division Arty (minus), and 31st RCT in reserve, because it had suffered the greatest losses at Chosin Reservoir. The 3d ID was shifted over to I Corps and the 2d Division and 187th ARCT (both now along defensive Line C) came under X Corps control. The 1st Marine Division reverted to 8th Army control and followed the 7th northward.

The road was in bad condition and some bridges had not been repaired, so there were bypasses near some of the larger towns. The bridge at Andong was out and there was some delay in getting through the bypass. The truck ride was long, cold, and miserable, but some heat was gathered from the packed-in bodies. A BAR gunner (BAR stood for Browning Automatic Rifle or, more frequently, Bad-Ass Ranger) and weapon were placed over each vehicle cab top in the ready position. Sergeant Tank Clarke was a BAR operator assigned to ride in Lieutenant Allen's jeep, along with SFC William Lanier, Communications Sergeant. According to Clarke, "The one thing most of the men will remember is the convoy north and all the refugee columns moving south, crowding the road, getting in the way, so that our vehicles could hardly move."

The distance covered was difficult and long because most of the route, which was rugged and in need of repair, had been designated one-way, with MPs posted to enforce the rules. Only at certain designated areas could convoys coming south to the supply depots pass by. At night, all units buttoned up because of guerrilla activity. Everything that moved beyond the outpost lines was in the free-fire zone.

As the convoy passed through the "S" curve of Tanyang Pass, Corporal Paulding noticed some American dead and a burned-out tank just off the road. One body was by the tank turret and another was beside the road. "When we got up to the schoolhouse, there were some dead near the latrine or a building in the back," Sergeant Estell recalled. "They were hanging up, head down, by their heels. First Platoon Sergeant James Freeman was getting us ready for the battlefield by having us view them."

PART II

War had taken a heavy toll on Korea by the time the 2d Ranger Company arrived on the peninsula at the end of December 1950. Fighting had been going on there since North Korean forces first crossed the 38th parallel on 25 June 1950. The South Koreans, completely unprepared for the assault, were initially routed. Seoul, the South Korean capital, fell on the third day of the attack, as the South Korean Army retreated across the Han River. Meanwhile, the United Nations took action. The Security Council condemned the North Korean attack and called on member nations to send military aid to the South Korean Republic. The United States responded by sending advisors and what land, sea, and air forces it had immediately available, but it too had not been prepared for the North Korean attack. The majority of the regiments on occupation duty in Japan were poorly trained and vastly under-strength. The 7th Infantry Division was sent to Korea about forty percent strength, and utilized South Korean citizens drafted by President Syngman Rhee, who was living in exile in Japan with about one million Korean citizens. In a letter to General Douglas MacArthur dated 14 July 1950, Rhee granted him "command authority over all land, sea, and air forces of the Republic of Korea during the period of the continuation of the present state of hostilities."[12] These forces helped slow the North Korean advance and establish a defensive perimeter around the city of Pusan, at the southernmost tip of the peninsula.

The war turned decisively in favor of South Korea and the United Nations on 15 September, when the X Corps, under the direction of General Douglas MacArthur, successfully landed at Inchon. This landing placed a large American force on the Korean peninsula behind the main North Korean army fighting around Pusan, forcing the North Koreans to retreat. Once the Americans and South Koreans had battered the enemy back across the 38th parallel by the end of September 1950, the decision was made to use the momentum of success to invade the North and reunite the Koreas.

Accordingly, UN forces continued the attack across the 38th parallel, and by 25 October had pushed the North Korean army as far north as the Yalu River at the Chinese border. It looked like the war would be over before the 2d Ranger Company completed its training at Fort Benning during the last week of November 1950.

It was then that the war took a grave turn for the free world when Chinese soldiers poured across the border to engage UN forces and aid the North Koreans in their fight. At this point the 2d Rangers were nearing completion of their training at Fort Benning. The assault forced UN and US troops to retreat steadily south, and by the time the 2d Rangers arrived in Japan the troops in support of South Korea had fallen back to the Pusan Perimeter. When the Rangers arrived in Korea, the combined Chinese and North Korean army continued pushing Americans, South Koreans, and other allied forces southward on the peninsula.

Chapter 4

First Combat Action,
Outside Tanyang Pass, 7 January 1951

"I have one criticism of Negro Troops who fought under my command in the Korean War. They didn't send me *enough* of them."

— General Douglas MacArthur[13]

"Americans are a different breed of cats from others, they have a sense of responsibility, pride, integrity, ability, that the Negro does not possess."

— General Edward M. Almond[14]

When the 2d Ranger Company arrived in Korea, the CCF Intervention, which began on 3 November 1950, was in its third month. The company's first assignment was to protect an important rail line running through central Korea at Tanyang Pass. This rail line allowed essential supplies to travel to the UN forces (specifically, IX Corps units) fighting farther north. Those units were battling to halt the Communist Chinese forces that were attempting to push UN forces off the peninsula and bring South Korea under complete Communist domination.

Before the trip to Tanyang Pass, 2d Ranger Company made some personnel promotions. Private Joseph L. Bruce, Jr., was promoted to Private First Class, and seven enlisted men—Thomas M. Burse, Norman H. Collins, Curtis Courts, Lester L. Garland, Walter S. "Ironhead" Gray, Ellsworth Harris, and Lawrence "Poochie" Williams—who were still listed as Ranger recruits, were promoted to Private (E-2). These were the first promotions made under combat conditions. The CO could promote men up to Private First Class. Most of 2d Ranger Company's promotions were made on 7th Division special orders. Although the company failed to take full advantage of the liberal promotion policy allowing troops to get promoted after thirty days of satisfactory action in a TO&E slot, promotions still worked out rather well, except for a few men who were already at the top of their TO&E positions.

Combat Action at Tanyang Pass

At 0730 hours 5 January, the Company boarded trucks and moved north to Changnim-ni. The unit arrived about 1000 hours after traveling a distance of forty miles. The unit was assigned a perimeter around the 17th Regimental Aid Station and just north of Tanyang Pass. At this time the Army was so short of doctors that the two surgeons assigned to the 17th Regimental Aid Station were Navy doctors on detached service from a Navy cruiser off the east coast of Korea. The Rangers' mission was to provide protection for the aid station, provide security on the northern flank of the MP outpost, and hunt down guerillas in the area who could raid the MSR. The company immediately took up position and platoon-sized patrols were sent out within a one-half to one-mile radius. The rules were no movement outside the perimeter, and no vehicle travel after dark except for strict, pre-authorized travel with specific route and time designations.

On the night of 6 January, 2d Ranger Company was in position in a small village known as Changnim-ri, just south of Tanyang Pass. At this time the company was assigned the mission of guarding the northern end of Tanyang Pass, which was a choke point on the MSR to the central front and the X Corps. When the Rangers arrived there, they were immediately sent out on patrols into the surrounding hills. Captain Allen and Lieutenant Queen reported to the 17th CP for a briefing. Their jeep, driven by Corporal Lester Garland, also carried Sergeant Lanier, Communications Chief, who radioed back to the aid station and the company. Nonetheless, when returning after dark, they were fired upon by the northernmost outpost. Luckily no one was hit, and everyone learned a lesson about movement in the combat zone and the importance of clear communication with outpost personnel.

Sergeant Herman "Cat Eyes" Jackson, 3d Squad Leader of 1st Platoon (under the command of 1st Lieutenant Bernard "Eyes" Pryor and Sergeant First Class James E. "Cigarette" Freeman) was assigned an outpost position with half of his squad. Jackson and his men had come in from patrolling the mountains and were very tired from the climb. The Rangers always made a point of patrolling from the highest point, so that if attacked they would have

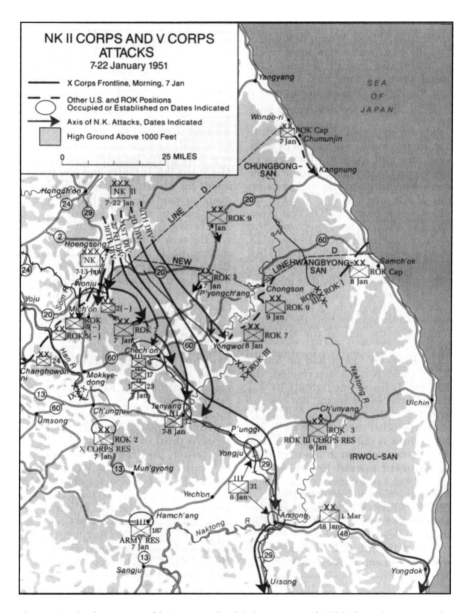

NK II CORPS AND V CORPS ATTACKS
7-22 January 1951

the tactical advantage of being on the highest ground. This location not only gave them a better view, but also provided a clear field of fire.

The sun was going down when Jackson's squad was ordered to defend the tunnel road. The tunnel was directly above the medical aid station and led north to the town of Tanyang. Jackson's squad was to protect the area at night. In addition to Jackson, the squad included James Carroll; Corporal Virgil J.

Collins, Assistant Squad Leader; Sergeant David "Tank" Clarke, BAR man; Sergeant Curtis Courts, radio telephone operator; and Corporal Richard H. Glover, rifleman. The men moved into position and remained until about 2100 hours, when they moved back and joined the other half of the squad. The enemy had pinpointed their location. From this fallback position, they still had the tunnel in sight, and in fact could see through the tunnel.

Jackson sat at the head of the squad, his legs crossed and a rifle in his lap. He remained in that position for three hours until about 2400. In the early hours of 7 January, the 2d Ranger Company experienced its first contact with the enemy since arriving in Korea on 30 December 1950. The enemy was closing in to infiltrate the Tanyang area, block the pass, and disrupt the flow of supplies to the front. Glover, in position just a few feet from Jackson, spotted a Korean soldier crawling beside Jackson under the protection of the ditch that ran along the road. Glover lifted his rifle and fired, hitting the enemy at least twice.

A scattering of shots were fired. "Tank" Clarke threw a white phosphorous (WP) grenade. If he had thrown a fragmentation grenade, it would have hit some of the squad members in the ditch. The WP ignited the roofs of nearby shacks, lighting up the whole area. Glover and Courts leaped over the bank and joined the rest of the squad. There were now four men on the other side of the bank; Jackson was the last man to make the leap. Once on the safer side of the bank, Jackson counted his men and found everyone present. All around them, however, the crust of the frozen snow and ice was cracking with the sound of people running on its surface. Every Ranger in the squad knew the noise wasn't 2d Ranger Company moving; it was the enemy closing in on their position.

Jackson spread out his squad to form a line about ten yards long. When they were in proper position, enemy could be heard running toward their front and both flanks—the enemy was everywhere. Jackson's squad opened up, spraying the area with heavy fire. By now, it was between 0300 and 0400 hours. The heavy defensive fire held back the probing enemy infantry.

Sergeant Jesse "Babe" Anderson brought half a squad into the area to relieve Jackson. Once off the line, Jackson looked for the place where Glover had shot the enemy. They found blood and evidence that the enemy had dragged their wounded man away. Jackson and his men followed the red trail to the village, where Jackson interrogated an old Korean man, pointing to the blood on the snow that had led them to him. The Korean made a motion, shaking his arms like he was a chicken. Jackson knew this was a damn lie. All that blood in the snow could not have come from killing a chicken. The old man and his family were hiding the guerrilla! This guerrilla had gotten so close that if Jackson had stood up he could have touched the enemy soldier in the center of his back. That's how close the enemy was able to get to this squad of Rangers. In fact, when Anderson relieved Jackson's squad, he found two live enemy grenades lying nearby in the snow. Had it not been for Glover's vigilance and marksmanship, the whole squad might have been wiped out.

Sergeant First Class Isaac E. Baker's outpost was positioned near the road close to the old schoolhouse building. The only man with Baker was Sergeant Edward Posey, armed with a BAR. At the squad CP three other men were concealed in a large crater hole. About 0500 hours, one of the men noticed a light in a hut north of the outpost. The few locals remaining in the village had been warned about lights and movement at night, so Baker issued a warning and fired a shot into the hut to extinguish the light. Under the cover of darkness, Communist guerrillas had sneaked into the town to attempt a move along the ditch beside the road toward the Ranger positions. Now, they simply attacked the Company position, mainly from the north, where they had infiltrated between the Artillery and 17th CPs farther north along the road. Their fire was returned by the 2d Platoon, which was occupying that sector.

Baker and Posey left the squad CP and started moving forward down the road to reinforce the squad's position. They were promptly met by a number of enemy infantry pouring out of the village. Posey encountered two enemy, who opened fire on him and on Baker. Posey aimed his BAR, killed his first two enemy soldiers, and continued to the squad position on the road in front of the village. What Posey was unaware of was that Baker had been fatally wounded. He would only learn of Baker's death after the firefight ended. Baker died at daylight, just before a helicopter could fly to a mobile Army surgical hospital (MASH). Unfortunately, during these early days of the helicopter, its flight ceiling and weight capacity were very limited, especially in cold weather. Captain Allen and Lieutenant Queen, meanwhile, ran from the Company CP to that sector to assess the unfolding situation. First Sergeant Lawrence D. West was told to notify Regiment that Baker was dead, which he did with an SCR-300 radio. As the men learned the hard way, death came quickly in Korea.

The unit also learned the need for constant security at Outpost 3. This outpost was on a small knob, about 150 yards to the west and in the rear of the 17th RCT Aid Station. Sergeant First Class William Hargrove, as Assistant Squad Leader of the 3d Squad, 2d Platoon (Lieutenant Vincent Wilburn and Master Sergeant "Dude" Walker commanding), was stationed at the outpost, facing west. Sergeant Hargrove had with him Privates First Class (PFCs) Julius Victor, Wheeler Small, Jr., Craig "Lil Man" Paulding, and George Thomas. They had one LMG, two BARs, one M–1, and one carbine. Each Ranger also carried a .45 caliber pistol, and several grenades were at their position.

The mission for this group was to: (1) guard the rear approach down the railroad tracks, (2) guard the tunnel entrance, and (3) guard the trail over the hill into the village of Tanyang. Outpost reports were required every thirty minutes and were made by calling into the Company CP via power telephone land line. Some of the telephone lines were laid to each outpost on a common party line, so that most of the outposts could listen to, and talk with, each other. At this time Wilburn was on duty in the CP, receiving the reports.

About 0530 hours Hargrove reported that he heard movement in the vicinity of his position but could not see anyone. Wilburn checked with nearby Outpost 2, but they had nothing to report. About 0545, just as it was getting lighter, Hargrove spotted a group of enemy soldiers approaching from the direction of the tunnel. He opened fire with his machine gun and dispersed the enemy. The firing alerted the rest of the men in the company, who started moving into their positions. Meanwhile, Hargrove's LMG, however, froze up after it had fired the first couple of rounds. He instructed Small and Victor to open up with their BARs. Victor fired approximately two magazines before he stopped, frozen solid. (It was during this engagement that the Rangers learned that a regular coat of oil caused a weapon to freeze in very cold weather and that, contrary to normal procedures, weapons should be only lightly wiped with oil under intensely cold conditions.) With their automatic weapons frozen, PFCs Paulding and Thomas exchanged fire with an enemy force of unknown strength using their individual weapons. At least one of the enemy soldiers slipped in close enough to pitch a fragmentation grenade into the outpost position, wounding Small and Paulding. Small was hit in three places and Paulding was temporarily blinded by the explosion. Realizing that the enemy knew his exact position and outnumbered his crippled force, Hargrove ordered his men to withdraw to the reverse slope of the hill, and then quickly administered first aid to Small and Paulding. While all this was transpiring, Thomas began throwing hand grenades over the hill at the unseen enemy.

Meanwhile, Lieutenant Queen, Sergeant John "Rigger" Ford, Sergeant Marion "Mighty Mouth" Alston, Master Sergeant "Dude" Walker, and a litter team from the medics had worked their way from the rear of the aid station to the bottom of the knob. There they met Hargrove and his outpost group. The litter team carried Small, while Victor and Thomas walked to the aid station on their own. While under sniper fire from nearby higher ground, Hargrove returned with Queen's group to re-occupy the knob. The entire action lasted about twenty to thirty minutes.

About the same time, Outpost 5 and Road Block "Able" were also attacked. Road Block "Able," under the command of Lieutenant Pryor, had been taking intermittent fire all morning, and at daybreak the Rangers manning that outpost were forced to take to the hills with only light combat gear. When they tried to re-enter the perimeter without first calling in, the personnel of Road Block "Able" drew small arms fire.

By 0700 hours the company occupied the perimeter in force. The earlier enemy efforts were nothing more than light probing actions. The main attack arrived about this time from north of the village of Changnim-ni, adjacent to and north of the perimeter. At 0715 hours the 32d RCT around Tanyang Pass, in response to the 2d's reports, also reported that it was under attack. Enemy strength appeared to be as high as one hundred soldiers.

Road Block "Baker" had not been heard from since 0600 hours because its radio battery had succumbed to the cold temperatures and quit two hours earlier. (More lessons learned: during cold weather the radio battery's life was shortened by about one-third, the battery had to be changed frequently, and the radio operator could not set the radio down in the snow. In the future, the Rangers mounted the SCR–300 on a pack board to keep it out of the snow. This also allowed the convenient carrying of other essential combat accouterments, and enabled easier carrying and handling.) When the Rangers stationed at Road Block Baker were fired upon, they returned fire at the guerrillas attempting to slip into the village.

By daylight, about 0745 hours, the guerillas were driven off without any penetration. A patrol was sent into town. Heavy patrolling continued around the town and in the hills. Intelligence reports later indicated that the enemy had been of the 1st Guerrilla Division, 5th Guerrilla "Ghost Corps."

The Tanyang fight was 2d Ranger Company's first direct confrontation with the enemy. A declassified report[15] from the 32d Infantry Regiment of the 7th Infantry Division boiled down the Rangers' combat at Tanyang this way: "The main event of 7 January 1951, was the attack of the North Korean guerrillas on Tanyang. At 2345, 6 Jan., 20 unidentified Koreans approached Road Block "A." The Rangers fired on them and they dispersed. Then at 0530 small arms and automatic weapons fire started in the South part of Tanyang and shortly after fighting had broken out all over town."

For his part in the action, Sergeant Hargrove was recommended for the Bronze Star.

During the next few days several Rangers were hospitalized due to cold weather injuries. Ranger Wheeler Small, who was wounded at the railroad tunnel outpost, recalled:

> I was more concerned about riding the ambulance back down the mountain road than I was about the injuries. The road was so narrow that only vehicles going in one direction were allowed on the road, at any one time. Sometimes the convoys or any single vehicle was ambushed. I would not let them put me in the ambulance without my weapon. I was the only American in it; the others were Koreans. We got stopped several times by sniper fire. When we reached the field hospital, I was the only one alive.

But he *was* alive. Sergeant First Class Isaac E. Baker, however, was not. Baker was the company's first man killed in action (KIA)—which, as it turned out, he had predicted.

Baker's Prediction

In 1948, before going into combat in Korea, Sergeant First Class Baker taught drill and tactical field training for the dismounted soldier at Fort Bragg. He trained, among others, SGM William Bates of the 558th Medical Collecting Company. Judging that his best path to a promotion was with an airborne unit, Baker went to Jump School and found his way to 2d Ranger Company.

When the 2d Ranger Company landed at Yokohama and received passes from Camp Zama, Baker headed for the Cross Roads NCO Club in Yokohama. The 558th had left Bragg as a unit for deployment with the mission of taking all wounded soldiers on the flight from Korea to Japan. Baker knew that the 558th medics had arrived in Japan and would have found a friendly bar. Baker went looking for, and found, Bates. Baker told Bates he had no money because he had bought his son a dry cleaning business in the States as a source of income. Bates tried to buy Baker a drink, but he refused. He didn't drink anymore, he wasn't hungry, and he was really just there for the companionship. "I don't think I am going to make it back," he told Bates. "My time is up! If I don't go to

Korea on Wednesday, I'll see you back here on Saturday." But he went to Korea. And it was the last time Bates saw Baker alive.[16]

Majori-Ri

The declassified command report of the 32d Infantry[17] relates enemy activity on 10 January 1951. A division artillery aerial observer reported three companies of enemy infantry moving south through the mountains east of Tanyang. The 32d Infantry's Intelligence and Reconnaissance (I&R) Platoon exchanged long-range fire with ten to fifteen enemy near Pyongdong-ni. The 3/32 was relieved by the 1/31 coming up from the south near Andong by 1200 hours. The 3/32 was reinforced with a platoon of tanks, a 4.2mm mortar platoon, and Battery C, 48th Field Artillery Battalion, which moved to blocking positions northeast of Tanyang, to meet the 10th North Korean Division.

During the period of 11 to 13 January, heavy enemy contact continued around Tanyang, with estimated enemy strength at battalion-to-regimental-sized units. On 13 January, the 1/32, minus Company C, moved east-northeast from the aid station near Changnim-ni toward Majori-ri. The battalion came in on the move, with only a brief attack order issued. The order of march down the trail toward Majori-ri was Company B first, followed by the command group and the Rangers. Queen separated from 2d Ranger Company to guide Company A along the north ridge line in an attempt to outflank the village where an estimated enemy battalion was located. Queen knew the terrain because he had led patrols over that same route the previous week. His assistance was needed because Company A lacked maps and was unfamiliar with the terrain. Queen noticed that the unit seemed to arrive late and the men were carrying full field packs with pup tents attached. They did not drop any individual equipment, in stark contrast to Queen, who knew the advantages of traveling light and had only an M-1 with an extra bandoleer and a blanket cut like a Mexican serape for shelter. Queen did not see the battalion 81mm mortars go into position, and the trail was too narrow for 75mm Recoilless Rifle movement. The men of Company A had great difficulty climbing and moved in single file.

As the rest of 2d Ranger Company prepared for combat on that cold January morning, nearly every man was double loaded with ammunition because it was so difficult to re-supply in such mountainous terrain. As one of the 1st Platoon BAR operators, "Tank" Clarke carried his weapon and helped carry ammo for the 60mm mortar. The Rangers moved for a few miles along a railroad track that made it difficult to walk, which made the miserable march that much harder.

On the evening prior to the attack, a patrol of several Rangers moved up into the mountains and fired on some Koreans to their left front. The enemy did not appear to take any casualties. The men ate cold C rations before bedding down in the snow. According to Clarke, they were too cold and tired to try to chop through the frozen ground. The next day they awoke, stiff and freezing cold, and headed out to meet the enemy.

The Rangers followed Company B down into a valley, slipping and sliding all the way. Traversing the mountain single file, they came to a village. As they approached the small collection of huts, they passed some dead cattle and a few dead civilians. Either the civilians had gotten in the way of the conflict or they were dead guerrillas from the previous days' air strikes or artillery fire—it was impossible to know which. Making their way up a ravine, the Rangers came upon some young civilian men. The word was out: young Korean men who were not in the army or in uniform were either guerrillas or deserters. Some of the men from Baker Company or Battalion were ordered to guard them closely and, if in doubt, shoot them. The Koreans were shot down while trying to escape, and the Rangers never gained any intelligence from them, which they would later regret. What Battalion headquarters did not know was that the enemy may have been watching as their men were killed.

The squad that Clarke was with moved farther up the valley while Baker Company started to climb the slope toward the huts. They had just seen some North Koreans killed while hiding behind a haystack. Without warning, a sharp small arms fire broke out and hit Baker Company squarely in the front. Private Frank King, Jr., was sitting on top of a rock eating a can of beans when a bullet struck him. Tucker heard Koreans screaming "Banzai! Banzai!" as King keeled over. Private First Class Herman L. Rembert was a few yards behind Sergeant Jackson, who was leading 1st Platoon. Rembert was hit in the chest and killed. Sergeant Harold Johnson, assistant squad leader to Sergeant First Class Daniel Boatwright, 3d Platoon, was hit in the helmet and right leg. With one man killed and several wounded in a handful of seconds, Jackson, Clarke, and the others took cover behind a large boulder. They could not see the enemy, but they could hear his gunfire. With a large rock protecting them, Clarke and about six other men in his group took stock of their situation and returned fire.

Sergeant First Class Freeman, 1st Platoon Sergeant, yelled "put some fire on the hills!" Clarke and Corporal Lawrence "Poochie" Williams did as ordered, blazing away with their BARs. Clarke removed the bi-pod from his weapon during the firefight because the enemy always went after the automatic weapons; his BAR was a less conspicuous target without the bi-pod. Members of the squad set up the mortar as best as they could without a base plate and dumped all the rounds toward the enemy on the surrounding hills. Despite the heavy return fire, bullets rained down around the boulder position, which did not give as much protection as the Rangers had hoped. As they also quickly discovered, some of the enemy fire was coming from behind the boulder.

It was at this time that Williams was struck in the head. He was killed immediately. His corpse almost dropped on top of Clarke, who heard Jackson yell, "Sergeant Freeman, Poochie got hit in the head!" There was nothing they could do for him. The bullet that hit Williams entered the top of his head and came out in front of his eye. Williams hated wearing a steel helmet, and wasn't wearing one when he was hit. Some of the men wondered later whether a helmet might have saved his life, but there was no time to think of such things in the heat of battle. Shortly after Willams was killed, Jackson had a bullet rip open the tip of his chin, and Glover, who was on Jackson's left, was hit in the neck. Glover was soon hit a second time in the neck, this time fatally. Just then another man near Clarke, Private First Class Robert St. Thomas, was struck in the foot. His feet were so cold that he could hardly feel the wound. St. Thomas peeled back his shoe-pack and asked Clarke, "Is that a bullet hole?" Clarke assured him that it was indeed a bullet hole.

With two men killed and several wounded, the squad spread out because its position behind the boulder was drawing too much enemy fire. By this time Clarke had used up all but one magazine of ammo and had lost contact with the ammo bearers, one of whom was Corporal Isaiah Woodard. Men were still being hit all around Clarke. He had saved the last magazine to use for covering fire in a retreat. That time arrived when some of Company B came down the valley yelling *everybody out!*

Clarke was certain that St. Thomas had gotten out safely, but he was mistaken. As he would later learn, St. Thomas was killed in action. The last time Clarke remembered seeing him alive was when he commented on the bullet hole in his foot. Moving back, Jackson ran across a rice paddy as enemy bullets sprayed the ground around his feet. When he spotted a large ditch he jumped into it for safety and crawled up the bank. Standing no more than ten yards from him was a Korean shooting to his left. The enemy soldier did not see Jackson, who leveled down on him and squeezed off two rounds before his carbine jammed. Jackson later recalled that St. Thomas was positioned in the direction the enemy was firing; he was sure the Korean was shooting at St. Thomas.

The shower of enemy gunfire continued. During the withdrawal Clarke passed Corporal J. T. Holley, who had been hit in the back and could not move. Holley was asking Clarke to help him to cover (he refused to leave the fight) when Sergeant Boatwright was hit twice. Clarke helped Boatwright gain shelter beneath a ledge but, thinking they would regroup and counterattack, left Holley where he was. Unfortunately, they did not regroup as Clarke expected. Instead, the North Koreans moved in and executed the seriously wounded—the same way they perceived their own men had been executed at the start of the skirmish. Although Rangers are not supposed to leave their wounded behind, the CO had ordered their immediate withdrawal. On the way out, Dude Walker was providing covering fire with an M-1 rifle, yelling, "Come on out. I got you covered!" Clarke realized his error regarding Holley too late to rectify it. It was a mistake that haunted him for a long time. Had he understood the situation, they could have tried to drag Holley out against his wishes.

Up on the ridge, the Rangers regrouped and gathered some of their walking wounded. Lieutenant Bernard Pryor, 1st Platoon Leader, staggered up. He had been hit at the top of the head and blood was streaming down his face. The bullet had gone through the top of his helmet and skimmed his scalp. The Rangers tried to get him on a litter but he refused. After a few moments, he collapsed and several South Korean porters carried him to the aid station.

After they broke contact with the enemy, the Rangers began to dig in for defense. They knew the Koreans would counterattack. Clarke, who was still out of ammo for the BAR, began to empty M-1 clips to fill BAR magazines. They dug in and the fighting went on into the night as the enemy counterattacked, but Company B held the enemy off with machine gun and small arms fire.

At the Aid Station

Weathersbee, who had badly sprained an ankle during an earlier patrol, was due to be evacuated but received permission from Lieutenant Allen to stay on light duty at the aid station. When the aid station was attacked, he and others repelled the enemy. Before the attack, Robert St. Thomas, one of the Company's cooks, had come in, loaded himself down with ammo, and yelled,

"I'm going up into the mountains." He volunteered for the mission and did not return. Once the wounded started coming in, Sergeant Teedie P. Andres moved from man to man, performing his duties as a medic. Weathersbee heard him say, "They are all dead." One of the dead was St. Thomas.

Much later, William "the Ghost" Washington arrived at the aid station with an injury to his hand. He told Weathersbee that he had had to play dead while North Korean guerrillas stripped him of his boots and tried to cut his wedding band from his finger. As artillery shells started falling, the Ghost—true to his nickname—got up, returned to friendly lines, and made it to the aid station.

When Lieutenant Queen heard of the firefight over the radio and learned that Captain Allen was wounded, he rushed back from Company A, which never got into the fighting. Queen went to the aid station to pick up those Rangers who had been left behind or who, like Washington, had been treated and were ready to go back into combat. He also picked up all of the ammo at the aid station and took command of the company, placing the 1st Platoon on the ridge line perimeter facing east, where he had left Company A.

Wounded men such as Pryor were evacuated by helicopter, which set down about five miles from the aid station where the altitude was low enough for it to land. The less-seriously wounded were sent by ambulance to the closest MASH.

The next day, the Rangers learned that sixteen men from Company B had been killed at Majori-ri, and one wounded soldier from Company B was carried from the fighting with his guts protruding from a wound and tied to a pole, but miraculously survived his injuries. Eight Rangers were declared KIA: Corporals Richard Glover, J. T. Holley, Milton Johnson, and Lawrence Williams; PFCs Frank King, Jr., Charles Scott, and Robert St. Thomas; and Private Herman L. Rembert. Both Pryor, who was shot in the head, and Estell, whose right arm was seriously injured when a bullet shattered the bone, were removed from the area and evacuated by helicopter.

The Morning Reports made out in Division Rear and signed by Warrant Officer Junior Grade Pilgrim listed eight 2d Company Rangers among the wounded: Sergeants First Class (SFCs) Daniel Boatwright, Harold Johnson, and William Lanier; Sergeants Teedie P. Andres, Lawrence Estell, and William E. Thomas; and PFCs Legree Aikens and James R. Davis, Jr. Not included were Corporal James Fields, who was evacuated after the Majori-ri firefight with delayed frostbite, and Lieutenant Warren Allen, CO, who was seriously wounded. Allen was taken to the aid station but chose not to be evacuated. He remained at his post with the company while his wounds were treated by the company medics.

In Special Order Number 11, the 32d Infantry awarded the Combat Medical Badge to four medical aid men of the 2d Ranger Company and the Combat Infantry Badge to five officers and 108 enlisted men of 2d Ranger Company. On 16 January, the Rangers were attached to the 2/31st after just forty-eight hours with the 1/32d Infantry. As they marched out, they passed a lot of dead communists.

Many of the WACs who had traveled on the *Butner* with the Rangers of 2d Company, including Corporal Lorraine West, were stationed at Yokohama and would see Rangers when they were on R&R or, if wounded, at the Yokohama hospital. According to West:

> The Korean Conflict became a reality when the wounded arrived. The first casualties were frostbites. There were very few WACs who were not touched by the loss of friends or loved ones. The Rangers came to Yokohama for R&R in varying shifts, so we kept in touch. It was always a reunion and it was always a good time, but they had changed. The skin was ashy, the Mohawk haircut gone, no longer sleek, the eyes dull but alert. The tone was quieter, with little or no discussion of battles. They told about the severity of the weather, the usual chow comments, the terrain, and how good it felt to have the comforts and pleasures Yokohama offered. The fatigue remained. The camaraderie remained. The pride remained. They were warriors.[18]

Through Tanyang to Chechon-Ni

The Morning Report of 17 January relates a twelve-mile march made in four hours from Changnim-ni north to Tanyang, which has to be an error. It is unlikely we averaged three miles per hour with winter combat gear, in extreme cold vapor barrier rubber boots (called Mickey Mouse boots) while battling such cold weather. The real distance is estimated at three to five miles, which is a much more realistic movement by foot under those conditions.

The Morning Report of 19 to 20 January shows that the Company trains (Supply and Mess Sections) joined the Company at Tanyang when, in reality, they had arrived almost two weeks earlier (7 to 8 January) at Changnim-ni (aid station). By 24 January, the Company was still in Tanyang and had more non-battle casualties going into the hospital—primarily colds, pneumonia, and frostbite to hands and feet—than wounded returning. So the present-for-duty strength was soon down to seventy enlisted men. Errors and delayed entries were common in the Morning Reports because they were made out by Division Rear every day, while the report made out in the Company tactical CP was disregarded. Since Division Rear based the Morning Reports on medical admissions and discharge reports that were frequently incorrect, the Morning Reports often did not reflect the true status of the Company.

The declassified Command Report of the 32d Infantry for 29 January[19] indicates that the 2d Rangers moved from attachment to the 32d to attachment to the 17th Infantry, when they moved on to Chechon. Upon reaching Chechon, Weathersbee came off quarters and rejoined the 2d Platoon, which went into the mountains with a Korean unit. Unfortunately, the South Korean unit moved out of the area during the night without notifying anyone—including the Rangers.

Many Rangers reported that soldiers were evacuated through the 144th Field Hospital for frostbite. (Being in a combat action, they were considered later to have been WIA.) This was becoming a widespread problem.

The Korean Frostbite Dilemma

By January 1951, the 8th Army had suffered 1,791 cases of frostbite, and the 121st Evac Hospital, Youngung-Po, had handled 850 cases. The incidence rate among the troops was 34 per 1,000. It soon became necessary to open a cold injury treatment center at Osaka Army Hospital, Japan.

Black soldiers suffered more than whites, even in integrated units where the differences in motivation, training, and discipline were minimal. Lower-ranked soldiers, especially privates and privates first class, suffered beyond their proportional numbers. There were more casualties in combat units than in support units. Also, younger (eighteen to twenty-four years) soldiers appeared to be more susceptible than men over twenty-five. This may have been due to the lack of self-discipline and false beliefs. Soldiers from the warmer states were more subject to cold injury than those from the colder and northern states. The winter cold also took a heavy toll among the Chinese POWs, of whom ninety percent appeared to have varying degrees of frostbite. American footgear, the shoe-pack, didn't provide the protection needed during active combat because

use of dry, clean socks, insoles, and foot massages were impossible to carry out, either on the move or at temporary, uncertain halts for those in the foxholes.

The weather was bitterly cold, fed by the bone-wracking wind from the north that penetrated the combat clothing left over from WWII. The 7th Division at the Chosin Reservoir area treated one hundred seventy four frostbites, of which eighty-three were from the 31st Infantry. The 1/32d attached to the 31st suffered the most casualties, although only eighteen of them were unable to quickly return to combat. More than two hundred men were hospitalized by the U.S. Navy medics. A typical case of only twelve hours' exposure might require toe amputations, closure, and grafting, with up to one hundred days' hospitalization.

Water-soluble medicines froze; plasma had to be warmed for almost an hour to be usable. Even Colonel Chauncey E. Dovell, 8th Army Surgeon, suffered frostbitten feet while visiting the 2d Infantry Division. Senior medical officers knew the same thing had taken place during the Battle of the Bulge in the winter of 1944-1945, when some 46,000 Allies fell victim to the weather. The Far East Command knew of the severe Korean winters from the American Occupation Forces' experiences in 1945-1946, but was still unprepared.

Buffaloes Move Farther North with Another RCT

Second Company remained at about seventy percent strength present for duty during the period of 1 through 10 February. The company was in Chuch'on-ni, Korea, having arrived there via a motor march of twenty miles in six hours from Tanyang. On 11 February, the 2d got its first completely new man, Sergeant Stewart Strothers, who was neither a Ranger nor a paratrooper. An ordinary soldier who arrived via the regular Army pipeline, Strothers was originally from Pittsburgh, Pennsylvania, and had been a pre-med or pharmacy student. The first non-jumper assigned to the unit, 2d Ranger Company made him third medic and was glad to get him because it was so under-strength.

On 6 February, a request for a spot check of Ranger performance from the Pentagon reached Eighth Army and was passed down to the appropriate division CGs. Major General Claude B. Ferenbaugh followed it up with comments regarding 2d Ranger Company on 30 July, 1951:

> During this period you were faced with many difficult and daring assignments. You participated in steady, large-scale advances, tactical

withdrawals followed by counter-attacks and pursuit of the enemy, and countless patrols.

You were handicapped at times by the lack of replacements for your combat losses but at the same time willingly accepted responsibilities of the missions normally assigned to an infantry rifle company with twice the number of personnel.

It as by virtue of superior leadership, unusual courage, and dogged determination on the part of each of you that you were consistently able to accomplish each mission and secure each objective with dispatch, honor and distinction.

Your outstanding cooperation, devotion to duty, aggressiveness, and esprit has been a constant source of satisfaction to me ever since I assumed command of the Division. Your departure is a distinct loss and will be felt keenly by all of us who remain.

[11 Feb 51] GAINS
Strothers Stewart ER 13259657Pvt2300 RaceN
Dtd of enl Jun 48 term of enl 3 yrs ETS Jun 51 O/S sv 11 dt elig ret
US Aug 52 asdg & jd fr 7th Repl Co 7th Inf Div APO 301 Par 33
SO 38 Hq 7th Inf Div APO 7

[18 Feb 51] RECORD OF EVENTS
Reld fr atchd 32rd RCT and atch 17th RCT departed Chechon by mtr march arrived Kum-a-ri approx 1000 hrs distance 8 miles

[20 Feb 51] GAINS
Buford, David TRA16180797Sgt5745
Asgd and jd eff 17 Feb 51 fr 7th Repl Co 7th Inf Div APO 7
Par 35 SO 34 Hq 7th Inf Div APO 7 dtd 16 Feb 51 add Info unk

RECORD OF EVENTS
Departed Kum——ri ———- hrs Arrived village of Chunchon-ni 1100
Hrs Advance with 17th RCT village of Chuchon 0900 hrs
Entered village 1100 hrs slight enemy resistance 2 enemy troop killed

On 22 February, the Rangers were attached to C Battery, 49th Field Army Battalion, for its security as they advanced north together. The company departed Chuch'on-ni about 0730 hrs. in a motor march, riding on ammo trucks whenever possible. The snows were melting and the streams and rivers were flowing very rapidly. What had been a small stream only days earlier was now a raging torrent of water that presented unanticipated dangers. On the way back to the front line, when crossing onto an island in the Pyongong Ang River, Corporal James Oakley, BAR man, lost his footing in the river and was swept rapidly downstream. Men from the 2d ran downriver and tried to, but could not, catch him. Another hour was spent searching the banks downstream for about a mile, to no avail. Oakley's body was found several days later by another unit. His loss was greatly felt, not only because he was well liked, but because his was not a combat-related death. In the midst of the dangers faced by the Rangers, it was tragic to lose a man because of the weight of the equipment he was carrying, none of which he was able to jettison into the river in time to save himself from drowning.

The battery moved on and took up a position with the remainder of the battalion and conducted its fire mission all night. The concussion from the muzzle blasts shook the squad tents so much that sleeping was almost impossible. During the setting-up and reconnaissance of the position, the Rangers found a lot of human bones that had been covered up by the snows and were only now becoming visible. They figured they were the remains of enemy civilians, because no uniforms or equipment were found.

While in this area on 24 February, the orders for Sergeant First Class James Freeman's battlefield commission finally came through. He was now a Second Lieutenant. He had been acting as the officer leading the 1st Platoon since Lieutenant Bernard Pryor was evacuated on 14 January. The day before, 2d Lieutenant Cliette (3d Platoon leader) had been promoted to 1st Lieutenant, so appropriate insignia for 2d Lieutenant Freeman were available within the company. His parachute and glider qualifications were noted on the Morning Report. We couldn't have too much of a promotion party because the booze that we had stashed in the company field desk was never found, and Class 6 rations (i.e., whiskey) had not started. Freeman received his promotion in the hospital.

The Morning Report for 25 February shows the following census: Asgnd–108; Duty–65; and Abs/ LD–43. About this time, Mary, Lieutenant Allen's wife, learned of the seriousness of the wound her husband had received on 14

January at Tanyang Pass, and wrote inquiring about his condition. He wrote back to her, saying that he thought he had told her about the thirty stitches in his chest and that he was not in the hospital. Little did she yet know of her role in his survival: the prayer book she had sent him the previous December while en route to Korea had deflected the bullet that entered his chest. The book's metal cover saved Allen's life. He also told his wife that Major General David G. Barr, commander of the 7th Infantry Division, had made some awards to the men, and he had received a Silver Star. Reporters from *Our World* and *Ebony* had taken pictures. As always, Allen reported to her about the men, particularly that Private First Class James Allen, from Fayetteville, was now in the unit. In the aftermath of Warren's injuries, Mary decided to begin planning their house; this would give both of them something to think about besides the war.

About the same time 2d Ranger Company received a warning order to send an advance party to Eighth Army (Rear) in Taegu. Queen took a company jeep and Weathersbee, Corporal Glen Jenkins, Jr., and two other Rangers with him. They traveled through the day because the roads were now much safer than before. According to Weathersbee, the advance party stopped at the 1st Ranger Company CP (attached to 2d Infantry Division) and learned from one of the CP guards that the unit was down to 27 men present for duty. The advance party arrived in Taegu the next day and reported into G-3, where they were housed in a dormitory-type building and learned that 4th Company, their sister unit from training days at Fort Benning, was in town.

Morning Report
[27 Feb 51] RECORD OF EVENTS
Reld atchd 17th RCT departed Chuchon by mtr march 0700 hrs Arrived Taegu 2000 hrs distance traveled approx 200 miles billeted R - R Gen Taegu Korea

The members of the Rangers' advance party to the Eighth Army parked their truck by the PX, which was open, but they could not go inside because they were too dirty. The soldiers in the compound were very clean, but the Rangers were filthy and looked like they had been in the field for six weeks—which is exactly where they had been. An MP went into the PX and bought beer and candy for them with the money the Rangers had brought over from Japan. When Queen returned, the advance party awaited the arrival of the rest of the company.

All during the month of February, 2d Ranger Company had been operating with a company strength varying between 61 to 70 percent present for duty, with some of those sick in quarters. On 28 February, when the company was attached to the 187th ARCT, APO 301, Lieutenant Antonio "Red Horse" Anthony arrived with a group of 32 Ranger replacements. The majority of these replacements came from the 80th AAA Battalion and were well known to the men of 2d Ranger Company. Lieutenant Anthony's red hair and large head—so large that his helmet would only fit properly if he first removed the helmet liner—gave him his nickname. Anthony had received a battlefield commission while serving with the 92d Infantry Division in Italy during World War II. He had trained these replacements as part of the 7th Ranger Company, which had been so designated in the second and third cycles but later was converted to replacement training. They did not take the special winter training at Camp Carson, Colorado, with the 3d, 5th, and 8th Companies, because there was not enough time—they were needed in Korea because 2d Ranger Company was so under strength. The Rangers who arrived as replacements included Corporals Homer Bush, John E. Nunley, Carl D. Hall, James Taylor, and Uthel Morris.

The company was billeted in squad tents in an apple orchard northwest of K-2 Airfield, Taegu, Korea. At the same time many wounded men returned from the hospital. Some of them had heard the rumors about a possible combat jump and eagerly made their way to rejoin the unit. Assigned strength was now up to 125, with 100 ready for duty. The 2d Ranger Company established and operated its own mess in the Apple Orchard marshalling area. Lieutenant Pryor returned to duty and took over as Assistant XO. Pryor's return meant Queen could shed some of the extra duties he had been performing: handling operations, performing XO duties, and acting as administrator. Pryor was still a little woozy on his feet and, like some officers, had to ride the company trains into the forward combat area.

The food received during the billet in the orchard at K-2 was eatable. Some of the Buffalo Rangers ate so ravenously that First Sergeant Lawrence West established "The Combat Greasers Badge"—a chow hound award for the heaviest eaters. He awarded several badges, all displaying a GI mess-type spoon with a wreath around it like the CIB or CMB. Some of the awardees were Herculano "Heavy Duty" Dias, McBert "Leave Nothing" Higginbotham, and William "Greaser" Weathersbee. Between combat missions the Rangers of the 2d Company enjoyed what they had, and continued to display the camaraderie that others on the *Butner* had noticed during their trip across the Pacific.

The 2d Ranger Company soon had enough men to reorganize into three rifle platoons, plus a mortar section, under Lieutenant Anthony. Lieutenant

Pryor took over duties as the Assistant XO and Allen was promoted to Captain on 1 March. The 5 March Morning Report finally mentioned James Fields' 14 January evacuation after the Majori-ri firefight to Michigan Veterans' Hospital.

The company began serious physical conditioning during its stay in the apple orchard. A guard was posted at the entrance, but the units ran up that dusty road for a couple of miles each day. During the first week of March, some of the Rangers got their hard-earned and well-deserved promotions, as follows:

[2 March 1951]

Collins, Norman, Corporal
Gordon, Andrew, Corporal
Hargrove, William, Sergeant First Class
Hodge, Roland, Corporal
Lofton, Matthew, Jr., Corporal

Company Order #3 Promotion to Private First Class (E-3) UP if AR 615-5 and SR 615-5-1:

Adams, Edward D., Private First Class
Arnold, Eugene V., Private First Class
Carrell, James E., Private First Class
Gibson, Culver V., Private First Class
Gray, Walter S., Private First Class
Hall, Carl D., Private First Class
Holland, Floyd, Private First Class
Morris, Uthel, Private First Class
Plater, James, Private First Class
Scott, Samuel, Private First Class
Strothers, Stewart, Private First Class
Taylor, James, Private First Class
Whitmore, Joseph, Private First Class

Reduced to Private (E-2): Peteress, James Jr.

[13 Mar 51]   Prcht jump was made by members of the unit on 7 & 8 Mar 51, No casualties. Asgd: 125   Duty: 105

[22 Mar 51] Special Orders received from 7th ID and 187th ARCT

Andrade, Anthony, Private First Class
Alston, Marion, Sergeant
Carroll, James, Corporal
Courts, Curtis, Corporal
Higginbotham, McBert, Sergeant
Lesure, David, Corporal
Murphy, Jack, Sergeant First Class
Plater, James, Corporal
Rhodes, William, Corporal
Woodard, Isaiah, Corporal

Modified Jump School

The 187th ARCT received unqualified replacements as airborne troops, including specialists such as Captain James Miller, a surgeon from 2d Battalion. He needed to become qualified for the pending combat jump. All members of the 2d, whether cook, surgeon, or BAR man, had to be qualified paratroopers, so everyone needed the right training and certification. The regiment set up a week-long course of conditioning and practiced landings from the back of a cargo truck. The candidates made three jumps at that height and were awarded their wings. Captain Miller returned to the 187th ARCT and served with distinction in combat. Two others, Floyd Holland and Stewart Strothers, also completed the program, as announced in the Morning Report of 24 June 1950.

SO 38, 23 Hqs 187th ARCT — UP AR 600-70, Change 4, dtd 24 Jun 50 . . . are rated qualified and awarded the Parachute Badge, having completed the modified jump course, as per VOCG.

2d RANGER CO
Holland, Floyd   ER13259651   Strothers, Stewart   ER33724491

[17 Mar 51] RECORD OF EVENTS

A prcht jump was made by members of this orgn on 16 Mar 1951 Two (2) EM lightly injured.
Herculano Dias Sergeant and Kirk P. Adkins Sergeant

Queen remembers only one other black replacement in addition to Doc Miller in the 187th ARCT. Sergeant First Class Menny Mosby from the 503d/80th AAA was in the S-2 (Maps) Section. Mosby later became a First Sergeant and retired as a Warrant Officer–3, in charge of the Walter Reed Army Medical Center Commissary, Washington, D.C., in the early 1980s.

Liberating Needed Materiel

The Rangers of 2d Company knew the good times between combat were not going to last forever. With various materials in short supply, they indulged in some moonlight requisitioning. Sergeant John "Pop" Jones, the 2d Ranger Company's Mess Sergeant who had volunteered for the Majori-ri attack and received the Silver Star for outstanding bravery, attested that one of the most important duties of mess personnel—beside being able to fire up the stoves and put out a hot meal within an hour—was to scrounge, beg, borrow, or steal rations. The company ordered rations, supplies, and ammo on a two- to three-day cycle through the Regimental S-4 of the unit to which it was attached; but by the time the requisitions came in, 2d Ranger Company had often moved on to another regimental attachment without its supplies. This brought on the frequent necessity for members of the company to moonlight requisition vehicles to transport their own supplies, lest they end up without any after a couple of days. The 4th Rangers had similar experiences, and had to be fed by other line units. Second Company never sent its kitchen/supply train with the attached unit's train, but kept it up near the tactical CP, close to the 60mm mortar positions (except on the Munsan-ni jump).

Moonlight requisitioning was easy in Taegu. The area was loaded with dumb, friendly non-combat units that utilized vehicles to visit the PXs and the whores of the local "cathouses." The occupants were careless and the Ranger units were in need of transportation—especially jeeps and larger ¾-ton trucks. The trucks were easy to steal but harder to hide, so the Rangers replaced them with more appropriate jeeps that could make it over the rough front-line trails.

Corporal William Tucker and Sergeant First Class Norman Collins couldn't tell the difference between the American and British vehicles. A jeep is not just a jeep: the British jeep of this era had a more square shape and was slightly larger than its American counterpart. Also, the jeep that Tucker and Collins "requisitioned" had the British Union Jack insignia painted on the sides of the hood! A British MP challenged them because neither looked like Her Majesty's soldiers. Lieutenant Freeman, who could pass for white, told the British officer to take the damn jeep and get moving. Needless to say, this avoided possible courts-martial for Tucker and Collins, who did not make that mistake again.

Garland, who drove for Allen, managed to get at least one jeep, and Corporal Glen Owens liberated two ¾-ton vehicles, which were then used as weapons carriers. Second Company had the stencils and markings ready for Master Sergeant Robert Watkins, 3d Platoon, who was a sign painter in civilian life. By the time the 2d Ranger Company returned to the front, their motor pool had grown large enough to need a Motor Corporal/Mechanic to operate. The 2d Ranger Company left Taegu with three jeeps, two weapons carriers, and two deuce- and-a-halves—a good haul of much-needed equipment and a testament to the Rangers' ability to infiltrate and evade. Later, Sergeant Watkins also made helmet stencils that looked like parachute wings, and the 2d Rangers began to stand out among the troops in their dress.

False Alarm

About the second week of March, word arrived that 2d Ranger Company would jump behind the lines to capture Hill 303, overlooking Chunchon, in the central jump. It was a joint mission with 4th Company. Our DZ was on the north side of the Imjin River, about 100 yards wide but "shallow." Queen was a little worried because we had already lost one man (Oakley) in water in what was supposed to be a small stream. He also knew from experience that any type of water landing was extremely hazardous. Once Hill 303 was captured, the Rangers were to hold it until contact (link-up) was made with the 25th Infantry Division or 1st Cavalry, which were coming up from the south. The jump, however, was called off when the 1st Cavalry and 1st Marine Division reached Chunchon ahead of schedule, with less resistance than anticipated.

Around 20 March, Weathersbee was told to report to Captain Anderson, 4th Company. Weathersbee and another sergeant were given a map of Chunchon and asked to make a sand table (a miniature replica of the terrain using dirt or sand and symbols representing forces) of the planned Chunchon operation ("Operation Ripper"). But when they finished, they learned the mission was cancelled. Instead, they were handed a map of Munsan-ni and told to get to work.

Chapter 5

First Airborne Assault Near Munsan-Ni, 23 March 1951

"If a man has a tent roof of caulked linen twelve braccia broad and twelve braccia high, he will be able to let himself fall from any great height without danger to himself."

— Leonardo da Vinci[21]

Tactical Comments

The model Ranger Infantry Company (Airborne) had been set up under TO&E No. 7-87, dated 17 October 1950, Department of the Army. But it is doubtful that any actual company followed the TO&E to the letter. One of the advantages a Ranger commander received was that he could organize and table the unit to fit the mission. Most of 2d Ranger Company's missions were *infantry in the attack*, so this is what we sought to do.

If this was our primary mission, the disadvantage was the lack of sufficient manpower to sustain an attack for a prolonged period because of a lack of trained replacements. Second Company was forced to rely on the good graces of General Ferenbaugh, 7th Division commanding general, to draw some of the colored troops that the 2d's commanders knew of from both the official and unofficial pipeline. The segregation policy gave 2d Ranger Company access to replacements that ordinarily would not have been available—meaning *if* the system actually had been open, in keeping with President Truman's Executive Order 9981. The reality was that in those years—after the declaration of Executive Order 9981, but before the Army was in full compliance with the new ban on segregation—Army integration policy was often modified according to the interpretations of high-ranking officials who did not support desegregation.

General Edward M. Almond, commander of the X Corps, the unit to which the 2d Ranger Company was attached in Korea, was one such official. In a 1953 interview, Almond aired his views: "When you say you have to have ten percent Negroes [in the Army], you are lowering the combat efficiency of the Army." Almond defended these opinions, which were seen as racist by the black press and others: "People think that being from the South, we don't like Negroes. Not at all. But we understand their capabilities. And we don't want to sit at the table with them." When a division commander in Korea noted that whites and blacks trained together at Fort Chaffee in Arkansas, and asked Almond why he refused to mix black troops into the all-white infantry battalions, Almond continued to claim that blacks were incompetent, cowardly in combat, and so unreliable that they posed a danger to white soldiers.[22]

Another tactical disadvantage was that frequent movement of the unit necessitated increasing the size of the unit's administrative augmentation force. For every man placed in an administrative role, you have to rob the line of rifle strength. Some prime examples are cited below:

— Because SCR-300s were used in the platoons, instead of a PRC-6 used by the platoon leader, messengers became radio operators.

— With no mortar and/or artillery forward observers, another SCR-300 was required to contact higher headquarters, usually at the battalion or regimental level.

— Having no assigned vehicle drivers necessitated removing Rangers from combat positions to serve as drivers. Even in combat an informal motor stable is needed for preventative and routine vehicle maintenance.

— Without a company armorer to care for the myriad of weapons and ammunition, fulfill their need for repair or replenishment, and reserve weapons in standby for special missions, these roles fell to combat personnel.

— Air-to-ground radio and the AN/GRC-9 radio (use of which was a three-man operation) were operated without specialized personnel.

— There were no Assistant Platoon Sergeants or Section Leaders.

Weaponry provided another tactical disadvantage. The most prevalent Ranger weapon was the BAR, which was used to counteract the Burp Gun (a Chinese sub-machine gun or AK-47). Second Company did not get Thompson submachine guns, which were comparable to the Burp Gun—with the exception of Lieutenants Pryor and Anthony, who had captured ones. The weight of a BAR and its ammo was more than the M-1, the standard-issue U.S. Army rifle in Korea. Contrary to the Geneva Convention, Ranger medics carried carbines. Queen frequently had to order Sergeant William E. "Rabbit" Thomas, company medic, to fall back behind the second squad so he would not get involved in the firefight before he could care for the wounded.

Ranks were not always matched to positions. A squad leader might be a Staff Sergeant or Sergeant First Class, while a *good* BAR man might be a Sergeant and was almost always a Corporal. A rifleman, an assistant BAR man, could be a Corporal. Constant casualties created frequent vacancies, and requests for promotion orders were rarely turned down by headquarters. The authorization of relatively high ranks in a Ranger company did cause a few problems later when the units were inactivated and the men were sent to the 187th ARCT, because of a lack of vacancies and doubt in the minds of some about their abilities. But the Rangers did not have to take a reduction to private, as the "Triple Nickelers" did after the initial cadre was trained.

An Open Secret

The news of an impending airborne operation was an open secret because the 187th and the Rangers remained in the marshalling area adjacent to the Taegu Airfield (K-2) for almost three weeks, from 27 February to 23 March 1950. The Rangers who were hospitalized in Japan and Korea also guessed as much because many of the doctors discharged them early. Rumors spread by a slip of the tongue through the troops and the local civilians involved in the preparations. Lieutenant Cliette reported back to duty on 3 March, three days after the unit arrived in Taegu, after he had been hospitalized on 20 February and promoted to 1st Lieutenant on 23 February. Returning from the hospital via troop train to 2d Ranger Company, Cliette reported that the military police riding on the trains received word to have all 187th Paratroopers and Rangers unload and get on the first available transportation to Taegu.

In addition to the replacements Lieutenant Anthony brought from CONUS, the 2d had returnees from several other hospitals, including Rangers George Rankins, Clinton Cleveland, Jude P. St. Martin, Herman C. Jackson, Anthony Andrade, Charles O. Lewis, Edward L. Posey, Edward D. Adams, Harold Johnson, Roland Hodge, Smead H. Robertson, and Robert S. Gray, as well as Craig Paulding and Wheeler S. Small, Jr., who had been wounded at Majori-ri but talked their way into an early release from the hospital after hearing the rumor of an upcoming combat jump. This would be the first combat jump ever made by U.S. Rangers and by all-black troops.

The tents in the marshalling area were lined up to form a company street, among the remnants of the apple orchard. Except for keeping the units within the orchard, there was no attempt at camouflage because the North Korean "Bed Check Charlie" aircraft had not gone any farther south than Seoul. The U.S. Air Force had established air superiority, and there were elements of the 80th AAA Battalion from 82d A/B Division around the airfield, as well as Eighth Army (Rear) in Taegu.

Weathersbee recalled that one day when the unit went out for a practice jump, he saw Ted Williams, the famous baseball player for the Boston Red Sox. Williams, a reserve aviator, had been recalled to active duty as a major in the Marine Corps, and his unit was flying a mission out of K-2 airfield. Weathersbee went over to say hello and shake his hand. While there he also saw Captain Forrest Walker, formerly 3d Battalion, 505th, who was being rotated to the States from the 2d ID. Captain Walker had served with distinction and been awarded the Silver Star by General Ridgway, although the award had been ordered stopped by General Almond, and Walker was reassigned to the 3d Battalion, 9th Infantry.[23] Men like Weathersbee admired Walker for leading Company E, 9th Infantry Regiment, in the mid-January recapture of Wonju, on the central front. The fact that prejudice had kept Walker's well-earned Silver Star from him only made him more of a hero.

While Weathersbee worked on a sand table for the Munsan-ni drop (part of Operation Courageous) with a Sergeant First Class from 4th Company, the Rangers established a separate sand table because it was well known that the RCT table would be very busy with briefings. Besides, everyone was utilizing the talents found in their own units. The jump, part of Operation Tomahawk (23 March), would be at Munsan-ni, about twenty-four miles northwest of Seoul. Operation Tomahawk was the Eighth Army's new plan that, it was hoped, would cause a panicked withdrawal by the enemy. Operation Killer (21

February to 7 March) had failed to accomplish a rapid enemy movement, but after Seoul fell to UN forces during Operation Ripper (7 March to 31 March), the Chinese were pulling back. The 187th was to drop twenty-five miles northwest of Seoul and an armored column was to link up with it there. The ground unit would be Task Force Growden, led by the 6th Tank Battalion, 24th ID, with artillery and infantry. The 2d and 4th Company Rangers were attached to the 187th and both would participate in the jump. Second Company would be distinguished by yellow chutes with yellow strips, and 4th Company by yellow chutes with red strips.

Operations Order 1 from the 187th RCT detailed the jump for 23 March 1951 at 0900 hours. The drop altitude was approximately 900 feet. The plan assumed that the paratrooper drop, followed by a linkup with U.N. forces from the south and east, would cut off enemy units defending the approaches to Munsan-ni. There was only one main road leading northwest from Seoul, and that road passed through Munsan-ni. Escape or withdrawal routes from Munsan-ni required ferry and ford crossings of the Imjin River. Taking control of Munsan-ni would destroy the enemy's supply and communications routes from Kaesong to Munsan-ni and then southeast to Seoul. Second Company's mission was to seize and hold Hill 151 until control of the hill could be passed to the 187th's 2d Battalion.

The evening before the jump, the men of 2d Ranger Company went down to the airfield and fitted their chutes. The chutes were loaded onto the planes so they would stay dry, protected from any early morning dew. Each Ranger packed a duffle bag and a light combat pack with two days of C-rations, poncho, a 60-mm mortar round, and extra socks. No one carried a sleeping bag, but all had field jackets and a sweater or long-john top for chilly nights. Nearly everyone carried two hand grenades, one or two bandoleers of ammo, jump knives, and pistols. The leaders had flashlights and binoculars. Queen had the company telephone, an EE-8, and the air/color panel, along with a blanket fashioned and sewn like a Mexican *serape* that enabled him to sleep with his weapons-hands covered, but free to operate his M-1 without delay. Everyone carried toilet paper in more than one location.

That evening, the company had a regular dinner, but it was a quiet night in which no one went over to the airbase to visit any of the clubs. Many stayed up late to write a last-minute letter home and check weapons. The bundles for the mortars and the light machine guns were packed and the chutes fitted and marked. Some Rangers attended a church service.

Good Friday—23 March

The men of 2d Ranger Company got up early the next morning—which also happened to be Good Friday. Sergeant Parks, Mess Sergeant, had some scrambled eggs, pancakes, and fresh (reconstituted) milk ready for the Rangers: a hearty breakfast, but definitely not a condemned man's meal of steak, potatoes, and wine. Second Company's men repeated the chant "Buffalo— Rangers!" as they marched to the airfield and located the C-46s that would fly them to the drop zone (DZ). They packed their bundles and marked them with blue ribbon, because the yellow strips the 2d had been ordered to use were not available. The colored strips made it easier for the Rangers to know which bundles to look for when they hit the ground, and perhaps to recognize and locate them quickly.

After a shout of "Buffalo" the Rangers boarded their respective aircraft and started chuting up. The C-46 was a good plane to jump from because it had two doors and a slow speed for jumping. The flight crew was a National Guard unit that had been called to active duty. Before boarding, Allen called the unit

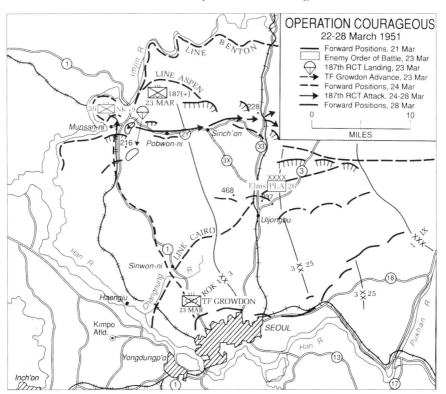

OPERATION COURAGEOUS
22-28 March 1951

together for a moment of silent prayer. Dias didn't have an appropriate jump-type chin strap for his helmet, so he tore up a bandoleer to make a chin strap. Even so, he lost his helmet in the "opening shock" and hit the ground without it. Over in the 1st Platoon aircraft, Allen was the jumpmaster. Lieutenant Freeman, platoon leader, was in one door of the C-46 and Corporal "Pretty Willie" Coleman, his radio operator, was in the other. Corporal Joe Wells and Corporal Cleaven McBride jumped with some of the 187th Headquarters and Headquarters Company men assigned to jump in one of the 2d Ranger aircraft. According to Dias, 4th Company Rangers A. B. Smith from Vidor, Texas, and Al Koop of Enid, Okalahoma, jumped with the 2d Ranger Company's 1st Platoon because their aircraft was out of space.

Wells said that McBride followed him out of the airplane door, and when they hit the ground General Ridgway was seen standing near a jeep. Both Rangers headed toward the mountains and Hill 151, with Wells nursing a sprained ankle. He recalled another injury worse than his own: one of the men from the 187th, a Puerto Rican, was shot in the hand while in the air. Wounded or not, he was just ahead of them.

Over on the 2d Platoon's aircraft, Paulding noticed that he had a black crew chief. It was the first time that he had seen one. The chief kept running up and down the aisle, passing out cigarettes. When the doors opened on the four-minute light, he took his position in the back of the aircraft, placed his headset on, and remained there. When the plane approached the DZ, each Ranger yelled "Buffalo" as he bailed out.

The jump was so low that after the shock of the chute opening and about two oscillations, the Rangers were on the ground. Once on the ground, the Rangers recovered their bundles without any difficulty.

The DZ was hot! After Posey and Anderson jumped from the 2d Platoon aircraft, both landed close together off the DZ, where an enemy's mortar was set up. Some of the enemy were firing mortar rounds into the DZ, while others were firing small arms at the paratroopers. Posey and Anderson were removing their parachutes when Posey heard Anderson say, "We're in the middle of this—let's go to work." Posey, armed with a BAR, and Anderson, with an M-1 rifle, concentrated their fire on the enemy's position. After killing all five enemy soldiers and destroying the mortars, they continued to fight from their primary landing position to the assembly area. Working as a team, they overcame two other enemy rifle positions before reaching the assembly area. While First

Sergeant West was assembling the company, Posey and Anderson took their positions with the 2d Platoon and prepared to move out for Hill 151.

By the time Weathersbee arrived at the assembly area, Rangers were knocking out one enemy emplacement after the other. Weathersbee remembers a machine gun nest on the edge of his platoon's area that West knocked out personally. According to witnesses, he "tippy toed" up to the nest, pulled a pin on his grenade, and dropped it in the hole. Every enemy emplacement the Rangers encountered was destroyed or captured.

Johnson, in the 3d Platoon, was the last man in his stick. Cliette and Boatwright were the stick leaders for that group. After their aircraft cleared the runway they headed north and flew over the ocean. The plane made a turn and flew over Seoul, heading for the Drop Zone. When the turn was made, the Rangers were given the red light, indicating that exiting the aircraft would begin within the next ten minutes. The jump light panel was beside the door at a level of about 4 ½ feet. Its red and green lights were operated from the pilot's compartment. It was the jumpmaster's duty to check the aircraft in his vicinity and the ground for safety configurations.

"Cat Eyes" Jackson was in the left stick, which would jump from the door on the left (if facing the front of the airplane). The men went through the usual procedure before exiting: stand up, hook up, check equipment. They were ready to go as they watched the red light, waiting anxiously for the green.

When the green light came on Cliette, the jumpmaster, was having trouble with a bundle that got stuck in the door cross ways because of the wind. The right stick completely bailed out before the bundle was cleared from the left door. As soon as it was wrestled free, the left stick cleared the plane. (Black paratroopers were famous for exiting—or, in airborne slang, *un-assing*—the aircraft quickly.) Concerned that the delay caused by the bundle would mean his stick would either land on a hill occupied by the enemy or some other place off the DZ, Jackson completely unhooked and crossed over to the right door just as the other stick started to move. He rehooked on the run but didn't have time to insert the safety pin in the static line snap fasteners. He moved to the door and jumped out.

According to Jackson,

> in a C-46, you expect to get a good, sharp, hard opening shock with the T-7 type parachute, as you count: one-thousand-one, one-thousand-two, one-thousand-*three*. I don't know whether I had a good or bad position,

but when that chute popped out, I just felt good about it—until, when descending, I saw that I had a couple of bullet holes in my chute! I'm thinking that people are shooting at us because we were late getting out of the aircraft. I landed in either a peach or apple orchard and my chute was tangled up in small trees. I heard a couple of shots—they were firing at us. I crawled into a nearby shack and was able to get out of my harness. After removing my chute, I started down the field to get our mortars. I picked up a couple of men that jumped with me: Adell Allen, Anthony Andrade, David Lesure and some others.

Back to the fourth aircraft: Queen jumped with Anthony's mortar section and six men from Headquarters and Headquarters Company from the 187th. Once the aircraft was loaded, they took off with the usual grunts and groans about getting the old, heavily loaded ship up and off the runway. Everyone yelled when they cleared the strip and the pilot raised the wheels. They joined the flight in a V-formation heading west out toward Seoul and the Yellow Sea. The airplane turned back east toward land after a couple of minutes over the water.

Queen was sitting in the rear of the aircraft near the radio operator's table until the four-minute warning, and then he came up to help with jumpmaster checks on the troopers at the rear. The old C-46 slowed down to about ninety knots and held it pretty steady in formation. As the airplanes approached the drop zone (DZ), sporadic machine gun and small arms fire could be heard from the ground. Jets from the Air Force had gone in and done some strafing of the DZ and suspected troop locations. The XO from Headquarters Company got his radio bundle hung up in the door and they almost passed the DZ. Anthony pushed out his mortar bundles but he didn't appear to follow them closely. Queen jumped last. He "swept the plane clean" to make sure no one was still aboard before bailing out.

By 0920 hours on 23 March, the whole company—six officers, two Korean officers, and ninety-five enlisted men—had landed via parachute north of Munsan-ni, Korea, with the mission of securing Hill 151. Hill 151 was approximately 2,000 yards north of the DZ, the dominating terrain feature in the zone of action of the 2d Battalion of the 187th. Queen policed the DZ for personnel and equipment and headed for the assembly area. There were only two noteworthy injuries among the members of the unit, all of whom had landed in the DZ. Queen found Corporal Jenkins unable to walk after badly spraining his ankle, and Private First Class Eugene Coleman had hit his head in some manner and lost his memory. The 2d Rangers, less their 60mm mortar section, were in their assembly area by 1000 hours and about seventy percent effective. Queen had landed near an orchard and picked up Lieutenant Lee, one of the Korean officers. Queen saw Allen on the road and sent Lieutenant Lee with him. Queen also saw Anthony, who had not recovered all his bundles but was trying to assemble his platoon.

In this jump Corporal Donald Wright, Company L, 187th ARCT, was also injured. Carrying the same heavy combat load as the Rangers—an SCR-300 radio, weapon, ammo, and combat pack with two days of C-rations—he landed against the wall of a stone dike. Jumping from an altitude of 600 to 800 feet, men were on the ground in twenty-seven to thirty-six seconds. With so little time to change flight direction and so many other jumpers to stay clear of, Wright had few options. He had intended to slip (change direction) and land on top of the dike. However, his sink (descent) rate was too fast and the dike appeared to move upward to meet him during his descent. He rolled down the dike and had to cut his way out of the chute. His injuries included a set of damaged and broken teeth as well as a busted hip and knee. But since he could still move, he continued to perform his function as radio operator.[24]

Jump and combat casualties were being handled by a Mobile Army Surgical Hospital (MASH) unit on the DZ set up by the Indian Army. Queen, who would find Jenkins and Coleman later, did a quick check of the area but found no Buffalo Rangers at the MASH unit. Queen also saw General Ridgway on the DZ, with his grenades taped to his harness/suspenders, as was his usual style. Ridgway was standing near an L-5 aircraft that appeared to have flown him into the air head. Queen stayed out of talking range because he didn't want to get mixed up in any media coverage by civilian correspondents who might be traveling with Ridgway. Queen looked up in the air and saw General MacArthur's C-54 or C-124 flying about 5,000 to 6,000 feet and circling the DZ on the south side of the Imjin River. Finally, Queen spotted the 1st Battalion jumping on the same DZ, when they should have jumped on another DZ about two miles south. Ridgway immediately caught the airborne operation errors.

Once Jackson oriented himself and got out of his harness, he began looking for the bundles marked with blue ribbon. He couldn't find them. Instead, he found two bundles with machine guns in them. When he and several others from the mortar section reached the assembly area, they picked up the rounds of mortar ammo each Ranger had dropped there. Every man in the company

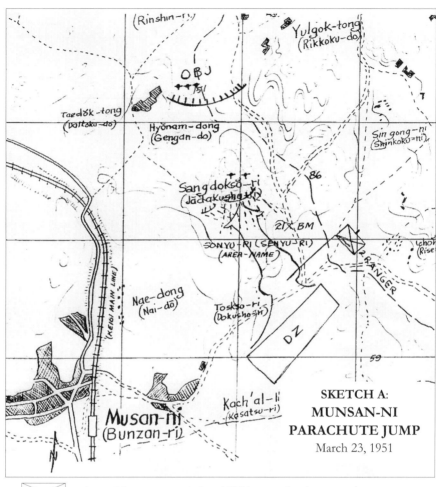

SKETCH A:
MUNSAN-NI
PARACHUTE JUMP
March 23, 1951

⊠ = Assembly area occupied at 1000 hours after heavy resistance.

parachuted in with at least one round in his pack. When they passed through the assembly area, they dropped that round, to be picked up by mortar section personnel such as Jackson. The mortars were to be mounted first in the assembly area, and then to support the company in the attack on Hill 151, as necessary. In the assembly area, Jackson and others put the machine guns down and found their mortars; other members of 2d Ranger Company had found the mortars and taken them off the DZ. There was plenty of ammo, and they loaded up. Jackson met Hargrove, a squad leader from the 2d Platoon, which had knocked out a Russian 82mm mortar by dropping an incendiary grenade in the tube to destroy it—but the men had kept the Russian sight. Hargrove gave Jackson the sight which, unlike its U.S. counterpart, was capable of rotating the full 360 degrees. This meant the mortar crew only had to set out one aiming stake. The mortar section fell in behind 3d Platoon. When they reached the first ridge, Captain Allen was there with the company command and Lieutenant Anthony.

Queen had joined Cliette, who was with the 3d platoon on a small knoll just off the road on the north side of the DZ. Most of the 3d was there and Cliette was concerned about an enemy soldier lying beside a 50-caliber machine gun mounted on an anti-aircraft tripod in an emplacement about four feet deep. Queen fixed the bayonet on his rifle and jumped in the hole, punching the soldier in the ribs. The soldier jumped up—to the surprise of everyone, who seemed to think he was dead. He was immediately taken prisoner and Queen manned the weapon. When he spotted North Korean soldiers fleeing up Hill 151 while being pursued by the remainder of the company, Queen fired the remaining ammo in the enemy machine gun in their direction. The heavy machine gun (HMG) was very primitive, with a rotating barrel like the old gattling gun of the Civil War era. The firing made a hell of a racket. Queen didn't think that he hit anyone because he didn't see anyone fall. When Hill 151 was captured, no one was found torn up by HMG fire.

The platoon moved behind a barrage of Anthony's mortars. The company was now attacking from the base onto the forward slopes. The order of the attack was 1st Platoon leading, with Headquarters Company following, 2d Platoon next, and 3d Platoon in the rear.

According to Jackson, the 3d Platoon crossed two small rice paddies to get to the upgrade slope of Hill 151. The 3d Platoon was hitting the left flank of Hill 151 at the same time the 1st and 2d Platoons were fighting for the top of 151. Captain Allen told the men to get those mortars into action to support the 3d Platoon moving across the rice paddies.

The Mortar Section mounted its mortars quickly and fired at a range of some 400 yards. Jackson stripped off all of the propellant charges except one, because the distance was so short. Each 60mm mortar round came with four propellant charges attached to the shell fin. The gunner would remove the extra charges according to the data specified on the mortar firing table. As a safety measure, the extra charges were usually placed in a storage pit about ten to fifteen yards away from the immediate gun position.

The Mortar Section dropped its rounds right in front of the 3d Platoon. They came pretty close, and Jackson was sure that 3d Platoon was thinking the Mortar Section didn't know what it was doing, and that some of the charges might fall short. Actually, the Mortar Section was watching from its position on the ridge and could see where every round landed. Its members fired a round from each mortar in sequence, then went down turns. *"Drop two turns, fire!"* *"Drop two turns, fire!"* They walked the fire uphill, just in front of the 3d Platoon.

After part of Hill 151 was captured, the mortars shifted position forward— almost to the top of the hill. By now they were receiving some sniper fire as well as five or six rounds of artillery fire. Thankfully, the artillery fire ended quickly.

First Sergeant West had been one of the first to arrive in the company assembly area. He and about five of his men ran into two enemy-manned 50-caliber, AA-mounted machine guns overlooking the area. (See Sketch A.) Realizing that this fire could stop the company from assembling and organizing, West charged the position. At the same time, Cliette arrived with his platoon to help. (West was supposed to be recommended for the Bronze Star for his decision and bravery, but was overlooked.) The company took two prisoners from this position, including the one who faked being dead until jabbed in the ribs by Queen with his bayonet. Two others were killed. Concurrently, Allen, with another squad, came across a group of enemy soldiers trying to change into civilian clothing.

By this time, rumors that nine troopers had been captured were starting to circulate. Supposedly, they had jumped late and landed past the DZ. Men from 2d Ranger Company saw some chutes in the hills to their flank, in the zone of the 4th Ranger Company. Also, the artillery had lost a few guns and trucks from the heavy drop due to malfunctioning chutes. There were riggers—troopers whose main task was to repair and pack all parachutes—out on the DZ after the heavy drop to recover parachutes for return to supply channels. Some riggers claimed to have accidentally fallen out of their aircraft during the heavy drop operations.

The company now prepared to attack and capture, as quickly as possible, a village named Sangdokso-ri, about one-third of the way to the main objective. (See Sketches B through D.[25]) The company moved out with two platoons abreast about 1030 hours, with Headquarters Section in support because the men had not seen Anthony with the mortars for about an hour. Freeman's 1st Platoon cleaned out the slopes leading down into the village, killing six and taking about twenty prisoners. Here they ran into Anthony and the Mortar

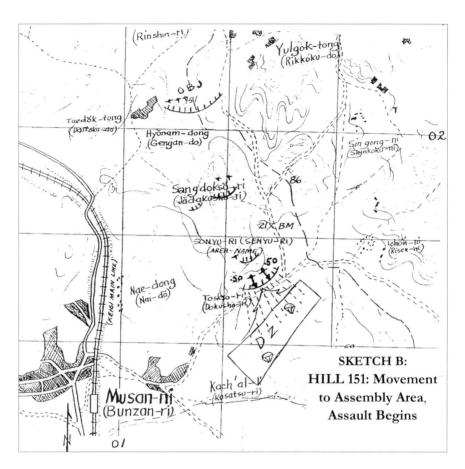

SKETCH B:
HILL 151: Movement
to Assembly Area,
Assault Begins

Section, which had come around the first knob and taken the road into the village. The houses and dugouts were searched, as were the slopes of the hill to the rear of the village. The two ROK officers, Lieutenants Lee and Pak, questioned and helped control the civilians found.

Two- or three-man fire teams from the assault platoons called to enemy personnel who might have been hiding in the dugouts to surrender. If no one appeared, the Rangers threw in a grenade to ensure that the dugout was empty or nothing dangerous was left waiting inside. They had learned that during fluid fighting, enemy soldiers would remain holed up unless forced out. Then, hours after being by-passed, they would creep out during the night to attack American positions or CPs.

After a brief reorganization, the company started its final assault toward Hill 151. (Sketch B) The Mortar Section took position on the high ground behind Sangdokso-ri village. The company moved out with Wilburn's 2d

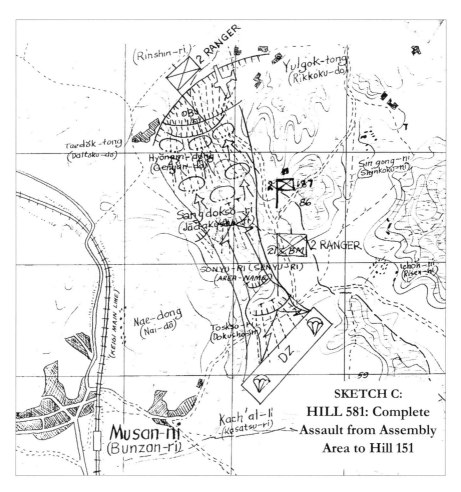

SKETCH C:
HILL 581: Complete
Assault from Assembly
Area to Hill 151

Platoon on the left and Freeman's 1st Platoon on the right. Queen started to go forward with Wilburn's platoon, but Allen called him to come back to the mortars. Wilburn's platoon advanced about 100 yards. He set up his LMG Team to cover his advance. Freeman was to the right and a little to the rear, but he quickly brought his platoon into line.

When the assault platoons were approximately 750 yards short of their objective, enemy troops estimated at company strength were seen withdrawing across the positions on the knobs, just ahead of the main objective. Queen called into the 2d Battalion's Fire Direction Center (FDC) radio net and put some 81mm mortar fire on the objective to hurry the enemy along. At the same time, 2d Battalion notified 2d Ranger Company that it had four P-51s on call, and asked Queen if he could use them. Queen directed them to strafe the back

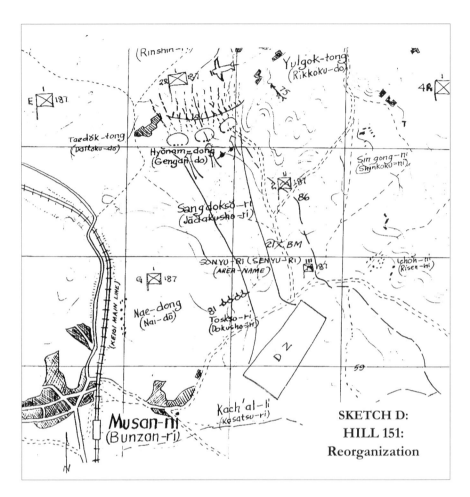

SKETCH D:
HILL 151:
Reorganization

side of Hill 151 and the village behind it. Within a few minutes, the P-51s were screaming over their target, causing Queen to lift the mortar fire for fear it might hit the planes. (See Sketch C) The Company advanced rapidly under this cover, and soon the P-51s had to be called off because their runs were too close to the advancing Rangers. The Tactical Air Control Point (TACP) or Forward Air Controller (FAC) had a little trouble contacting them because he was on low ground and his radio transmissions were masked. The Rangers had their fingers crossed for a while because some remembered the 1949 accidental bombing of Combine II at Eglin AFB, Florida, by B-29s. The company moved over the forward slopes of the hill and cleared it, finding six dead enemy soldiers there. An estimated twenty to thirty enemy soldiers were killed in the combined action this day.

Native American Private First Class William Van Dunk, a medic from 2d Platoon, was killed while clearing the forward slopes of the objective. He was one of the replacements brought over by Anthony in early March. Van Dunk was one of the first men on the objective when he was hit in the left hip/buttock. This was his first combat action, and it seems he got too excited. He was out in front of everyone else. Shock set in when he found out he was unable to move. His comrades only saw a small wound, but the bullet may have traveled up and hit his spine and caused internal bleeding. Van Dunk died on Hill 151 in less than ten minutes.

It all happened before the Rangers could do anything or get him down to the aid station or the Indian MASH unit. A silent wave went through the Buffalo ranks; one of their new men had been killed so suddenly and by such a seemingly small wound. Van Dunk's death hung like a cloud over the Buffalo Rangers. His handsome, pale face, with chiseled features that reminded you of a movie star, was suddenly silent. Who had ever seen a first-time-in-combat-medic leading a Ranger attack? It was a sight to behold.

Action with the Prisoners of War

The Buffalo Rangers must have been one of the first units to take prisoners. Sergeant West was directing traffic in the company assembly area. As the company topped the first ridge and captured the heavy machine gun overlooking the DZ, several prisoners were taken there. Freeman, 1st Platoon, assigned Weathersbee to take them back to the edge of the DZ and deliver them to the prisoner of war (POW) compound, an open-air jail where captured enemy were collected and quickly interrogated by intelligence personnel for useful information. Weathersbee had four POWs when he started toward the POW cage. Corporal William Tucker, another Ranger from 2d Ranger Company, was in front of Weathersbee on the road guiding three more prisoners. Tucker stopped, waited until Weathersbee reached his position, and said, "You have more than I have." With that he walked away and left his three prisoners, one of whom was wounded and being carried by the other two. Weathersbee now had eight POWs to escort to the compound. He had all of them take turns carrying the wounded prisoner, but by the time they reached the POW compound the wounded prisoner was dead.

A major at the compound looked at Weathersbee and exclaimed, "This SOB is dead! Why are you bringing me a stiff? You should throw him in a ditch or something." The Major was acting as if Weathersbee was the enemy.

Weathersbee's thoughts flashed back to Tanyang Pass, when Jenkins had encountered enemy soldiers playing dead. Intelligence School had taught him that wounded or frightened prisoners were good sources of information, and the Major's attitude made him angry.

Tucker, who was the second Ranger to share the prisoner escort duty, said that he saw the 187th Engineers using bulldozers to dig a trench. They were putting up barbed wire around a compound cage with concertina-type barbed wire strung out by the military police and the engineers. The engineers had dropped some heavy equipment on the first day in anticipation of taking prisoners.

On his way back to the unit Weathersbee met up with Pop Jones, who had three more prisoners. Jones told him that Van Dunk had been hit. The company was assaulting Hill 151 when Weathersbee rejoined it. When he spotted Van Dunk's body, he looked it over to see where he had been shot, but didn't see any blood. Machine guns were firing over the heads of the Rangers as they walked up the hill yelling "Buffalo!" Weathersbee rejoined his platoon.

After taking the hill, the company was subjected to some high-velocity artillery shelling, as if it was coming from a self-propelled or anti-tank gun across the river. There was no sign of the gun's muzzle flash or smoke. It seemed to be hidden in a fold of a roadway running between two hills. It either was firing from partial defilade or firing and moving back into defilade after each shot. The shells skimmed the top of Hill 151 and landed on the DZ in the rear. Weathersbee later heard these shells inflicted some casualties among the gun crews set up in that area. The riggers had to scramble because they were still collecting parachutes and other equipment from the DZ.

Weathersbee's platoon also received some sniper and small arms fire from across the river. Bullets whined overhead, just like in old cowboy movies. The Company Observation Post (OP) was right up in the front lines where the Imjin River and a small village on the north side of Hill 151 could be watched from the prone position. Boatwright was standing up near the Company OP when he was hit in the hand by sniper fire—anyone standing up would draw sniper fire. Queen rushed to Boatwright and offered him a cigarette to calm his nerves. Boatwright later teased Queen about the incident, because he thought Queen had seen too many John Wayne movies, where the hero takes a drag on a cigarette before immediately heading back into the thick of battle. Robertson was also wounded about the same time. A bullet bounced off the pistol in his shoulder holster and knocked him down. When he stood up, an artillery shell exploded next to him. The force of the blast picked him up and threw him to the ground. He never returned to duty with the unit. When some of the Rangers visited him in the 4th Evac Hospital, he still couldn't hear too well.

Jackson, in the Mortar Section, recalled what he witnessed just before the company made the final assault on Hill 151:

> We received a barrage of five or six artillery rounds. Suddenly, it stopped! I saw this big cloud of dust in the direction of Seoul. That cloud of dust was the movement of armor. Tanks breaking through, coming to our DZ, linking up with the paratroopers. These were our tanks that were breaking through the enemy lines, giving us some support and relief. The enemy shifted their fire from us, the 2d Rangers, to the tanks. The tanks were breaking through. We moved the mortars to the top of Hill 151 and dug in for the night.

After Hill 151 was captured, the three platoons held a line along the crest of the hill, from right to left as follows: Company CP on the right, 2d Platoon in the center, and 3d Platoon on the left, with the mortars in the center about fifty yards behind the CP. (See Sketch C.) When Queen realized that 4th Company had not been able to seize Hill 205, he suggested to Allen that 2d Ranger Company get permission to attack the enemy facing 4th Company from their left flank. 2d Ranger Company, however, was attached to 2/187th, while 4th Company was attached to 3/187th. Allen didn't act on Queen's request because neither Regiment nor Battalion had requested any other information or action since the "Buffalos" had reported the capture of their objective.

Later in the afternoon, after the "Buffalos" began to dig slit trenches, Queen led a small patrol down to locate the 2/187th CP and get some LMG and 60 mortar ammo; but none was available. Queen saw Captain James ("Doc") Miller, the only black officer assigned to the 187th, at the aid station and he asked Miller to send a litter jeep up the next morning to collect Van Dunk's body. Miller had gone through a week's jump training in the Taegu marshalling area, and the Munsan-ni combat jump was only his fourth one.

Queen also went to check with the Commo Officer and S-3 to see if a phone line was to be laid to the Company CP, because he had jumped with the EE-8 telephone for the hook-up. He offered to guide the wire team to the CP, if needed. But he did not receive a response and there seemed to be no specific plan, so he headed back to the CP on Hill 151. Most of the company was dug in by the time he arrived. The CP area was too crowded, so Queen found an abandoned enemy hole about twenty-five yards down the hill, between the CP, OP, and the mortars. He didn't like the position at all. He would have to remain awake all night, or take the chance of being killed or maybe left out should any heavy action take place during the night hours. Queen carved the hole a little longer and put a seat in it. He made good use of his light pack and the Mexican-fashioned blanket, for nodding off during the chilly night.

Sergeant Alston, the Commo Chief, had laid wire to all of the platoon CPs utilizing some company wire supplemented by abandoned enemy wire found on the hill. Each platoon carried a sound-powered telephone for this purpose, and all were hooked into the Company CP on a common circuit. The Ranger on radio watch would also man the phone. A whistle or a click using a battery would alert the operator on duty.

That day, the Good Lord had blessed the Buffalo Rangers in the Munsan-ni action:

— They made history as the first all-black Airborne Ranger unit to make a combat jump. The Buffalo Rangers demonstrated the great potential of black troopers. The 555th Parachute Battalion, America's first all-black troopers, were not committed to combat in World War II because some doubt existed in the minds of the highest-ranking military officers about the black serviceman's fighting ability and performance. Black volunteers during the Battle of the Bulge were overlooked. The time for the black soldier to prove himself didn't come again until Korea;

— They had not taken heavy casualties, as they had at Tanyang Pass;

— Within the *first 30 minutes*, sixty percent of the unit was in the assembly area, and 1st Sergeant West was already taking aggressive action;

— The Buffalos were able to execute their mission within two hours after "un-assing" their aircraft;

— They were the first unit to capture their objective—Hill 151.

[23 Mar 1951] RECORD OF EVENTS SECTION

Departed Taegu Korea by plane 0750 hrs.
Destination Munsan-ni Korea.
Prcht jump on Munsan-ni made 0915 hrs.
1 EM killed in action.
2 EM wounded in action 2 EM lightly injured in action.
Mission accomplished. Morale of troops excellent.

In a letter to his wife dated 31 March, Allen wrote the following:

> By now you will have read where the 187th and Ranger companies made a
> jump behind the enemy. The 2d Rangers were a part of the operation. It
> marks the first time in history that a Negro unit has made a combat jump.
> For the entire period that we were engaged, our casualty rate for the
> Company was one KIA and four others wounded slightly.

During the night, the enemy did not attempt to infiltrate 2d Ranger
Company positions. About 2300 hours, submachine gun fire was heard in the
right rear of the company position, down near the 2/187th CP. Flare shells were
fired by the mortars and artillery units during the night. C-47 aircraft flew over
the surrounding area and dropped huge flares. The moon was out and shining
brightly, and the visibility was about 100 yards in our company sector. The
temperature dropped steadily during the night, and Queen wished that he had
brought the wool insert of a summer sleeping bag instead of his blanket. But he
still would have been afraid to zip it up, lest he be unable to get out of it fast
enough (plus, he wouldn't be able to keep his rifle in hand inside a sleeping bag).

At first light, about one hour before sunrise, some squad-sized, small fires
were built on the reverse slope of the hill to warm the assault rations. The
enemy didn't attack or fire on our positions until about 0830 hours.

Theater Action after the Jump

Since the litter jeep didn't come at daybreak on 24 March, Queen gathered a
carrying party to take Van Dunk's body to the aid station. At the same time
search parties searched from the mortar position to the DZ for stragglers,
ammo, and equipment. It was estimated that 2d Ranger Company had killed
thirty enemy soldiers, wounded ten, and captured sixty on 23 March.

The enemy apparently had an OP on the opposite side of the Imjin River
on Hill 191. However, his guns, either 75mm or 105mm, were masked or his

observation limited to such a degree that he could not place fire directly on our position. The shells, which flew about ten feet overhead and sounded like a small freight train, hit back in the DZ area.

At 1300 hours, 2d Ranger Company was notified that it would be relieved of its position by the 1st ROK Division before 1800 hours. Queen remained in position with a covering squad from each platoon while Allen took the remainder of the company to report to 2/187th CP. About 1400 hours, Queen made a mistake and withdrew the remainder of the company, which was serving as the covering force. His orders, however, were "to remain in position until relieved," so Queen had to return to Hill 151 with his men. While they waited for the South Korean soldiers to relieve them, the Rangers tested their rifles by firing at some ruins on the road along the Imjin. Queen, meanwhile, settled down inside his foxhole where, under slightly cloudy skies, he caught up on his sleep. About 1700 hours, when no relief column had arrived, Queen got a call from a messenger to hurry along and rejoin the company.

Queen reached the DZ road, where he met up with the remainder of the company. They had mounted the tanks of "C" Company, 6th Tank Battalion. The orders were to push twenty-six miles east to try to cut off a division of Chinese. There was one squad on each tank. By 2400 hours, the Rangers had moved only about six miles. The roads were too narrow and the tanks were unable to proceed. The company was ordered to remain with the tanks and protect them from infiltration by enemy infantry.

Meanwhile, the rest of the RCT had passed on. They had cows pulling carts, as well as Koreans and POWs helping to carry the equipment. It was reminiscent of the good old American ingenuity that the 82d A/B had used on its jump into Sicily during World War II, overcoming the lack of transport by confiscating and requisitioning all available farm animals, especially the small, stubborn, but hardy Italian donkeys.

Queen slept on the back deck of one of the cold tanks. The rear deck of a tank is a very warm place to sleep as long as those twin gas or diesel engines are running. Once the engines stopped in Korea, however, it got as cold as the South Pole. Queen didn't seem to mind. The men were sent out about fifty yards to the flanks of the tank column to provide security against an enemy ambush or infiltration. They didn't unroll their packs because no one knew when the word to move out would come down.

The 2d Ranger Company left the 6th Battalion tanks in place at daybreak on 25 March to join the remainder of the RCT. It started to rain pretty heavily. The

Rangers caught a ride on some artillery trucks. They only made it about one mile before the trucks began to bog down in the muddy road, which was more like an unimproved wagon trail than anything else. They took off on foot again and marched to the village of Sinchon, where they arrived about 1200 hours. The 2d Ranger Company took up a position south of town on ridges overlooking the village of Chana-don, with the mission of guarding the RCT's right flank and looking for a relief tank battalion coming from the south that would be its next link-up. Queen received some different colored flares that he gave to Wilburn, as the 2d Platoon was deployed forward. These flares were to be used for identification purposes and to mark front line positions. The Rangers settled into some old enemy foxholes and began preparing a meal using the last of the two days' worth of C-rations.

The company CP was established in a hole about 4' x 4' x 4', with a foxhole-type entrance. It would have been a good hole for two men, but there were now five in the CP group: Captain Allen, Queen, Lawrence "Top Kick" West, Alston (Commo), and "Doc Rabbit" Thomas, medic. In addition to the packs and weapons, there were two SCR-300 radios (one SCR-300 radio was on the RCT operations net and the other was on the company command net), with EE-8 and sound-powered telephones as well.

The Rangers received more fuel for fires from the village, but their fires were soon doused because of the rain and for security reasons. Cliette's 3d Platoon was on the left, Willie Coleman's 2d Platoon in the front and forward, and Freeman's 1st Platoon held the right. Anthony had the mortars around the CP. To the rear of 2d Ranger Company were the Indian MASH hospital and the RCT CP. Farther to the rear were the 4th Ranger Company and the RCT Security Platoon, which provided local security to the RCT Headquarters Company. Later in the evening Queen went to the RCT CP to try to get some fresh batteries for the SCR-300 radios and a telephone line to the CP. The helicopters were coming in during the rain to evacuate the wounded. Coleman's platoon tried to get all of the people out of the village, but they wouldn't move until one of Anthony's mortar rounds, with which he was plotting nighttime concentrations, fell short within the village. Then everyone "got hat" and left in a hurry. During the afternoon and night no enemy contact was made.

Second Company remained in reserve until about 1000 hours on 26 March, when it was attached to the 3d Battalion. The battalion had orders to attack to the east. Queen stayed back with the 2d Platoon and a mortar squad to guard the aid station and wait for the tanks. The armor came through about 1500 hours. There were only about six tanks; the rest had been knocked out by mines or had developed mechanical failures. The aid station moved east while Queen and the 2d Platoon moved on the tanks. This group caught up with Captain Allen and the rest of the company about 1730 hours. Allen had skirted the right flank of the RCT and gone on a separate mission to contact the 64th Tank Battalion, 3d Infantry Division. The contact was made, and Allen would later tell Queen that he was never so glad to see anyone as he was to see the 3d ID.

The company advanced as far south as the Sam-chan River Bridge. About 1830 hours, just as it was getting dark, Allen ordered Queen to take Wilburn's 2d Platoon to a hill he pointed out on the horizon, and ordered him to dig in there facing northwest. Queen was told that once he had his men in position, he was to move along the ridge line to the southwest until he met back up with Allen, who would give him further instructions at that time. Queen wanted to know more about the mission and the disposition of the other units, but Allen was adamant: "Hurry up and get them the hell into position!" Wilburn and Queen took off with nothing in mind except getting to the hill. It was already dusk and they wanted to be in position before it got completely dark.

The 2d Platoon advanced through a small village that was all boarded up. It looked as if everyone had gone on vacation. It took a short but steep climb to reach the top of the hill. Everyone was glad they did not have to fight for the high ground that night. Later, Wilburn remarked that he had seen some people running off the hill, but didn't say anything at the time. When they reached the hilltop, the Rangers didn't find any holes or abandoned equipment. The platoon spread out thinly and began to dig in. The soil was sandy and easy to excavate. Company CP was much farther away than anticipated, and Queen couldn't find Allen—but he could raise him on the radio. He notified Allen that he would remain with Wilburn's platoon for the rest of the night; even though there was a full moon, it was completely dark by this time. Queen, Wilburn, and radio operator Willie Coleman crowded together into a single hole. Little did Queen know that his night was just beginning.

After a short time, Wilburn and Queen decided to walk down the line to Freeman's platoon, which was quite a distance away, to try to figure out what was happening. They soon discovered that Freeman didn't know any more about the tactical situation than they did. He had no idea where the remainder of the company was, but he had received instructions over the radio to send a squad and contact Anthony's mortars. When Freeman asked Queen to take

Hargrove's squad to the mortar position Queen, who had been hoping to find Allen and get a situation briefing, reluctantly agreed.

It took about an hour of struggling through the woods and calling "Buffalo" before they finally found Andrade, who led them to Anthony's platoon CP. "Red Horse" didn't know anything either, and he pointed to Cliette's position, which seemed to be about another mile away! It was about 2200 hours before Queen returned to Wilburn's position. A radio message from Allen was waiting for him: he would meet Queen the next morning.

About 2300 hours, a harassing and interdicting white phosphorus shell hit behind 2d Platoon's CP, but no one was hurt. It was not until later that the Rangers learned that one of the battalions had had to evacuate a position after taking it during daylight hours. The unit had to make a night attack and retake it without additional assistance. A hell of a firefight broke out in front of the 2d Platoon that lasted about three hours. With the drama and exhaustion of the day behind him, a frustrated Queen finally sacked out with Wilburn and Plater in what appeared to be an abandoned winter wheat field.

On 27 March, the company was attached to the 1/187th at 0900 hours. Queen left 2d Platoon and moved down the hill and finally located the Company CP in a hut on the edge of the village facing a huge field of green rice or wheat. The large field consisted of about five acres, with growth more than two feet tall. Queen was still angry at Allen's failure to meet him the night before. However, a hot cup of chocolate from First Sergeant West smoothed over the situation. At 1000 hours, the unit moved into a reserve position on the left flank of Hill 148, west of the Sinchon River. About 1400 hours, the Rangers crossed the river and joined Company C, 64th Tank Battalion. The area along the river bank was being shelled by what appeared to be a 75mm self-propelled gun off to the north. No one was hurt crossing the river, and contact was made with the tanks.

The harmless shelling continued intermittently for approximately thirty minutes. Farther south, about one-half mile down river, the engineers and P&A (Pioneer and Ammunition) Platoon built a ford for vehicles. The tank-infantry team moved forward to occupy a circular defense, with the Rangers dug in between the tanks. Friendly artillery fire was plotted in and around the team's position. No contact was made with the enemy during the remainder of the day or during that night. The tank-infantry team was the all-black 758th Tank Battalion from the 82d A/B Division. The battalion had moved first to Texas, and then Georgia, and was redesignated the 64th Tank Battalion. Company C was commanded by Captain "Acie" McLain, with whom Captain Allen and Queen had served at Fort McClellan, Alabama, in late 1945. The Buffalo Rangers recognized, greeted, and visited briefly with many old friends from Bragg.

The company occupied its position on Hill 125 throughout 28 March, where it was reinforced by the 4th Ranger Company about 1300 hours. The 1/187th launched an attack just as the 4th Company moved into the line. The Rangers of 2d Company were ordered to hold their position until the small knob to the north was captured by 4th Company. The tanks supported the attack on Hill 507 by the 1/187th. The 4th Company, minus tank support and the 2d Ranger Company's mortars, attacked and captured Hill 279 at 1500 hours. The 4th Company had only two platoons with it at the time because others had been split off for different missions. The battle was short but well fought by 4th Company. A 4th Company BAR man seemed to spark the attack. The enemy grimly held on to the reverse slope of the hill, showering the assaulting platoon with hand grenades. Jackson, of the mortar section, recalled the fire support missions and remarked, "I remember 4th Company attacking this mountain top; it was full of Chinese. It appeared as if every Chinaman in Korea threw grenades at them. And, after they threw the grenades, they ran like mad!"

According to Queen, it was a spectacular fight of platoon-sized units. Lieutenant Waterbury, platoon leader, was wounded several times but continued fighting until the hill was captured. Queen talked with Waterbury as he was on his way to the aid station in the rear. He was grinning about winning the Purple Heart. The entire unit was in high spirits, as they had been itching for a fight after having been misused as CP guards for so long.

The Buffalo Rangers moved into battalion reserve on Hill 148 east of the Sinchon River at 1700 hours. The company had hardly started to dig in when a blinding rainstorm blew up, forcing everyone to the nearest hole for cover. Queen slept in the sitting position in a half-dug cave with Lieutenant Chum and Lieutenant Kim, two Korean officers who were serving as interpreters. Chum seemed pretty unhappy because officers had to dig foxholes in the American Army. He was unhappy in 2d Ranger Company in general, and sought to rejoin 4th Company when it returned to Taegu. Two prisoners were taken during that day's action, but no further contact was made with the enemy.

On 29 March, the Buffalo Rangers continued holding their position on Hill 148. At 1130 hours, Company A, 7th Infantry, 3d ID, passed through the company position to attack to the north. Officially relieved, 2d Ranger Company assembled within the 1/187th vicinity. All assembled personnel were moved quickly by trucks at 1330 hours. The RCT was officially relieved by the 3d Division at the same time.

Land-Tail Out of Munsan-Ni

The exact date, time, and place that the RCT company trains linked up and entered the air head are not shown on the Morning Report. No one remembers them physically being available until the 187th RCT was relieved and started the motor march back to Taegu. The men in 4th Ranger Company constantly complained about the lack of food, so 2d Rangers must have been in the same condition or had resorted to more "moonlight requisitioning." On 26 March, First Sergeant Way of the 4th Ranger Company wrote in his diary, "Road march to Hill 146. Company getting just a bit hungry."

[29 Mar 1951] RECORDS OF EVENTS
Departed the Village of Sinchon Korea about 1430 hours
29 Mar 51 by mtr march Arrived in Suwon Korea about
2000 29 Mar 51 trp psn were relieved by element of the 3rd
Inf Div Morale of troops excellent
Asgnd: 113Present for Dy: 105 Sick: 1Hosp: 6KIA: 1

[30 Mar 1951] RECORDS OF EVENTS
Departed Suwon Korea approximately 1100 hours 30 Mar 51
Arrived in Taegu Korea approx 0530 hours 31 March 51 Morale
of troops excellent

The 4th Rangers, after relief, started back to Taegu via truck and rail. The 187th RCT returned to Taegu in army service. The 2d Rangers arrived back in Taegu about 0530 hours on Saturday, 31 March 1951. Sergeants David T. Buford and Herculano Dias were admitted to the hospital. Corporal Donald L. Felder was admitted to the hospital but would return to duty on 3 April. Corporal John W. Gould was assigned and joined from the 187th ARCT. Sergeant John "Pop" Jones was admitted to the hospital on 2 April and would not return.

In the Aftermath of the Historic Jump—Racial Booby Trap or Act of Sabotage?

[4 April 1951] Morning Report
RECORD OF EVENTS
  Reld fr atch 187th RCT atchd 7th Inf Div Ltr TWX Eighth US Army (EUSAK) dtd 28 Mar 51 Departed Taegu Korea by rail at 1030 hrs arrived Andong, Korea 2400 hrs distance traveled approx 80 miles.

The 2d Ranger Company now had seven officers and ninety-five enlisted men available for duty. It continued northward, departing Andong about 0100 hours on Thursday, 5 April, and arrived at Chunchon at 1000 hours. The distance traveled was approximately seventy-five miles. The Buffalo Rangers billeted and rationed with the Netherlands (Dutch) Battalion that had been attached to the 38th Infantry, 2d ID, since December 1950 because of the division's heavy losses.

The Buffalos reached the 7th Infantry Division Replacement Company at Chechon-ni and picked up fifty-two "leg replacements" on temporary duty for two weeks of training for possible formation of another Ranger company (or battalion). These men were a big, big surprise to everyone. The company strength for duty suddenly shot up by fifty percent (from 103 to 155). The two weeks of training were recorded on the Morning Report, but Special Order 96 stated that these men were assigned "for an indefinite period for training."[26]

There were many suspicious thoughts about this surprise, as the regular wartime planned replacement system was just beginning to function and furnish timely replacements to the 8th Army. First, only the Negro replacements to the 7th Division were sent to 2d Ranger Company. Second, there was no advance notice of these replacements. Third, their military occupational skills (MOS) were extremely varied, including infantry, artillery, drivers, mechanics, and cooks. Fourth, they were neither airborne-nor ranger-qualified soldiers, nor were they volunteers for the same. Finally, they remained assigned to their regular units, but were on temporary duty "for training"—after having just completed thirteen weeks basic and advanced training.

The area around Chechen was chosen for billeting and training. At the same time, 2d Ranger Company also received a few triple volunteers or shove-outs from the 187th ARCT; these, too, were not expected. They were airborne- qualified but had not gone through Ranger training. The 187th ARCT already had a few Negro paratroopers and at least one black officer, Captain James Miller, 2d Battalion Surgeon. The question discussed among the veteran Rangers was whether these guys were quitters or eight balls.[27]

Terrell, John Jr.RA13348307 PfcMOS: 7475
Vails, Robert A. Jr.RA12327222 PfcMOS:7475

On 12 April, the company received another 113 Negro EM for training purposes. The company strength was now up to 269. These replacements were not only more infantrymen and artillerymen, but also included combat engineers, ordnance men, artillerymen, military police, quartermasters, and even a bandsman (a trumpeter who brought his personal instrument with him). On 16 April, another 78 EM were attached for training, so the company's nominally authorized strength was now assigned. This group also included more infantry, engineers, ordnance, and a bandsman. Second Company was very glad to get the bandsman and taught him the American and Chinese bugle calls. He imitated Chinese bugle calls during combat training, and was used to jazz up the Buffaloes' walking fire-attack. Throughout April, as fast as more black replacements were received, they were sent to the Buffalo Rangers. By the 23d of the month, the Company had 404 enlisted men. Numerically speaking, this strength easily constituted enough manpower to form nearly three companies (except for the lack of officers).

Background and Perceptions of Racial Pressure

Within the Buffalo ranks everyone felt that General Ferenbaugh was a pretty straight shooter and fair in his reports about the unit's service and combat performances. There were no records of courts martial, AWOLs, or poor performances under fire. On 6 February, he had reported that 2d Ranger Company was performing its assigned missions although at only sixty-one percent authorized strength, and praised its members for their specialized training and high *esprit de corps*. What Ferenbaugh didn't know was the burning desire of the Buffalo Rangers to erase the myth—particularly among officers from the South—about black troops being unable and unwilling to fight except under white leadership. These feelings were directed primarily at General Almond, who had always blamed and castigated his black personnel for the World War II failures of the 92d ID in Italy.

At this time the Buffalo Rangers did not know that an evaluation and review was being performed by then-Lieutenant General Ridgway. The general had reached the conclusion that the expectations of Ranger companies to conduct long-range penetrations and raids on hostile installations were highly unrealistic. He believed that using Rangers in this manner was beyond their capabilities and invited their destruction. When Ridgway succeeded MacArthur as Far East Commander, he passed his views on to Lieutenant General James A. Van Fleet, who assumed command of the Eighth Army in mid-April 1951. Van Fleet ordered his G-3, Brigadier General Gilman C. Mudgett, to carefully survey and report on the Ranger situation. Within a month, General Mudgett reported the "conclusion that a Ranger battalion at Army level would meet with general approval."[28]

Concerned about the employment of the Ranger companies under divisional control, Colonel Van Houten sent Lieutenant Colonel James Y. Adams to Korea as an observer of Ranger activities. Van Houten felt that each of the six companies was being deployed in a variety of what he considered faulty ways. In a personal letter to Major General Maxwell D. Taylor, Office of the Assistant Chief of Staff G-3, Van Houten expressed his concern about forming the companies into a provisional battalion under 8th Army control and attached to the 187th ARCT for operations, training, and logistical support.[29] Ranger units should not be placed under the 187th ARCT's operational control, he argued, because they would likely become just another airborne infantry battalion because the 187th was in need of replacements. Van Houten insisted that Rangers could still accomplish the missions visualized by General J. Lawton Collins *if* they were an independent unit under the control of Eighth Army.

On 12 May, one month after assuming the Far East Command, Ridgway reached the conclusion that too much attention had been placed on airborne missions. Van Houten submitted a draft TO&E for the Ranger battalion, a proposal he wrote to the Department of Defense in Washington to provide several recommendations about the Army's racial situation involving the complex and touchy issue of black soldiers in the Eighth Army. Ridgway felt that the 24th Infantry Regiment should be deactivated and replaced with the 14th Infantry. The black personnel of the 24th would be integrated into other units on an individual-MOS basis. Ridgway concluded that the members of the other black units, the 3/9 (2d ID), the 3/15 (3d ID), and the 64th Tank Battalion, should be integrated with white personnel. Finally, Ridgway also moved to integrate the service units, as well as the 40th and 45th National Guard Divisions being deployed to Japan.

Ridgway took the high moral ground that it was un-American and un-Christian for free citizens to be taught and subjugated in the manner we were. Plus, the change might ensure an *esprit de corps* that a fighting army needed. Ridgway's idea was neither foreign nor a complete surprise to the Pentagon high command. Two other Army studies of blacks in Korea had recommended the same thing. The top leaders, Major General Anthony C. McAuliffe, G-1, and Taylor, G-3, also had endorsed and favored this "full" desegregation move. However, Secretary of the Army Frank Pace's advice was to move slowly and carefully. Once the complete desegregation gate was opened, he cautioned, it would be harder to retreat should it not be fully successful. Only General Wade H. Haislip, in the Department of the Army, strongly opposed it.

Word soon spread via rumors within the 8th Army that desegregation had met with the approval of Van Fleet, and that many of the senior generals favored it. A few others opposed it, notably General Almond of X Corps. The wheels of complete desegregation turned very slowly, and it was not until 1 October 1951 that the 24th Infantry was inactivated.[30]

None of this information was known to the Buffalo Rangers in April 1951, when they received the mission of training for combat survival. Although the task came as a complete surprise to the Buffalo Rangers, they were glad to get fresh manpower from which they hoped to create additional Rangers after the Munsan-ni jump. Since the replacements had received only seven weeks of basic training on individual weapons and had no training on the bayonet (which was Captain Allen's favorite Ranger weapon), the 2d Ranger Company's first task was to get them in top physical condition. It was approaching springtime, so bare-chested road runs, speed marches, and bayonet training were the order of the day. Training stressed self-sufficiency of the lowest unit and drilled the concepts of movement to contact; fire and movement; support fire; assault with marching fire; capture of objective; reorganization; preparation for counter-attack; inspection of personnel and equipment; and signals/communication. The typical day began with a road march in the approach formation while carrying light packs, weapons, and ammunition to the training site. Replacements were mixed in with the regular troops. The men started with a squad in the attack and worked up to the company in the attack.

Queen was worried that 2d Ranger Company would be committed to a mission destined for failure. He knew it was rumored that these units had not passed their Army Training Test (ATT) and were incapable of providing close support combat fire to the infantry units without too many errors (short rounds). Failures of this sort would provide the opportunity for Corps to send in some white officers to get promotions and awards . . . at the expense of black Ranger fodder. Almost daily, from 6 to 24 April, a red-headed major driving an X Corps headquarters jeep observed the training exercises. He arrived about 0900 hours and parked on a hill overlooking the training area, observed what 2d Ranger Company was doing, and took a few notes. None of the men of 2d Ranger Company remember him introducing himself or visiting the company CP to explain his actions or purpose.

Without warning, on 24 April the Buffalo Rangers were relieved of their special "leg replacement" training mission.

Morning Report
[24 April 1951] RECORD OF EVENTS
VOCO relieved from training mission of 7th Inf Div and attached 31st RCT for employment unit departed Hangyee, Korea approx 1345 hrs via mtr march Arrived 7th Division Forward at 1500 arrived 31st RCT 1600 hrs distance traveled approx 20 miles rec'd mission to defend the high ground (Hill 613 in the vicinity of UT 265 070). Morale of troops excellent.

Not until 1994 would men from the 2d Ranger Company—including its officers—learn that Almond had gotten his racial policy endorsed and implemented by Ferenbaugh as follows:

> Colored troops who arrive in this division, if they have the proper MOS's, will be assigned to the 2d Ranger Company. Others who are assigned by error will be returned to Eighth Army Replacement Battalion. Personnel will not be mixed within units. If Ranger Company becomes greatly over strength, another company will be formed.

In other words, any black soldiers coming into the 7th Division with an infantry MOS (4745)—the most common MOS coming out of basic training and in the replacement pipeline—would be assigned to 2d Ranger Company with no consideration for their lack of Airborne or Ranger qualifications. More importantly, these replacements would not be volunteers—despite the pleas of Airborne and Ranger recruiters. This was the inauspicious beginning of the era of complete racial integration.

It was well known that troop commanders up to the rank of Brigadier General feared the immediate wrath of General Almond. He had relieved the commander of the 31st Infantry, Colonel Richard P. Overshine, after the Inchon landing. He shook up Major General David Barr, division commander, and put the skids under him after the Hungnan evacuation. Several other commanders had risked mission failure rather than face Almond's verbal outbursts. It is a wonder that Ferenbaugh skirted Almond's order by keeping all of his black troops stashed in the 2d Rangers, regardless of MOS (including quartermaster, ordnance, artillery, MP, and bandsmen), rather than sending them back to 8th Army. Perhaps Ferenbaugh guessed that the 7th Division soon would be moved from the control of X Corps, or that MacArthur, Almond's benefactor, would soon be relieved by President Harry Truman.[31] This shift of the 7th Division to the IX Corps, when it happened, was a blessing for the Buffalo Rangers. In retrospect, the fact that 2d Ranger Company remained attached to the 7th ID—a division to which black troops had never before been assigned—and under the benevolent command of Ferenbaugh was downright miraculous.

When the Army began integrating its personnel, men of all races had the opportunity to analyze and respond to myths fabricated by society and examine stereotypes firsthand. Predictions such as Van Houten's *"You people* won't fight when you get to Korea!" were disproved by valiant service in combat. On an individual basis, soldiers began relating to people of different races and began realizing that our main concerns, challenges, and problems usually were very similar. Families, the future of our children, and coming home safely were the top priorities of nearly every soldier—regardless of the color of his skin. Soldiers were beginning to construct their own opinions. As time passed, the Buffalo Rangers dealt with traditional, or alleged, stories that had been told of people of a different color. Direct knowledge and experience provided explanations for those things that previously could only be imagined. We lived and died together, formed friendships together, and established lifelong relationships—particularly with those men of our sister unit, 4th Ranger Company—that often knew no color.

On 1 July 1951, General Ridgway's proposal to deactivate the 24th Infantry Division and begin integrating the U.S. Army in Korea was approved by the Department of the Army. In order to ensure across-the-board desegregation, the service established a goal that every Army unit in Korea should contain an equal percentage of African American personnel. Within a short time, however, the laudatory goal presented the Army in Korea with a problem: if a disproportionate number of black soldiers were sent to Korea, what should be done with the additional black personnel? The solution was obvious to proponents of desegregation: they should be distributed among and integrated into units throughout the Army worldwide.

Supporters and opponents of integration alike realized that merely desegregating the portion of the Army that was fighting in Korea was logistically impossible. If the military's system of deployment, training, and personnel rotation was to remain operational, distinctions based on race would either have to be maintained everywhere or nowhere. Thus, barring the cessation of integration entirely, it was only a matter of time before desegregation occurred throughout the Army. Additionally, the success of desegregation in Korea made arguing that integration should not occur elsewhere impossible. With that in mind, the U.S. Army's European Command in April 1952 began implementing a plan to integrate all of the troops under its jurisdiction, using the Army in Korea as a model. The desegregation of Army units around the world gradually followed. Ironically, as painstakingly slow as this process seemed, by the time the U.S. Supreme Court ruled segregation unconstitutional in its landmark *Brown v. Board of Education* decision on 17 May 1954, the Armed Forces had already pioneered the road to integration.

Chapter 6

Attack and Defense of Hill 581, 20-21 May 1951

"Ranger Bill Weathersbee and some of his friends were cleaning their weapons when a rifle company from the 7th Infantry Division came through their positions to continue after the Chinese. The rifle company commander was astounded at the level of carnage he found. He halted his company and asked the Rangers questions about the action. The company commander then faced his unit and said in a loud voice, 'I want all of you to look around. This is what happens to the enemy when soldiers don't panic.' The company commander then faced the Rangers and said, 'Gentlemen, I salute you.' With a snappy salute, he moved his men on."

— *Rangers in Korea*[32]

The battle for Hill 581 was one of the largest that 2d Ranger Company participated in while attached to the 31st Infantry Regiment. The 31st was nicknamed "The Polar Bears" because its regimental crest contained a polar bear standing in the upright position, with the unit motto, *pro patria* ("for country" in Latin), inscribed below it.

During its first five months of service in Korea, the 31st Infantry had three commanders: Colonel Richard P. Overshine, who was relieved by General Almond; Colonel Allan D. MacLean, who was killed at Chosin; and Colonel John A. Gavin, a 1932 West Point graduate who didn't appear to have the "fire and brimstone" needed at the time. In early March 1951, General Almond sent Colonel William J. McCaffrey, who had served on Almond's staff in the 92d Infantry (Buffalo) Division in Italy during WWII, and was the current X Corps Deputy Chief of Staff, to command the 31st. Although the regiment appeared to be the weakest of the three, its regimental colors carried emblems of historic service from Philippines/Siberia (1916-1920), Philippines/Shanghai (1921-1945), and Japan/Korea (1946-1949, extended to 1953).

Second Company departed Hill 210, Chipon-ni, by foot march at 1700 hours on 17 May 1951. It arrived at the rear area at 0600 hours on 18 May. Its mission was to attack and hold Hill 581. The attack would begin at approximately 1500 hours. A roster of personnel departing on R&R leave showed only three officers, but actually four—Captain Allen and Lieutenants Pryor, Freeman, and Anthony—departed, with eleven enlisted men. This brought the strength available for line duty down to three officers (Queen, Cliette, and Wilburn) and fewer than eighty men. Wilburn remained with the unit rear detachment to coordinate all supply, mess, and administrative duties, and also to act as XO.

The Rangers were attached to the 1/31st for the attack. Queen doesn't recall meeting the Battalion CO or anyone from his staff for the attack order. The terrain was familiar to Queen because this was the same hill from which he had executed a night withdrawal about two weeks earlier. The Rangers didn't have any attachments from the Heavy Weapons Company or a forward observer (Artillery or Mortars). There was only enough manpower to form two platoons, each of approximately 32 men plus a Ranger medic; a 60mm mortar squad; and a small command group. Each platoon had a three-man LMG team with about six BARs per platoon. Queen put Cliette in the lead with his 3d Platoon, followed by the command group, then Master Sergeant George Rankins with a combination 1st/2d Platoon with the mortar squad in the middle of it. The point fire team in Cliette's platoon contained Privates First Class Isaac Grasty, Jr., Winston M. Jackson, James Hardy, and William K. Mathis. Some of these men were part of the group of ten leg replacements General Ferenbaugh had allowed to be transferred in from the group of more than 400 who were sent to 2d Ranger Company for special training in early April. The ten who remained with 2d Ranger Company made up a fire team trained by Higginbotham. Grasty called Mathis "The Get-Away Man" because he could run so fast. Mathis had been a college track star before enlisting, and his speed made him an asset as a radio operator because his ability to outrun others helped keep the radio secure. Radio operators often had to be close to an advancing enemy force in order to radio their exact position back to other Army units, so they sometimes had to make a hasty escape after establishing their position in order to keep themselves and their radio out of enemy hands.

The advance was made in column of platoons. Sergeant Marion Alston, Communication (Commo) Sergeant, was carrying an SCR–300 on the battalion command net. Corporal Ray H. Rhone, Jr., radio operator for Cliette, was also on the battalion command net. During platoon-sized long-range patrol operations along the COPL (Combat Outpost Line), the platoons frequently operated in this manner because they were almost always out of Company range.

Queen remained near the combined platoon because it did not have an officer—not that he had any doubt about Rankins' ability. But this was the first time that the ten new legs were going into heavy action. Thus far they had performed in a satisfactory manner.

About 1000 hours, Battalion notified Queen that an air strike using P-51 or P-47 aircraft would hit the forward (northwest) slopes of Hill 581. The general direction of the attack was toward the southwest. Mathis put the air-ground identification panel on the back of his pack because his fire team was in the lead. "The Get-Away Man's" task was to outrun any aircraft that came too close. The air strike was performed by three aircraft that came directly over the long axis of the company's formation and advance. The air strike dropped napalm about a third of the way up the hill.

The company had worked its way about two-thirds of the way to the top when the point team was surprised by an outpost of two or three Chinese. The enemy popped up only forty yards away and managed to run over the crest and disappear. Queen looked at Mathis, the point man, and exclaimed, "Before the day is over, you are going to regret passing those enemy soldiers!"

When the Rangers reached the top of Hill 581, they reported in to Battalion. The firefight started a little after noon when both sides met at the top of Hill 581. The lead Ranger platoon pushed over the crest and was greeted by a fusillade of automatic fire, mainly from burp guns. The initial flurry of bullets skimmed through the trees at shoulder level, clipping off leaves and branches. The lead troops hit the ground and returned fire. Several men were wounded. The most seriously injured Ranger was Sergeant Kirk P. Adkins, who was hit in the chest and dropped to the right front of the command group. Queen rushed over and dragged him back while Alston ran up to the front, using his M-1 to provide covering fire. Sergeant Leroy White, who frequently carried a camera, also ran up to provide covering fire. Queen gave up Adkins when Rankins and Courts arrived to carry him away. Because 2d Ranger Company lacked attached forward observers, Queen would have handled the fire missions while Captain

Allen deployed the company. Since Allen was absent, Queen performed both functions.

Queen got Alston back to his side and radioed Battalion. From a prone position with his field glasses he looked across the front and down into the valley falling away to the south. What appeared to be an enemy battalion was approaching the hill from the southwest. Doc Rabbit (Thomas), the company's medic, was working on Adkins, whose chest wound was so severe that if he did not get back to the aid station for helicopter evacuation he would likely die.

The firefight continued with small arms through most of the afternoon. Neither side was able to advance, and the enemy seemed to be testing out the Rangers's strength with advance units. The main force, estimated at battalion strength, was moving into an assembly area for the main attack. While simultaneously attempting to control and deploy the company, Queen called fire missions in to Battalion over the command net by relaying the coordinates and asking for harassment and interdiction fire to break up the enemy firepower.

Unable to advance, Queen was ordered to hold the company in position. He placed Cliette's 3d Platoon up on the line to the right of the combination 1st/2d Platoon. The 1st and 2d Platoons were located in a heavily wooded area with dense undergrowth. Runners from the 1st Platoon reached the Company CP by walking behind their positions to the left because of the dense vegetation. Cliette warned Queen about an unmarked minefield in the right rear of his position. Cliette remembered the field from a previous mission when 2d Ranger Company had been a covering force for the withdrawal of another battalion. The 1st Platoon covered the left side of the hill. Since this area was open, the mortar squad was placed behind 1st Platoon within Queen's voice range. The mortars were deployed on a shallow ridge on the reverse slope of the crest. There was no company reserve.

When the Rangers began running low on ammunition, Queen remembered that 2d Ranger Company had buried some extra ammo in the 60mm mortar pits on the hill about two weeks earlier. All he had to do now was find the pits and hope the ammo had not disappeared or been dug up by the enemy. While waiting for a re-supply from Battalion, some machine gun and mortar ammo was found and distributed. Queen told the Rangers hauling the wounded back to the aid station to return with ammo. He didn't expect the laborers of the civilian Korean Army Service and Labor Corps (KASLC) to come up to their positions because they were non-combatants. He believed that when they saw all of the wounded 2d Ranger Company had suffered, non-combatants would balk at approaching the front unless they had some very close and forceful escorts. With his front spread thin and ammunition running low, Queen tried to organize the men in groups of two or three for mutual support, because no word of weapons attachment had been received or was really expected. Grenade booby traps were rigged to provide a warning to cover any remaining gaps in the line.

The volume of enemy fire and length of contact convinced the experienced Queen that he was facing a reinforced regular enemy battalion and *not* a guerrilla battalion, and that the enemy was employing a two-company pronged attack. Reinforcements and artillery support would be needed if the enemy mounted a sustained or heavier attack. The ridge was too narrow and steep for a jeep to climb, and it would take another company two to four hours to make a flanking move to support 2d Ranger Company. There was, however, another rifle company behind 2d Ranger Company's position, and some of the enemy small arms fire was passing over the 2d's position and hitting the rifle company and Battalion Headquarters strung out behind them lower down on the ridge. Queen contacted Battalion and called in artillery fire to defend the 2d's flanks. Supporting artillery positions were situated in the valley to their left flank, meaning they fired at a right angle to the 2d's position. A lot of this fire was either too long or short because of the steep and narrow ridge line where the Rangers had set up their positions. Queen tried to plot pre-arranged defensive concentrations, but to do so he had to close the sheaf (concentrated) or zero in one gun and then have the remainder close on it. Otherwise, the result would be a scattered battery time on target (TOT) that would almost certainly rain friendly fire into the company perimeter. By dusk, Queen had made good adjustment of fire to cover the front and right flank of the 2d's positions.

During the fighting, Corporal Ralph W. Sutton was shot in the left side of his chest. He died quickly. Sergeants Posey and Weathersbee were detailed to remove Sutton's body from Hill 581 and take it to the aid station. When they arrived with Sutton's corpse, they found a re-supply point next to the aid station and a number of Korean laborers with carrying racks—A-frame packs used to carry items on their backs. Posey and Weathersbee loaded the laborers with small arms ammunition, machine gun ammunition, grenades, mortar rounds, and C-rations and departed for Hill 581. When they arrived at the company's position, they passed out ammunition and food just before dusk fell and returned the Korean laborers to a safe point away from the firing line. The enemy started a series of probing attacks just as the sergeants regained their former positions. The attacks would continue all night with great severity.

About dark (1900-2000 hours), a sergeant from the Battalion Weapons Company reported into the Company CP (a two-man foxhole) with a Machine Gun Section of about eight men. He either had two LMGs or one LMG and one HMG with LMG tripods. Queen told him to take a position in the center between the two platoons along the hill's crest. During the first hours of darkness, the enemy continued to probe 2d Ranger Company's lines, mainly on the right in Cliette's platoon area. Cliette needed help and called for it, so Queen moved the artillery rounds closer and closer until the shell bursts sent shrapnel into the trees in their immediate area. Although pressed hard, Queen hesitated to call for an air burst because they had not had time to dig in very deep—just slit-trench positions—or to erect overhead shelter. Despite the intensity of the fighting, the 2d suffered only a few light small arms casualties. Not everyone was so fortunate. By midnight, the sergeant from the Battalion Weapons Company made his way to Queen, told him all of his men were wounded, and that he was pulling out.

About 0300 hours, Cliette reported that the enemy had infiltrated into some of his positions. Queen ordered him to pull back to the ridge line by going to the left behind the combined 1st/2d Platoon. Queen then ordered 1st Platoon to draw back on a line with the Company CP (about twenty yards). The enemy was mounting an all-out attack, but without mortar support. Earlier, Queen had gone down to the 60mm mortar position and told Andrade to drop some rounds to the immediate front and over to the front and flank of the 3d Platoon. The mortarmen fired so rapidly that the base cap on the mortar tube blew off and disabled it. Wells, a light machine gun man, discovered his weapon was so hot that the rounds went off as soon as they entered the chamber—without his having to pull the trigger. Wells had fired his weapon from the hip and most of his ammunition was now gone. With his position in peril, Queen gave the word for the company to withdraw down the ridge line to Company A's area because it was time to call artillery fire in on their current position. All this time Queen's calls for artillery were being sent over the Battalion Command Radio Net and relayed to the Artillery Liaison Officer. Queen knew he was located close by because he could hear him repeat what he had said. The lieutenant, into whose area Queen had withdrawn, seemed a little frightened by the chaotic nighttime events. Queen's withdrawal might have looked to him as if the Chinese had broken through. The unnamed lieutenant told Queen that he had taken some casualties from the enemy fire that passed above 2d Ranger Company. Corporals Jacob Mason and Carl Hall manned an LMG on the right flank of 3d Platoon and provided covering fire for the platoon during the Chinese assault and subsequent platoon withdrawal.

Queen spread the company out in front of the new position. He had his platoon CP in a shallow hole about 4 x 6 feet and put his two-man command group (Alston and himself) in the hole. Queen redistributed weapons and ammunition, giving his M-1 rifle to someone whose weapon had jammed. Queen still had his .45-caliber pistol, which he would later use to lead the counterattack.

Queen passed the word that they were going to mount a counterattack to take back the hill at first light (about 0500 hours), about an hour before the official dawn (0600). He knew that the members of 2d Ranger Company couldn't afford to fail, regardless of their small numbers present on the line. They had to dispel and kill forever the myth that had hung over "black combat soldiers" about their willingness and inability to fight. They were not going to be pushed off that hill because it would have meant that they would have to retake it the next day. The shame of losing the hill without being annihilated would be too much to bear. Queen hated the idea of prepping for another attack after the loss of so many men in the initial assault, but he called for artillery on their old positions to prevent them from being overrun by enemy forces as they moved out to retake the high ground. Adjusting the artillery fire to brush up against 2d Ranger Company's position was a risk worth taking to hold enemy forces back.

The platoon from Company A remained in position as 2d Ranger Company rushed back up the hill in a walking firefight. A distance of forty to fifty yards separated 2d Ranger Company from Company A. During this assault Sergeant First Class Eugene Jennings was wounded and evacuated.

When 2d Ranger Company retook Hill 581, the early sunlight revealed scattered enemy corpses in their former positions on the reverse slope and crest of the hill.

Looking Back: Five Different Views from Foxhole Level

Private First Class Isaac Grasty, Jr.

Hill 581 was where I had my first big combat action or exposure. A couple of nights before the action, we had to withdraw from the same hill. We ran an all-night "strategic retreat," as we called it. On May 20th we went to retake the hill. We received no enemy heavy fire from the side we went up, even though we expected heavy fire. Once we reached the top and got halfway down the backside, all hell broke loose. We hit the ground right where we were. Legree Aikens was to my right sitting in an upright position about three yards away, firing his BAR, resting it on his knees with the bipod folded back. The main reason I was so near Aikens was that I was his assistant, with extra magazines for the BAR. Aikens was hit in the legs during the exchange of fire. Corporal Ralph W. Sutton was to my left in a standing position behind a tree. He asked me and Aikens to cover him while he went down the hill a little farther so he could get a better firing position. After Sutton left Aikens told me that he had been hit again. He handed me his BAR. About this time, we were ordered to pull back to the top of the hill.

I got the order to go down and help bring a wounded man back up. I got down there with three men and found that Sutton was the wounded Ranger. Each of us grabbed a limb in order to carry him. I had his left arm, under which there was a hole big enough to put your fist in. He had been killed instantly! After we got him to the top and covered him with a poncho, we were told to dig in for the night. Usually Aikens, Sutton, and I would dig in together, but this night I don't remember who was with me.

The firing started again just before daybreak. Lieutenant Queen called in artillery and told everyone to pull back. When I got out of my hole to do so, I was hit in the upper left arm and shoulder.

Because of bad weather at this little airfield somewhere in South Korea, I could not immediately be evacuated to a hospital for proper treatment. This was on May 21st. By the time I could be airlifted gangrene had set in, and it required an emergency operation. They saved my arm but left me permanently disabled, with only partial use of the limb. About ten days later I was evacuated to the USAF Hospital in Nagoya, Japan.

If there was anyone deserving an award, I would say Sutton did. Too bad he never got a chance to start the chicken farm he had planned when he got back home.

Sergeant Herman C. Jackson

We had buried some ammunition on Hill 581 before but we didn't know that one day we would return and use it. We had been patrolling when they decided to give us rest. This was a short rest period when we pulled back from the line.

They put up these showers, like we had never seen before. They had a pile of clean clothes on the ground when you came out of the shower. You could pick out anything decent to wear that would fit. We had been in the mountains so long that our clothes were shredded. It was a relief to get some clean clothes; some of the uniforms were in good shape.

We had put up a supply tent and several Rangers were cleaning weapons. We had some extra weapons on the supply truck that had to be cleaned. We started cleaning the weapons after taking a shower and changing clothes.

The sun was out and it was very hot. Captain Allen came in the tent and he saw this Korean sitting down. I don't think that he knew who the Korean was. Anyway, this Korean was helping us clean weapons, and that didn't seem too strange. We had a couple of young Korean boys working in the field kitchen with Sergeant First Class Parks. Just about every outfit had a few Koreans, somewhere. This Korean person had a field jacket on and the hood over his head, in the tent, on this hot day! Captain Allen said, "It's hot. How in the world can you sit there wearing that field jacket?" Captain Allen reached over and pulled the hood down, and all this hair fell down! It was a woman! Boy was Captain Allen surprised! He pitched a bitch! We all had a laugh, but the company commander didn't think this was very funny. He had her kicked out of the area and we finished cleaning the weapons ourselves.

On our way back to Hill 581 we climbed the mountain and saw some Koreans below us. As we passed toward 581 our pilots were bombing in the vicinity. Fighting was going on everywhere. As soon as we got to the top we made contact with the enemy. We were leap-frogging platoons into position. After we completed one leap, we ran into heavy rifle fire.

I remember Corporal Sutton was with me during this time. He climbed a doggone tree to get a clear vision of the enemy. I was about five yards from him, as I had just moved forward. I said, "Come on. Let's get these mother f***ers!" The next thing that I remembered is that I was hit! I was hit in the stomach, the right thigh, and right wrist. I fell forward to the ground. In just a minute or so Doc Rabbit (Thomas) came up. Rabbit said, "Damn, Jack, you are hit pretty badly!" He gave me a shot of morphine. As a matter of fact, he gave me two more shots. I guess he thought I would die in comfort. Rabbit cut my cartridge belt off me. I had two pouches of grenades and I was carrying an M-1 rifle. Rabbit cut off all the stuff that I was carrying.

I started moving back a little piece, then some medics came up and started walking me down the hill. They walked me to the aid station where I was placed in an ambulance and went to Division Evac. From there I was moved to a MASH unit. While there, I was surprised to see some Korean or Chinese being treated. They operated on me and I was moved to another MASH unit, and from there I was moved to a hospital in Japan.

I remained in Japan for some time. They were getting ready to return me to 2d Ranger Company in Korea. We went before a board of medical officers, test-fired our weapons, and were ready to leave for Korea. As we approached the time to move out, a sergeant told me and another soldier to wait. He ordered us to turn in our equipment. "*You* are going home!"

Samuel Payne, Jr.

On Hill 581 we took a pounding but secured the hill. Sergeant Aikens got hit, he was taken down; but we continued on the attack. Our platoon pushed through the 3d Platoon on the way to engage the enemy, who was preparing to do battle. As members of the 2d Platoon, we did not hesitate; we were committed. We fixed bayonets. One of our men did battle with an enemy using the bayonet, killing him. I cannot remember the name of the Ranger. We charged up the hill screaming, "Buffalo——Mother——!" This was our battle cry throughout our stay in Korea.

After securing the hill, we began to dig in, expecting the Chinese to counterattack. They did counterattack, and they seemed to bring every small-arms weapon and ammunition, including the kitchen sink, toward our hasty defensive positions. We could see the Chinese marching in column, coming toward us. Lieutenant Queen called in artillery fire from division. The enemy still continued to move forward.

Sutton was hit just before dusk. When one of the enemy dead fell nearby, we knew he was Chinese by the strong smell of fish and garlic. We knew they were nearby because of that smell.

My BAR fire team's mission was to protect the machine guns. My BAR team was dug in beneath the machine gun manned by Wells. The enemy tried many times to knock the machine gun(s) out, but we kept grenades raining down on them. A few of them got killed or wounded and pulled back. They couldn't stop our machine guns. I know that he [Wells] killed ten to thirty. Orders were passed down not to fire until we had a target. The enemy had overrun some of the 3d Platoon positions and wounded Rangers. But all of our people walked out or were helped out. We were told by our platoon Sergeant, Dude Walker, to hold our positions, and to cover the withdrawal of the 3d Platoon.

By daylight the enemy had faded away, taking what wounded or dead were left. The 2d Ranger Company would not budge! We sent out contact patrols but located no living enemy soldiers. We, as a fighting unit, had fought with regiment after regiment in the 7th Division. We had fought with all three outfits (17th, 32d, and now the 31st Regiment). What we saw was living proof that the 2d Ranger Company had held and could hold its own with any fighting machine that they threw at us.

Wheeler S. Small, Jr.

[Note: Ranger Small was wounded at Tanyang Pass and returned to the company after getting a ten-day R&R from the Osaka hospital. He said that he got a twice-daily massage with oil from the nurse because of his extremely dry skin. He went higher in "Buffalo Heaven" for ten days while on R&R from the hospital: "You should have seen me," he said, "a black man horseback riding in Japan!"]

On 20 May, the entire 2d Ranger Company was in a firefight. Hill 581 was a tough hill to take. I think that we slept on the forward side of the hill. I dug a spot and covered up with my parachute because of the rain. We went over the hill that afternoon and dug in to defend our positions. We got attacked for about six hours. To me, this was the longest engagement with the enemy that we had. It was a rough time for me because I had diarrhea and I couldn't leave the foxhole. Bullets were flying everywhere. I was firing my rifle and shitting at the same time. It was quite an ordeal!

They were overrunning our position. We were forced to pull back and set up on the opposite side of the hill. Lieutenant Queen called in the artillery. He kept telling them: "Drop closer! Drop closer!" until the enemy was forced back.

At daybreak we went back and cleaned up and secured the hill. We found out later that 2d Ranger Company was the only outfit that stayed on Hill 581.[33]

Sergeant George Rankins

[Note: Sergeants George Rankins and Curtis Courts were the two Rangers responsible for saving Kirk P. Adkins' life, along with a medical miracle.]

All hell broke loose! Shortly thereafter, Lieutenant Queen ordered us to rejoin the main group at the top of the hill. When we arrived at the top he conversed with Lieutenant Queen, who asked: "Rankins, are all your men present?" I replied, "Yes, sir, except [Kirk P.] Adkins. He is at the bottom of the hill dead!" Lieutenant Queen snapped back, "I don't give a damn if he is chopped up into little pieces. You get him and bring him up here!" This was a little scary because Queen never used profanity. I replied, "Yes, Sir!" and hauled ass back down the hill with Curtis Courts and Iron Head Gray.

We found Kirk there, alive, though shot to pieces. His intestines were spread out on the ground. We actually pushed parts back inside and securely wrapped him, as best as possible, with my field jacket. We started to drag him up the hill, then down toward the aid station. A helicopter landed close to us. The pilot was slightly lost and looking for a certain unit. We told him that this was not the unit, but we did have a comrade who was very seriously wounded. We wanted him to take him to get medical aid. He replied, in no uncertain terms, "NO!" I insisted, and he again said, "NO!" I put my .45 to his neck and informed him that Kirk was going in that chopper, or else! We loaded him into the chopper. There was no doubt in my mind that the pilot tried to turn us down because of color.

We went back up to the company and were hit hard that night. The enemy tried to walk into and around our positions. Read military history and you will find a West Pointer received the Medal of Honor in 'Nam for the same type of action.

This Was Truly a Purple Heart Hill

Within the next twenty-four hours, Captain Allen and the large group on R&R returned for duty. They hurried to the top of the hill because the battle news had spread. Nonetheless, the number of our men present for duty in the foxholes dropped by almost twenty-five percent in just one day! In the battle of Tanyang Pass, the 2d Ranger Company had suffered more killed in action casualties, but not as many wounded in action. By the beginning of June all those seriously wounded had been transferred to station hospital, put in temporary rehab programs, or moved stateside and dropped from the rolls.

There may have been Purple Hearts for Rangers who were treated on the spot and remained in position until 2d Ranger Company was relieved. In any case, on 19–20 May 1951, the following Rangers of 2d Ranger Company received the Purple Heart:

Private First Class Legree Aikens—Seriously Wounded in Action
Sergeant Kirk P. Adkins—Seriously Wounded in Action
Sergeant Eugene V. Arnold—Lightly Wounded in Action
Sergeant Clinton Cleveland—Lightly Wounded in Action
Private First Class James K. Conway—Lightly Wounded in Action
Corporal Donald L. Felder—Lightly Wounded in Action
Sergeant John E. Ford, Jr.—Lightly Wounded in Action
Corporal John W. Gould—Seriously Wounded in Action
Private First Class Isaac Grasty, Jr.—Lightly Wounded in Action
Corporal Walter S. Gray—Lightly Wounded in Action
Private First Class James Hardy—Lightly Wounded in Action
Private First Class James E. Harvey—Seriously Wounded in Action
Sergeant Herman C. Jackson—Seriously Wounded in Action
Corporal Emmett L. Johnson—Seriously Wounded in Action
Private First Class Ralph Leggs, Jr.—Seriously Wounded in Action
Corporal William G. Rhodes—Lightly Wounded in Action
Corporal Jude P. St. Martin—Seriously Wounded in Action
Corporal Ralph W. Sutton—Killed in Action
Corporal William Tucker—Seriously Wounded in Action
Private First Class Joseph Whitmore—Lightly Wounded in Action
Sergeant Henry Wilson—Lightly Wounded in Action

The subject of criteria for awards was totally neglected in Ranger orientation. The company executive officers performed both administrative and combat duties while on the line. The fact that Rangers could recommend others for awards was never broached. Almost all of the awards in the company were recommended by the 2d's officers. At no time did battalion, regiment, or division turn down an award that was recommended; however, no utilization was made of the Bronze Star for meritorious service or the Commendation Medal for outstanding service. There were too many Rangers who didn't receive awards, but should have. BAR men, such as Sergeant Culver Gibson, were the firepower backbone of the unit on Hill 581.

Many times Rangers—such as Sergeant First Class Orrie Tucker, Supply Sergeant; Sergeant First Class Nathan Parks, Mess Sergeant; Sergeant George Jackson, Jr., Personnel Clerk; and Corporal Glen Jenkins, Jr., Motor Corporal/Mechanic—operated without close supervision. Their successes at keeping the unit supplied, fed, and rolling, regardless of the mode (including moonlighting without being apprehended), were miracles because of the many frequent attachments and moves.

Many Rangers were cited for bravery for their actions on Hill 581. General Ferenbaugh came down to the company area and bestowed the awards personally. The following Rangers were recognized for bravery:

> First Lieutenant James C. Queen—Silver Star
> Master Sergeant George Rankins—Silver Star
> Sergeant Curtis Courts—Silver Star
> Corporal Anthony Andrade—Bronze Star with "V" Device
> First Lieutenant Albert D. Cliette—Bronze Star with "V" Device
> Sergeant Culver V. Gibson—Bronze Star with "V" Device
> Corporal Joseph J. Wells—Bronze Star with "V" Device

Wells' Bronze Star states that he distinguished himself by heroic achievement near Sang-Kwiryang, Korea, on 21 May 1951:

> On this date, when the left flank of the 2d Ranger Company was overrun by a numerically superior enemy force, Corporal Wells, light machine gunner in the company, and his assistant were directed by the platoon leader to cover the withdrawal of the 3d Platoon to high ground within the 1st Platoon's positions. The machine gun had been damaged in a previous firefight and was low on ammunition. In spite of these obstacles Corporal Wells effectively covered the withdrawal of his unit. While in his exposed position, he was subjected to fire from three enemy machine guns, but he remained in position, constantly applying immediate action to his gun to keep it in operation until all ammunition was expended. Corporal Wells then threw hand grenades at the enemy until told to withdraw by the commanding officer. The heroic actions displayed by Corporal Wells reflect great credit on him and the military service.

MORNING REPORT
[25 May 1951] Record of Events
Enemy killed 50. Enemy wounded approximately 90. 1 EM killed. Morale of troops excellent. Company attacked by Chinese troops estimated regiment size approximately 2300 hours 20 May 51. Fight continued until approximately 0545 hours 21 May 51. Estimated enemy killed 60 wounded. 10 EM wounded hill secured. Lt. Queen cited for heroic action in the face of enemy. Morale of troops excellent. Company relieved of Hill 581, 1300 hours 22 May 1951. Departed area 0630 hours by motor march for Honchon area. Arrived Honchon for Hill 246 mission to relieve elements of 7th Marine (Regiment). Mission accomplished approximately 1500 hours. Morale of troops excellent.

In Hindsight

Throughout the ensuing years, Queen has harbored some festering thoughts about what sparked him and the Buffalo Rangers in the battle for Hill 581. No doubt, many other participants have had some of the same thoughts. We know that the main thought of each infantryman in battle revolves around his desire to survive and to hope the same for his buddies. He wants to avoid becoming a coward, being injured or killed, except maybe to get the "million-dollar wound" that doesn't show or hamper any normal body functions. When the fight is over, he wants to be justly recognized and rewarded for his efforts. He feels a sense of elation and exhilaration when his unit accomplishes its objective. Queen recalls some of these same thoughts and others that have dwelt on his mind and come to the forefront during the company reunions since the war.

Chapter 7

Assault and Occupation of Hill 545, 11 June 1951

"The term 'Rangers' connotes small, highly trained elite units executing raids, patrols, or other operations behind enemy lines. The term also elicits images of intense *esprit de corps* and proficiency in unconventional warfare; it originated in the colonial period of US history when special troops 'ranged' between frontier posts."

— *Encyclopedia of the Korean War: A Political, Social, and Military History*[34]

On 28 May, 2d Ranger Company departed Hill 246 with the mission to secure Hill 545 in the area around Yononchanga. The Rangers would do so without some of their key members. Badly wounded Sergeant Kirk P. Adkins would remain at 3d Station Hospital for an indefinite period, so he was dropped from the rolls. Sergeant William "Doc Rabbit" Thomas and Corporal Willie "Pretty Boy" Coleman went on R&R to Japan. Sergeant Clinton "Crying" Cleveland and Sergeant First Class Donald West were evacuated to the hospital on 1 June. On 4 June, Corporal Julius Victor, who had been a driver for Major Tenza, Executive Officer, 3d Battalion, and Corporal Ramon West, a member of Anthony's replacement platoon who would become a damn fine BAR man, rejoined the company through the 7th Replacement Company's normal procedures.

When the company left Hill 581 and moved on to Hill 246, records show that it was briefly attached to the 17th RCT, then the 2d Battalion, 32d Infantry. While with the 17th RCT, the same battalion that had suffered heavy losses at the Chosin Reservoir and Tanyang Pass, the Buffalo Rangers learned the good news that the severely wounded soldier who had been evacuated at Tanyang, by being carried on a pole, with his hands and feet tied like a hog ready to be roasted, had survived! The 1/32d now had many new replacement personnel, including the Battalion CO.

Morning Report
[4 June 1951] RECORD OF EVENTS
Reld atchd fr 2d Bn 32th RCT & atchd 1st Bn 32d RCT Departed area DS823133
2300 hours by mtr march arrived area DS860182 2400 hours distance trv 6 miles.
Morale of troops excellent.

During the first two weeks of June, the company's present-for-duty strength hovered between 100 and 104, less mess, supply, and motor personnel, or about ninety to ninety-five for duty in the trenches (counting West and the company clerk). The company was operating in the Sanying-ni area, northwest of the Hwachon Reservoir, near the Kansas Line.

It was here that Joe Russo,[35] aid man with A Battery, 15th AAA Weapons Battalion, 7th Division, joined the Buffalo Rangers. Russo arrived in Korea in May 1951. He got into the service by lying about his age and joining his neighborhood buddies in the 696th Armored Field Artillery Battalion, 112th Field Artillery Group, part of the New Jersey National Guard. Russo was nineteen years old when he arrived in Korea. Here is how he described what he found when he arrived:

> The Kansas Line was being reinforced and bunkers were being built. I didn't have too much to do and I don't know if we were in the IX or X Corps area. I was placed on DS with the 2d Rangers. I asked our Company Clerk, "What does that mean?" and he said I was attached to them for medical support in camp. It also included going on patrol if I was needed. The Ranger Company's CP was located across a stream that ran off the Pukhan River. Battery A was on one side of the stream and the Rangers on the other side. A detachment of the 7th Signal Battalion and 17th RCT were also nearby. A temporary POW compound was set up near Battery A's CP. We experienced a lot of monsoon rain during this time.
>
> It was during the period June-July when I put in for the Soldiers Medal for saving the life of a cook who was asleep in a burning tent. Myself and another fellow drove a jeep through the enemy area at night to evacuate him because he was that badly burned. Many years later, after I was discharged, I did receive the Army Commendation Medal.

Movement North and Combat Action

The Morning Report of 4 June shows the company's senior aidman, Doc "Rabbit" Thomas, going on R&R to Japan, and Russo joined the Company to replace Thomas during this time.

Second Company was constantly on the move, creeping northward. On 5-6 June, the company moved to the vicinity of Yunokchong at 1100 hours, a distance of some ten miles. The Rangers were in a stand-down condition when word was received to secure the high ground to the north, which was covered with heavy forest and Chinese troops. This was a joint mission with the 1/32. The Rangers were to attack up the left (west) ridge while Company C attacked up the right (east) ridge.

The 2d Platoon, led by Freeman, was the lead platoon, with the Company Command Group following in single file. The ridge line was very narrow, heavily wooded, and steep, consisting of red clay-like soil similar to that found at Fort Benning. The Chinese were very well dug in, and our artillery shells were bursting on treetops because of the heavy vegetation. This was old growth forest, and the tree trunks were anywhere from one to three feet thick.

Second Company and Company C were almost abreast of each other during the attack. Queen, who was listening to the battalion command net, knew what was happening in Company C almost immediately. The lieutenant in the lead platoon had been a Platoon Sergeant in Company C, just like Freeman, before receiving a battlefield commission. He was using the fire support of the 4.2-inch mortars to support his assault. A couple of short rounds fell in the platoon area and the Lieutenant was seriously wounded in both legs. He took off his belt and tied a tourniquet around his legs, saving his own life.

There was a narrow, uphill ridge that sloped down on the left and right sides of the hill. The 2d Platoon attacked from the bottom of the hill while the enemy was throwing grenades and firing down on the platoon. Private First Class James Peteress, Jr., led the attack, pressing forward using fire and movement, vigorously employing his BAR. The enemy was dug in and using American-made Thompson submachine guns and 60mm mortars against the Buffalo Rangers. Peteress was wounded and instinctively tried to fall to the prone position. The extra pair of pack suspenders attached to his heavily laden BAR belt caught on a branch of the tree that he was leaning against and hiding behind. Others tried to pull him down, but the limb would not immediately give or break. He was hit multiple times while caught in that position and died shortly after evacuation. In a company formation the day before, Queen had awarded Peteress, an extraordinary BAR man, his third Purple Heart.

With Peteress dead, Posey moved off to the left of the ridge in the hope of getting into position to relieve the enemy pressure from the attacking 2d Platoon. Once in position Posey opened fire on the enemy with a carbine. The enemy immediately picked up on Posey's position and responded with grenades and return fire that struck Posey in the right arm. The wound rendered his arm useless and he was unable to fire his carbine, which fell to the ground and tumbled down the hill. Thinking fast, Posey used his left hand to pull his .45 out of its holster. With this as his only weapon, he charged the enemy from the left side as his squad charged forward from the right. Behind Posey, the squad routed the enemy from their positions, killing all enemy soldiers in the area. Only after checking the men in his squad did Posey allow his wounds to be treated. For these heroic actions, he was later awarded the Silver Star.

Queen was using artillery to suppress the enemy fire on their ridge line. The short rounds on Company C threw an air of caution into the situation. Queen was notified that no TOTs of battalion size would be fired closer than 500 yards to the unit's front line. This was a problem, because he knew that the artillery unit firing his missions was a National Guard or Reserve Corps Artillery Unit, and he didn't trust the firing accuracy of these groups.

The opposing two sides were so close that Queen could hear the enemy's 60mm mortars' propellant shell cartridges fire when the shells were dropped in the tube. The shells were falling to the side of the very narrow ridge because of the lack of clearance for firing. Both sides were handicapped by the lack of overhead clearance for mortar firing. Queen's dilemma was to get artillery onto a hilltop less than 100 yards from his lead squad. He called in the coordinates but neglected to provide the location of the company's front. When asked, he replied "five hundred yards," and asked, with Allen's permission, for battalion TOT. Because the attack was stalled on the right ridge, the mortar fire support was approved. Actually, on the Ranger ridge, both U.S. units were occupying the same elongated, waist-deep trenches that crisscrossed the hill. The TOT came in on time and the company moved forward and captured the hill.

The unit took a couple of prisoners. The first man captured asked for an American cigarette and a chance to go to Formosa to join Chiang Kai-shek's army. His face was pocked with bumps, and it was one of the few times during the war that Queen felt like abusing a prisoner. Peteress—a damn good man and the second most-wounded Ranger—was dead because of his aggressiveness, and this POW had the audacity to ask for a cigarette while offering to change sides, all with the same breath.

Post-Battle Events

The lightly wounded Rangers in the action on Hill 545 were Sergeant Edward L. Posey, Sergeant Henry Wilson, Sergeant First Class Jack Murphy, Corporal Homer Bush, Corporal George Bynum, Jr., and Private First Class Otis Williamson, Jr.

As the company moved north, a few promotions followed:

James E. Freeman, First Lieutenant
David "Tank" Clarke, Sergeant
Jose A. Escalera, Jr., Corporal
Otis Williamson, Jr., Corporal
Lester Garland, Corporal
Scherrell Smith, Corporal

The Morning Report for 23 June reflects that 2d Ranger Company made another move within the 32d RCT at this time.

[23 June 1951] RECORD OF EVENTS
Reld fr atchd 1st Bn 32 Inf Regt on OP Hill 660 Approx 20 enemy troops sighted 19 Jun 51 enemy dispersed by artillery barrage no further contact with enemy Morale of troops excellent

Starting in late June the records began to include additional information about all of the men returning to 2d Ranger Company from the hospital: their dates of arrival in Korea, and their dates of eligibility for rotation (usually six months later, regardless of hospitalization periods). For example:

James R. Murray RA45 041 010 Cpl. MOS 34745

Race Negro, term of enlistment 3 years, Expiration of term of enlistment April 1954. Date arrival Korea, 30 December 1950. Date of eligibility for rotation to US June 1951. Assigned and joined from 3d Station Hospital, APO 301, paragraph 1, Special Order 176, Headquarters 3d Station Hospital, APO 301, effective 25 June 1951.

The Buffalo Rangers of 2d Company had a relatively easy time in comparison to some of the other Ranger companies. Over in the 24th Division, the 8th Rangers were part of Task Force Byrum, riding in M-39 personnel carriers with the 6th Medium Tank Battalion. On 19 May, the Task Force met a Chinese battalion that closed with and attempted to destroy the tanks in a defile. The Rangers, in conjunction with a company from the King's Shropshire Light Infantry Battalion attached to the 24th, fought them off.

Reports of these types of operations disturbed Colonel Van Houten. Although the Rangers' intended purpose was to operate behind enemy lines, they were being used by other units to spearhead their attacks for them—a function the units were supposed to perform for themselves. The mixed reports he received from the divisions to which the Rangers were attached were also disturbing.

For example, around IX Corps, 4th Company on many occasions was split into platoons or even squads to handle assignments. Sometimes its members unknowingly bivouacked within artillery gun placement areas, or filled in gaps between units, leaving their flanks exposed and vulnerable to attack. They were even attached to the 1st Marine Division, and a few individuals were sent to the 8240th AU (A US Army advisory and intelligence element supporting Korean partisans) for a short time for duty.

Medical Coverage

The Rangers were authorized only one aid man per company headquarters, with additional duty as "driver, truck, light" (i.e., jeep driver). Each platoon also had an aid man, and all were authorized a medical kit, as well as an individual and folding splint set. But no special training was provided for the aid men, in contrast to what is now done in the Army's Special Forces units, in which they receive at least one year of training before being awarded that MOS. Luckily, 2d Ranger Company received some medics who had already received basic aid man training while in the 558th from Sergeant First Class Baker, or in the 3d Battalion Medical Platoon under Lieutenant John Cannon and Master Sergeant Frank Barbee.

Several of the Rangers, including Corporal Donald Felder, one of the youngest and most inexperienced troopers taken into 2d Ranger Company, have felt a twinge of guilt since their days with 2d Ranger Company. Felder, who was a machine gunner in Pryor's 1st Platoon, puts it this way:

I became fascinated with airborne after watching the newsreel of the first black troopers in the military. Some troopers tried to discourage me from joining the Rangers. I saw my first action at the schoolhouse [Tanyang Pass] where I killed my first enemy. The experience had a devastating effect on me and triggered internal conflicts. I recalled on that same night moving away to be by myself, so I could pray and resolve my feelings about what I had done that day. I never knew that this internal conflict would rumble and roar within me for many years to come.

The next firefight was in the valley where Lawrence Williams, Charles Scott, J.T. Holley, and Herman Rembert were killed. [Eight Rangers were KIA in this battle, these four plus Corporal Richard Glover, Corporal Milton Johnson, Private Frank King, Jr., and Private First Class Robert St. Thomas.] The enemy was practically invisible, concealed on the high ground. It was during this battle that I witnessed the most heroic acts of my tour during the Korean War. One of the acts I observed was a Ranger—Lawrence "Poochie" Williams—who realized the situation the Company was in, and moved from a position of cover into the enemy's field of fire with a mortar tube minus its base plate, using the snow as a [base] plate and firing mortar rounds in the direction of the enemy's position. After firing several rounds, Williams was wounded.

Realizing this, Ranger Charles Scott immediately went to his side. Scott examined Williams' body, giving the sign that Williams was dead. It seemed Scott's next step should have been to take cover himself, but instead Scott continued going from body to body seeking out wounded soldiers of the 7th Infantry Division and administering medical attention to those soldiers who had been wounded but were still alive. He continued for some time until he, himself, was fatally wounded.

The heroic acts of these two Rangers were very obvious, as they were witnessed by many Rangers. I could never understand why these two Rangers never received any recognition for their heroic acts. As noted previously, the matter of awards was a neglected area of all the Rangers' orientation. The company's members' mental concept going into battle was to prove themselves as a group. The idea was that most of these acts were routine duties—until they saw the awards being made to many others—wheels—for far less audacious acts of bravery. In almost every war there are many who are not fully rewarded or recognized for their deeds. [The later revelation of these acts has been a catharsis for many Buffalo Rangers. It is currently impossible to rectify these omissions because the dates for recommendations have long passed.] I participated in most of the firefights where Rangers were recognized for their heroic acts; however, in my judgment the selfless acts of Williams and Scott were incomparable. They feared not for themselves, but for the safety of their fellow man.

My Ranger experiences made me think as an individual. However, I realized that becoming a professional soldier was not in the cards for me. It also made me realize how easily a life could be taken and how disgusting wars are. How can one justify the loss of so many lives and the suffering of so many human beings?

The most important lesson I learned from my Ranger experiences was never to let anyone become the master of your fate. And that education is the only route one can take to successfully take his place in society.

In that same vein of mature moral interpretation, some of the Buffalo Rangers have felt a twinge of guilt because they were wounded or injured early in Korea and did not return to the company for more combat. Ranger James Fields, a light machine gunner in Cliette's 3d Platoon, was in the Army for three years, nine months, and sixteen days. He was evacuated immediately after the Tanyang Pass–Majori-ri firefight for frostbitten feet. During those days, Fields recalls, "we were young men trying to find ourselves in a racist, segregated society. I don't know why it has been so difficult for me to write about my experiences in the military. I had set some high standards for myself and I met none of them," he continued. "Perhaps a feeling of guilt or a sense of failure for not completing the tasks I had set out to do: I had to leave the fight [in Korea] before it was finished. Perhaps, I let down some of my comrades."

It was not until 5 March, when Fields was transferred to the 155th Station Hospital, APO 503 in Japan, effective 24 February, that he was picked up on the Morning Report. Contrary to his own regrets, Ranger Fields didn't let anyone down—he distinguished himself at Tanyang and was awarded the Bronze Star.

Records—Rotation—Reality

No one remembers too clearly what duties the Buffalo Rangers performed during the last days of June. The Record of Events for the end of the month, recorded 20-30 June 1951, cites only the usual organizational duties. This could mean everything from local security and patrols to training and combat. The Morning Reports reflect a series of corrections ranging from status to strength and ranks and MOS's. The Rangers' MOS specialty designation prefix of "3" begins to appear in the Morning Reports at this time.

On 15 June, Captain Allen wrote to his wife, Mary:

> We have been on the move continually for ten to twelve days. It looks like we will now hold up for a while. The time for rotation is getting near but we can't get any definite plan for rotating the Company. I hope to get all of the men who are eligible out as soon as possible.

The other Ranger Companies were executing a variety of missions during this period, ranging from recuperation to task force battle, as follows:

> 1st Rangers, 2d ID: Captain Charles Ross assumes command
> 3d Rangers, 3d ID: Combat operations; Dave Rauls captured but freed by friendly fire
> 4th Rangers, 1st Cavalry: Operations on Task Force Croft
> 5th Rangers, 25th ID: Operations on "Objective Sugar"
> 8th Rangers, 24th ID: Reinforced Tank-Infantry Patrols

Chapter 8

Award of Combat Infantry Company Streamer and Start of the Journey Home, 4 July 1951

"At Beppu, in Japan, the 187th RCT submitted an addendum to its after-action report on the Munsan-ni Airborne Operation to Washington, D.C., dated 12 July 1951. It should be of special interest to the members of 2d and 4th Ranger Companies; i.e., I Company, 187th was credited with material captures attributed to 2d Ranger Company in the 187th Journals, and the 4th Company never did take their objective at Munsan-ni."

— *Korean Nights: The 4th Ranger Infantry Company*[36]

The Morning Report data indicate that by early July 1951, the Buffalo Rangers were still in the Army Reserve near Todon-ni, Korea, which was not too far from Chunchon City and an unimproved airstrip. Things were going pretty slow, as evidenced by Captain Allen's letters to Mary in which he wrote, "We are still in reserve. I saw Jack Benny and his USO troupe." The USO shows were usually held in the reserve regiment and the heavy artillery locations. They were near enough to the front lines so that the performers could brag about hearing the fighting (artillery firing) and still draw a large audience.

Somehow, during the time the unit was in Eighth Army Reserve, Queen came upon the Army Regulations pertaining to the unit award known as the Combat Infantry Company Streamer. The basic requirement for this award was that at least 65 percent of the company needed to have been awarded the Combat Infantryman's Badge and have at least thirty days on the line, with enemy contact. Special care had been taken through the rotation of jobs to ensure that even Sergeant George Jackson, Personnel Clerk at Division rear, had met that requirement.

[4 July 1951] Morning Report
Unit awarded the Combt Inf Streamer per GO 390
Hq 7th Inf Div APO 7 dtd 4 Jul 51

Thanks to Queen, the Buffalo Rangers now had the Combat Infantry Company Streamer Award—but on paper only: physically, they had no guidon or streamer! The company had left Fort Benning before the Army had a guidon made, and the unit was never issued an official one. "Big Jim" Queen volunteered to take a four-day temporary duty (TDY) trip back to Taegu to have a guidon and streamer made. He knew that there were personnel from the old 80th AAA Battalion in the city, and he could shack up and eat with them while waiting for the guidon to be made by a local Korean tailor. With that, the Buffalo Soldiers took up a collection and donated their loose change, most of which consisted of Korean and Japanese money.

The Trip to Taegu and Beyond

Things were relatively slow, so Big Jim secured his TDY. He stayed with CWO Woods, Personnel Officer for the old 80th. Queen had taken his combat gear (i.e., M-1C rifle, pistol belt with .45 caliber, ammunition) and binoculars with him. He wore his steel pot, pack suspenders, and dirty combat uniform while in the Eighth Army (Rear) area. There, people were dressed in a more civilized fashion, so he stood out like a sore thumb. Since Queen's clothing was extra large and he could never find the correct clothing sizes at the QM shower point, he washed and dried his own clothing before putting it back on. Throughout his time in Korea, he kept the same clothing he had brought with him from the States because it fit and had been modified to reflect the Airborne dress (field jacket with extra pockets on the upper sleeves; reinforced elbows and trouser knees). The MPs didn't bother Queen, and everyone was cordial.

Queen rested and slept late for about three days. But he also used up some of the collected money on local entertainment, so when the guidon was ready he had to borrow funds from Chief Woods. Korean money was almost worthless, and cigarettes would get you further in a trade.

While he was gone, Queen learned that his old company commander, Captain Benjamin "Bennie" Redd, from the 81st Infantry Battalion (Sep), Aleutian Islands, Alaska, was commanding a medical unit near Seoul. Queen did not know the exact location of Redd's unit, but sensed that it was located up near the Han River, east of the capital. The Han River was on the far side of the battlefront. The best way to get there was to catch a ride by hitchhiking. He was not asking for any special favors, so most drivers were glad to have some company—especially a Ranger officer riding shotgun! Although it was relatively safe for a single vehicle to travel in the daytime through the corps or Army rear areas, no guerrilla agent would dare attack them now: Queen had all of his combat gear plus the guidon with him.

He reached the river line on an artillery ammunition truck and did not have too much difficulty locating the medical unit. Because it had nurses assigned to it, the unit was considered an evacuation hospital. Redd commanded a medical clearing or ambulance company that supported the hospital, and was the only officer assigned to the unit. It seemed they were short Medical Service Corps Officers, so Redd had volunteered for the assignment. Big Jim ribbed him for leaving the infantry and hiding in the non-combatant medics.

Because time was short, Queen only stayed for the evening. He ate a good meal with silver utensils and slept on a canvas cot for the first time in a long time. He caught a ride early the next day on another truck heading to the 7th Division, and arrived back without difficulty.

Company Jump School

Captain Allen persuaded Division and Army G-3 to grant permission to give parachute jump training to the ten "leg replacements" who had volunteered from the 7th Division's pipeline back in April. These men had fought with the company for slightly more than three months and deserved the chance to start and back-date their jump pay. Army regulations allowed a soldier to draw pay backwards or forward for three months after making a jump, under normal circumstances. In combat, a general officer could certify that the equipment and aircraft were not available and the jump pay would be continued for an indefinite period. At this time, jump pay for enlisted men was $50 per month and $100 per month for officers. This meant a back-pay package of $150 for these men, which was important because combat pay was not instituted in Korea until 1952.

Allen set aside a training cadre of Rangers from the 3d Platoon to provide the training, including Staff Sergeant John E. Ford, Jr., one of two qualified, black senior riggers who had performed duty in the 82d A/B Division. The entire company was undergoing refresher training because it was time for everyone to make a jump for normal pay purposes. The last company jump had been at Munsan-ni on 23 March, and it was now slightly more than three months later—time for a pay jump. There were no platforms to jump from and practice landing falls, so the deuce-and-a-half truck bed was substituted for that purpose. The ground was dusty and took the place of the sawdust pits. The company did road runs, push-ups, and practice landings from slowly moving trucks to simulate windy landings. Shouts of "ARE YOU HAPPY? ARE YOU GONNA JUMP?" echoed throughout the hills. This may have looked silly to the leg units in the area, but it meant dollar signs and was a morale booster for the Buffalo Soldiers.

In later years, three of the jump candidates remembered the training as follows:

Paul Lyles

We came back to base camp in Korea for a rest period—which entailed jumping from six-wheeler trucks in the process of learning to do a PLF. After a few days of this training we were supposed to be ready for our jumps. We were told that within the next days we were going to make three jumps to qualify as paratroopers and receive our airborne wings. Three of the men who made jumps that day were Washingtonians: Billy Mathis, Winston Jackson, and myself.

Isaac Grasty

We started training at once—jumping from the back of a truck, in order to learn how to make a PLF. I don't know if all these guys finished this training. I can only remember three: Mathis, another tall fellow—I can't remember his name—[Grasty is describing Paul Lyles, who measured about 6 feet 2 inches] who was assigned as the 57 recoilless rifleman, and myself. I do remember that all of us made the three qualifying jumps *in one day*. After this, the three of us were assigned to Lieutenant Cliette's platoon.

Winston Jackson

Our training by the company personnel started in July. As a youngster I had been hurt very badly in the ankle while playing basketball. On the first two jumps my old injured ankle began to hurt, to the extent that I could hardly walk.

Someone wanted to jump in my place, but I got extra advice about making a PLF on my last jump. I made it, but it hurt so badly that I was taken to the aid station. I was told that I just had a sprain and I was to be placed on light duty.

[27 July 1951] Record of Events
11 enlisted men[37] make qualifying parachute jumps at Chunchon, Korea. No casualties.

During this period, Captain Allen was writing less frequently to his wife. His letters contain no specific information about airborne training for the replacements or deactivation. On 13 July he wrote:

> I hope that the Commies act favorably on Ridgeway's latest proposal. We are taking things easy, conducting training, and straightening out property records. I am starting to gain back the weight I lost. I don't think that I'll be home for the beach season, but I'll try to get home for the World Series. I have never seen two major league teams play.

The Captain attempted to get in some last-minute promotions to deserving Rangers. Those promoted to sergeant or above were done by 7th Division special orders, while Private First Class and Corporal promotions were cited on company order.

On the Morning Report of 15 July there were several entries concerning Corporal James E. Carrell.

Carrell James E. RA17233881 Cpl.
…duty to R&R Japan effective 8 July 1951, paragraph 8, Special Order 188, Headquarters 7th Infantry Division, APO 7, dated 7 July 1951.

…R&R leave to confinement Post Guard House, Camp Zama, Honshu, Japan, effective 2140 hours, 10 July 1951.

The reason for Corporal Carrell's confinement remains a mystery to the men of 2d Ranger Company. However, on Special Order 210, Headquarters 7th Infantry Division, dated 29 July 1951, transferring the Buffalo Rangers to the 187th ARCT, Carrell's name is conspicuously missing, while the names of the other two men who went on R&R with him—Sergeant First Class William Hargrove and Corporal Jacob J. Mason—are shown.

At this time the beloved Company clerk, George Jackson, Jr., re-enlisted for three years. Unfortunately, he did not get any enlistment or re-enlistment bonus. He did upgrade his permanent rank and must have anticipated the significance of this move, because later the difference between a temporary and a permanent rank would become a critical issue. All other enlisted promotions recorded on the Morning Report for Sergeant and Sergeant First Class are listed as temporary. President Truman had already given an involuntary extension to all members of the Armed Forces in late 1950. Almost all officers in the company received category appointments or enlistments while in Korea. On 27 May, Lieutenant Antonio Anthony, who had arrived in Korea in late February, was extended in his category (voluntary term of service to Category III),[38] per special orders from the 7th Division. All of the other company officers whose birth dates were during this period of duty in Korea were also extended.

[15 July 1951] Morning Report
Jackson, George Jr. RA13291868 Sgt. MOS: 34816 Duty to honorable discharge, AR 615-360, Expiration of term of service and WCL 35093 effective 13 July 1951 (Department of Defense Form 214 attached).

Jackson, George Jr. RA13291868 Cpl. MOS: 34816 Race Negro Term of enlistment 3 years, ETS July 1954 Departed Zone if Interior December 1950, arrived Korea eligible rotation United States June 1951, enlisted in the Regular Army, assigned and joined, paragraph 24, Special Order 195, Hqs. 7th Infantry Division, APO 7 (DD Form 4, attached).

Jackson, George Jr. RA13291868 Cpl. MOS: 34816 Promoted to grade of Sergeant (E-5) permanent paragraph 24, Special Order 195, Hqs. 7th Infantry Division, APO 7.

As late as 24 July, Warren wrote to Mary:

I am waiting for the good news before writing. We are expecting a new Army Post Office (APO) by the end of the month. Rotation seems to be a dream. Who are all the people that I read about getting to the States? I hope that I can write soon with some good news!

Up to 29 July, the 2d Ranger Company was still making corrections on errors detected in the old Morning Reports. There were so many errors that Queen wanted to just substitute corrected reports and throw the old ones away, but that was not possible. It is impossible to say whether the reports in the National Archives today portray a true picture of the Buffalo Rangers' activity. What is certain is that the last man to leave the unit was Corporal Lawrence Williams, and he did so on 25 July.

[31 July 1951] RECORD OF EVENTS
NO CHANGE. 20-31 July 1951 Usual organization duties.

Order to Inactivate the Ranger Companies

During the period of 11-14 July, the 8th Company Rangers were attached to the 24th Division, and while still conducting combat operations with the 21st Infantry seized Hill 1118. Afterward, the Rangers repelled an enemy attack and directed artillery fire on Hill 581 while the 21st attacked. On 14-15 July, the 8th Company Rangers deterred a Chinese attack against their position. On 16 July, amid preparations for their next mission, Captain Robert Wesley Eikenberry, commander of the 8th, was notified by Division G-3 that the Rangers were being inactivated.[39]

On 24 July 1951, Colonel Van Houten sent all of the Ranger trainees back to their regular units or to other assignments. Within the Department of the Army the decision to inactivate the Ranger companies was reflected in Message 95587, dated 5 July 1951, which stated: "Deep patrol missions by small units, for which the Rangers are intended, are made most difficult in the Far East Command by reason of racial differences between the oriental and the Caucasian."[40]

This superficial reasoning omitted any references to 2d Ranger Company, which definitely did not fit the racial profile mentioned. Also omitted was the fact that the 8086th Army Unit (Miscellaneous Group) was currently conducting clandestine operations utilizing Caucasian advisers. In addition, whenever a deep (combat or reconnaissance) patrol gets so close to the enemy that racial features are recognizable, the issue is moot! Last, earlier in the Korean conflict almost every division had an indigenous force operating within its zone, and these forces were not too effective. For example, the Rice's Raiders unit (Benedas Force) at Tanyang, on 7 January met with almost total disaster.

There must have been some rumors before the order was given because in his 13 July letter, Captain Allen mentioned to Mary that the unit was "straightening out the property records," and it appears he saw the change approaching. Queen did not recall that this information reached the Buffalo Rangers, nor were they given the opportunity for transfers to 7th Division. Only one Buffalo, Corporal Joe Wells, remained behind after the unit was deactivated. Wells, who had been cited for bravery on Hill 581, remained for approximately another month while serving as a Catholic chaplain's assistant. When a replacement chaplain's assistant arrived, Wells, like all of the former 2d Ranger Company, was sent to join the 187th ARCT in Japan.

The final Morning Report gives no reasons why, but relegates the Ranger units to the history books.

[1 August 1951] Morning Report
Todon-ni, Korea 7 Officers and 117 Enlisted men relieved from assigned and transferred to 187th RCT (Abn) APO 51, paragraph 11, Special Order 210, Hqs 7th Infantry Div., APO 7, EDCMR 1 Aug 1951

RECORD OF EVENTS
Inactivated this date per General Order 584, Hqs Eighth U S Army, Korea. APO 301 dated 25 July 1951, no personnel assigned or attached. Final M/R.

General Ferenbaugh, 7th Division commander, wrote a Letter of Appreciation acknowledging the unit's performance during its seven months of attachment. At the end of the war, the South Korean government awarded its Presidential Unit Citation to all of the units in the 7th Division. Somehow, the Buffalo Rangers of 2d Ranger Company were left off the orders. However, in 1988 the South Korean government awarded the Korean Presidential Unit Citation to the Buffalo Rangers at the biennial RICA reunion, in Colorado Springs, Colorado.[41]

All across the Korean front the other five Ranger companies were performing a similar exercise. On 3 August, the 3d and 4th Companies left Inchon via train and picked up the 5th and 8th Companies at Yongdungpo. The 1st and 2d Companies had arrived at Pusan the day before via truck. It was the first time that all of the Ranger companies were assembled in one place. Many of the men were very angry and others, the late-coming replacements, were disappointed. No one knew what their fate would be in the 187th.

Camp Zama, Japan, December 30, 1950, prior to our movement to
K-2 Air Base, Taegu, Korea. *U.S. Army*

2d Ranger Company (Airborne) riding a ferry on San Francisco Bay in 1950.
Herculano Dias

Captain Warren Allen teaching bayonet training. Identified individuals include, from left to right: Private Anthony Andrade (holding rifle behind Allen's back—right—leg), Samuel Nixon (next to Andrade), William J. McPherson (face partially obscured by Allen's left hand), Roland Hodge (holding rifle with right hand), Jude St. Martin (right arm outstretched holding rife), and Earl Johnson (far right). *U.S. Army*

Members of the 2d Ranger Company (Airborne) reading a map in central Korea.
Herculano Dias

Artillery fire eases, allowing the men of 2d Ranger Company, 17th RCT, 7th Division, to advance across a stream northeast of Kumma-ri, Korea, on February 19, 1951. *U.S. Army*

Two wounded men of the 2d Ranger Company, attached to the U.S. 7th Infantry Division, are brought into the aid station in Ponji-ri, Korea, on May 21, 1951. Left to right: Pvt. Legree Aikens, B.A.R. man, 2d Ranger Company, U.S. 8th Army; Cpl. Jude St. Martin, B.A.R. man, 2d Ranger Company, U.S. 8th Army; and Sgt. Alphonso Camoesas, aid man, 32d RCT, U.S. 7th Infantry Division. *Carl W. Reeves*

Sgt. William "The Ghost" Washington, Korea 1951.

"He could weave a story around almost anything, if given
the right opportunity and circumstances."

U.S. Army

Author Edward L. Posey, in a photo taken in 1951.

U.S. Army

HEADQUARTERS 7TH INFANTRY DIVISION
Office of the Commanding General
APO 7

SCS 200.6   30 July 1951

SUBJECT: Letter of Appreciation

TO: Officers and Men of the
             2d Ranger Infantry Company (Airborne)
             APO 7

1. On the eve of your departure and the inactivation of your unit I wish to express my sincere appreciation and gratitude to each Officer and Enlisted man of the 2d Ranger Infantry Company (Airborne) for your complete cooperation and the outstanding combat services rendered during the seven months of your attachment to this division.

2. During this period you were faced with many difficult and daring assignments. You participated in steady, large-scale advances, tactical withdrawals followed by counter-attacks and pursuit of the enemy, and countless patrols. You were handicapped at times by the lack of replacements for your combat losses but at the same time willingly accepted responsibilities and missions normally assigned to an infantry rifle company with twice the number of personnel. It was by virtue of superior leadership, unusual courage, and dogged determination on the part of each of you that you were consistently able to accomplish each mission and secure each objective with dispatch, honor and distinction.

3. Your outstanding cooperation, devotion to duty, aggressiveness, and esprit has been a constant source of satisfaction to me ever since I assumed command of the Division. Your departure is a distinct loss and will be felt keenly by all of us who remain.

4. I am happy to have each one of you as a member of my command. You can be proud of the part you have played and the enviable record you have made. My regimental commanders and my staff join me in extending to you a sincere "Well Done."

                                   /s/ C. B. Ferenbaugh
                                   /t/ C. B. FERENBAUGH
                                   Maj Gen,   USA
                                   Commanding

A TRUE COPY:

WAITUS H. HARDIN
Major, AGC
Assistant Adjutant General

Letter to the men of 2d Ranger Infantry Company (Airborne)
from Maj. Gen. C. B. Ferenbaugh. *US Army*

Drawings by Ranger Joe Russo. "Musan-ni" (top), and Rangers Lt. Albert Cliette and Cpl. Glenn Jenkins, Jr. (bottom). *Courtesy Joe Russo*

The Korean Peninsula and a Ranger from 2d Ranger Company (Airborne).
Courtesy Joe Russo

The commanding officer of the compound where the Rangers were billeted announced that no one would be allowed to go on pass except the officers. This was a big disappointment to the men. The compound was situated on the side of a large hill with a chain-link fence going almost to the top of the hill. It was possible to climb the hill, walk beyond the fence and go to town, or to scoot under the fence beyond the immediate guard's post. The guards were relatively young soldiers who had not seen combat, so the intimidation and cat-and-mouse game of going to town started as soon as it became dark. Many of the men still had live ammunition! The Japanese colonel of the Joint Logistic Command (JLC) called out the MPs, but it was a hopeless battle.

All of the 2d Ranger Company officers left the compound together. Captain Harris, from Fort Bragg, had been the CO of the 666th Truck Company, which was assigned direct support duties for the 82d. Harris had a quartermaster truck company stationed in the city. It was an all-black unit that also had been billeted in the Spring Lake area, so it was like homecoming. The 2d Ranger Company men would visit him and help him drink up his booze while he brought them up to date on the latest news from Fort Bragg. Captain Allen remained there while his young and wild lieutenants set out to see the city. The normal curfew time was 2400 hours. Since the officers did not know the city, they just went down the street on one side and came back up on the other side. There were enough places to provide entertainment for a short period, and everyone was on the way back to the compound by 2400 hours.

By the time they reached the barracks, everyone was beginning to get a little tired. Red Horse and Bennie Pryor found a can of C-rations. They could not decide how to share it, so a loud argument erupted. Everyone else decided to hit the sack and sleep it off. The argument continued for a few minutes before the shoving started. The JLC Colonel and the Officer of the Day came in, and both men were pulled off shipment. Each had to spend about another week there while the Colonel placed Article 15 charges against them for disorderly conduct.

The next morning, the JLC Colonel held a mass formation of Rangers and cussed everyone out for their disgraceful conduct. Things were not all "peaches and cream" in other places within the compound, either.[41] Some of the men were still smashed from the night before. The Colonel couldn't expect, and didn't get, any help from the officers because he had handled the situation the wrong way from the beginning. He should have called an officer meeting and set some courtesy patrols with his MPs. He could have called for officers and senior NCOs to ride with the MPs. He should have pointed out the off-limits establishments. Instead he had both flaunted his authority and displayed his lack of combat wisdom, antagonizing the troops and escalating the situation. Certainly, each unit had enough non-drinkers and men of chastity to have handled the prostitute situations until 2400 hours. It was a known fact that many troops stationed in the town knew the local joints that were acceptable. Also, by 2400 hours all of the little money that the troops had would have been spent. The unit commanders would have emptied the houses of ill-repute and piled the men into trucks for a merry ride back to the compound. Some coffee and doughnuts would have made an excellent midnight snack before putting everyone to bed. Unfortunately, high rank does not always translate into know-how or common sense!

All ammunition was collected and the Rangers were transported down to the dock in open-bed, five-ton trucks (commonly known as cattle trucks) for loading onto the Japanese ferryboats for transport to Japan. Of course, there were imitations of cattle (mooing sounds) as the trucks traveled through the city. One Native American dove from the ferry into the harbor and started to swim back to land. It was lucky that he was not caught in the undertow or propeller wash. He was last seen being hauled back aboard the ferry, with cheers from all as they left Korea behind. The Colonel was probably happy to see them leave.

Chapter 9

After Korea: Life on Strategic
Reserve Duty in Japan

"The more I see of other veteran groups, the more I find that special bonds welded in extensive periods of hardship and in the life-threatening situations of combat in any form, create ties that last throughout life."

— *The Cold Steel Third: 3d Airborne Ranger Company, Korean War* (1950–1951)[42]

The ferryboats docked at Sasebo, Japan, about 0700 hours on 2 August 1951. The Rangers boarded a train and reached Camp Chickamauga, Beppu, about 1200 hours, where everyone enjoyed a big meal. The next day, the men were assembled with their duffel bags on the north side of the post at the Race Track, which doubled as a light airstrip and a parade field. Slightly more than 700 Rangers were present.

The Rangers were treated as replacements because Eighth Army had moved up the rotation criteria. There were so many troopers in the 187th ARCT with six months of duty in Korea that the shipment of all of them would have so drastically lowered combat readiness status that the unit would have been ineffective. The new criteria gave each month of combat service in Korea an equivalent of four points. Therefore, the 1st Rangers would have about thirty-six points, but the 4th and 2d Rangers would have only twenty-eight points. There were no extra points for married men or those with dependent children, as had occurred at the end of WWII. The number of points required for immediate rotation in August was increased to about forty-eight points. The new points earned by the troopers assigned to the 187th ARCT, now in Eighth Army reserve, was one per month. In addition, Eighth Army froze the rotation of qualified airborne personnel.

At the same time, the Far East Command conducted a purge known as Operation Flush, in which all qualified airborne personnel in non-airborne assignments in Japan Logistic Command and the Far East Command were involuntarily transferred to the 187th ARCT. There were a lot of disgruntled troopers, including some who had made both combat jumps at Sukch'on and Sunch'on on 20 October 1950 and Munsan-ni on 23 March 1951. Some of the older troopers from WWII thought they had performed their last airborne assignment before retirement.

Camp Chickamauga

Camp Chickamauga was named after a creek in northwest Georgia, the scene of a Confederate victory in 1863 during the Civil War, and had been a Japanese Army garrison prior to World War II. It was not large enough to house the entire ARCT, so the Pathfinders and Parachute Maintenance were moved to Camp Kashi, outside Fukuoka. The 674th Field Artillery Battalion, 4.2-inch Mortar Company, and Anti-Aircraft Battery were housed at Camp Woods, near Fukuoka. Housed at Chickamauga were Regimental Headquarters and Headquarters Company, Service Company, Medical Company, Military Police Detachment, and the 1st, 2d and 3d Battalions. To many troopers it was like old home week, because they had served with each other in the 11th A/B and 82d A/B Divisions in post-WWII assignments. Brigadier General Thomas T. J. H. Trapnell was now the CO, and his deputy commander, Lieutenant Clayman, was his former XO from the 505th AIR in the 82d A/B.

There were some disappointments among the troopers in the 187th who had longer service because the Rangers came in with a lot of rank. Many of these NCOs had been in TO&E slots and had looked forward to a combat-type promotion. Combat-type promotions were made on a temporary basis in Korea after thirty to sixty days of satisfactory service in a position. It was not too difficult to place the Ranger Lieutenants, but the Captains had to be squeezed in as assistant staff officers for a while.

According to Mighty Mouth Alston, Commo Chief, some of the Rangers assigned to 1st Battalion were assigned as follows:

> The Battalion CO was Major Mike Holland, who was very popular with the troops because of his free-will attitude. I was in Company D, 81mm Mortar Platoon, led by Lieutenant James E. Freeman (2d Ranger

Company). Our Platoon Sergeant was Wendell Russell (187th from Fort Campbell). I was a Section Leader, and other 2d Ranger Company Rangers included Squad Leaders (Staff Sergeants Adell Allen and Kenneth Moore). The other Section Leader was Sergeant First Class Mansfield Brown (Company M, 3d Battalion). Over in the Machine Gun Platoon were Platoon Sergeant Earl Higgins (4th Company) and Sergeant Howard Squires, Section Leader (2d Ranger Company). Colonel T.J. "Eagle Eye" Trapnell was promoted to Brigadier General while CO.

"I have been postponing this letter until I could give you a date to expect me," Captain Allen began a letter to Mary on 10 August. "We are now assigned to the 187th ARCT, in Japan. I am pretty high on the rotation list here; however, I don't know when I will actually get home. Colonel Trapnell, who was the commander of the 505th Regiment, now has this unit," continued Allen. "He said that he was glad to see the men and me from the 3d Battalion. I am assigned as one of the Regimental Assistant S-2s." Allen concluded his letter: "There are so many people here from the 82d A/B; it looks like old home week. Would you like to come to Japan? Colonel Trapnell asked if I wanted to stay."

Queen's Assignment

All of the 2d Ranger Company officers except "Big Jim" Queen were assigned to Camp Chickamauga. "Big Jim" was assigned as Reconnaissance Officer (XO), Company H. Lieutenant Rich MacAfee, Ranger, battlefield commissioned with the 5th Rangers, was the 81mm Mortar Platoon leader under Captain James "Hog" McPherson. Captain Mac was an old 504th Weapons Company CO from the 82d during WWII. Lieutenant MacAfee had been a Mortar Platoon Sergeant in Company H, 505th, at Bragg. Sergeant Gus Georgiou from 3d Rangers was the Reconnaissance Sergeant. The 2d Battalion CO was Lieutenant Colonel Christenson, with Major Musick as the Battalion XO. First Sergeant West took over Company B with a Hispanic commander. Captain Allen was later sent down to take over Company L. Ranger Winston Jackson, 2d Ranger Company, finally got his light duty assignment as a clerk under Captain "Moon" Mullins, in Regimental S-4.

The regiment began a heavy and steady training cycle, starting on the platoon level. The local training area was Mount Mori, located in the hills northeast of Chickamauga about seven miles distant. Blank ammunition could be fired there and there was no need to police the brass shell casings because the local Japanese scroungers were there to collect them almost as fast as they were fired. The Japanese melted the brass shells down and made items to sell, such as ash trays, belt buckles, and lamps.

Some of the men who joined the units at Camp Woods reported that they received a less-than-cordial welcome. William "The Ghost" Washington was assigned to the Regimental Counterfire Platoon. Queen, who had been awarded the Senior Parachute Badge in the 82d, saw a chance to build up his jumps for the Master Parachute Badge by volunteering to be a Rifle Platoon Umpire during the Army Training Test at Mori. The heavy weapons platoons were undergoing platoon training, so Captain Mac released him for this special duty. The exercise was about thirty-six hours long. It started at camp and involved taking a train ride up to Ashiya Air Base, jumping north of Mori, and making a cross-country march of about ten miles to arrive for a dawn attack in Mori. There were twenty-seven rifle platoons in the regiment, and "Big Jim" jumped with about half of them. He was awarded his Master Wings in the 187th ARCT. Later, the regiment had a regimental-size exercise in Mori, and Queen was captured along with the mortar platoon.

Queen and Captain Mac were roommates in a small BOQ. "Big Jim," "Willie" (Vince Wilburn), and "Lieutenant Rich" hung out together. On Fridays from 5:00 to 6:00 p.m. the Officers' Club had Happy Hour, a military custom during which all drinks were half-priced. This trio could usually be found at the end of the bar, trying to see who could drink the most vodka in that hour before going to supper. They drank vodka because it didn't leave a headache or trigger a hangover the next morning. Like Trapnell, Rich had also been a Japanese POW at the end of WWII and spoke the language very well. The Officers' Club bartender was a young Japanese named Tiny. He knew how to keep the trio supplied and when to skip payment. Rich liked to sing a Japanese folk song when he got drunk. No Japanese girlfriends were allowed in the club, but could be met at the bar that Lieutenant Colonel Christenson had selected.

There were a couple of hotels up in the hills about two to three miles from town by bus. Willie and Jim went up there on a weekend for a good meal and some rest, away from the very small town with its one main street leading down to the wharf. According to Japanese custom, guests at the hotels were to leave their shoes at the door; but once a soldier had his boots stolen he soon learned to take them into the room and sleep with them nearby, or he would have to walk back to camp in stocking feet. Sergeant Barbee had the medic jeep drop them off at the hotel. Somehow they lost all of their money and almost had to walk back to town. Luckily, they had stashed some money in "Big Jim's" boots for just such an emergency, and were able to ride the bus back to town.

Waiting To Go Home

On 19 August, Captain Allen broke the news to Mary about the new and "unfavorable" rotation policy:

> I have unfavorable news. The new rotation policy: as of 1 September, you need 36 points to be eligible. The travel of dependents to the Far East is being resumed. Would you still like to come? I have 31 points and I can't get on the list until December. It will be the end of December or early January before I can expect to be home. I am very disappointed. But we'll need more money because of expenses (khakis and winter clothes). I went over to Korea as a courier and I saw Major (William) Gott. I will be out in the woods for a week on an umpire detail.

During the last two weeks of August, Allen picked up in his writing to Mary. In sharp contrast to Queen, who enjoyed the umpire detail because it kept a soldier out of trouble and passed the time, Allen complained that it was the most worthless time that he had spent in the Army, that there was nothing new happening in the unit, that his morale was rock bottom, and that the peace talks were going much too . . . slowly.

Part III

Personal Memoirs and Important Information

This section acknowledges all of the Buffalo Rangers of 2d Ranger Company who trained at Fort Benning and / or joined the unit later and served in Korea. Although the roster that appears in the appendices consists of those men who were aboard the USS General H.W. Butner, *this entire section provides a more complete view of the Rangers who served in 2d Ranger Company throughout the war, including replacement troops who served faithfully with 2d Ranger Company but were not aboard the* Butner.

This section provides a snapshot of where life has taken each man to the turn of the new century. All efforts have been made to ensure accuracy as of that time. It was compiled with the help and research of many Rangers and RICA. To any Ranger who may inadvertently have been excluded, I apologize for such a terrible oversight and please know it was unintentional. Readers should be aware that over the years there have been numerous individuals who have tried to claim involvement in 2d Ranger Company but do not appear in official records or were not known by me or other Rangers. Every name in this section belongs to a soldier who is not only in the official records for 2d Ranger Company, but is known to other Rangers who served with him in Korea. I have been careful to include all soldiers who deserve the recognition of serving as a 2d Ranger Company Ranger during the Korean War and to exclude those whose claims, although persistent, cannot be substantiated. If I have omitted any Ranger with a valid claim to service with 2d Ranger Company, I apologize for the mistake.

To our Buffalo brothers: I appreciate the service and sacrifices that you made. May the Good Lord continue to watch over the Rangers of 2d Company and bless you and your families.

Chapter 10

As I Remember

Recollections of Samuel "Shorty" Payne, Jr.

A Few Anecdotes

So many things come to mind. Do you remember Escalera sleeping under that tank and we could not revive him right away? Do you also remember when we had moved into the school yard position and he dug a slit trench instead of a foxhole? Then we started receiving artillery and small arms fire and he had no place to go but in a hole with one of the other guys, and the old man chewed his ass out!

The Buffalo Rangers, 2d Ranger Company (Airborne),
Prior to the Jump: March 22, 1951

We were interviewed by *Stars and Stripes* at the airfield before the first Ranger parachute jump in history. They took pictures of some of the guys in the company. Also, one of Posey and me I call "the tall and short of it." I tried to get a copy of the picture; they said copies were sent to the home states.

My platoon was Jump-47, because most of our company jumped from C-47s or C-46s. We assembled and moved right into the attack. A Medic got hit just as we landed; he died from shock.

A whistle was used to assemble the men.

We got some small arms fire from the hill, but a lot of the sons-of-bitches were running. We caught them by surprise. We were moving pretty fast and had orders not to take any prisoners because we did not have time to stop.

Like I have told many guys, they were looking at history. I was there and I participated in it, and I am very proud to have been a member of the first black Airborne Ranger company, not only as a Ranger, but as a black one. I am so sorry that we did not have the public relations that the Marines or the 187th had. But we shall survive and live on. To all of the original members of the 2d Company, we know we were the best. And we proved it from day one when we got to Korea.

I will never forget the night patrol with the heavy tank battalion. We were the spearhead company that was sent out to make contact with elements of 15th Regiment, 3d Division. The first thing we ran into was an element of the tank battalion. We linked up and continued off onto the attack. Went on a tank patrol, a bunch were heading down the draw to the valley.

We were moving so fast that we passed over the top of some well-kept camouflaged holes that the gooks had dug and were hiding in. So the old man sent for some stick charges and started blowing them out. We started digging in. While doing this we began to get intermittent artillery fire from across the river. The gooks had a forward observer calling in artillery. Then we started getting support artillery from 8th Army Field or Corp Heavy gun.

Yes, we were to patrol one mile in front of our position, keeping a eye on the house, which we learned was a Forward Observer post that we helped destroy. I am glad I was a part of the history-making jump.

Hill-581: May 20, 1951

We had been taking on small arms fire and had just moved into the position. Corporal Sutton was hit by fire while sitting on the side of the hill. We were digging in our position pending an attack that we were expecting. We had seen the enemy moving rank and file down the draw. We called in artillery fire off and on. Also supply brought up to the position crates of hand grenades, ammunition, and flares. We were stockpiling. They did not attack us until early in the morning. They had been sending out patrols, testing and feeling out our position. I was a BAR man protecting the machine gun position. We could hear and smell the sons-of-bitches right below our position. They probed the position all night. We threw hand grenades every so often.

When the Chinese overran the 3d platoon position, our machine gunner beat off the gooks, killing many. He deserved a lot bigger award than he got. I believe he received a Bronze Star; should have been a Silver Star or better. I cannot think of his name. He was from New York. My memory of names is bad; faces yes, but names I stink as far as memory is concerned. We had an assortment of all types of individuals: top of the shelf, so to speak. A very proud bunch of men that really was obedient to the 2d Ranger Company and to the job at hand.

We ran daily patrols, both contact and combat. We would patrol at night about two hundred yards in front of our position. We set up ambushes a couple of times out and would come back about daylight.

June 11, 1951

Our platoon had been given the job of knocking out a machine gun on the knoll overlooking a man-made path. Earlier we had been pushed off this same hill; I think more out of anger and frustration, we started back up the hill. Peteress was the BAR man. For some unknown reason he started up that path; the gook had it zeroed in before we were halfway up the knoll. We were caught in a crossfire from the front and right flank. Peteress still pushed ahead. Then the gooks opened up, cutting him half way up the chest and the left side of his face. After he fell, Lieutenant Freeman gave the order to push the position straight ahead. We killed two of the enemy who were left to protect the machine gunner: they were chained to the machine gun and gave up smiling, but were shot dead.

We dug in for a hole-type thing. We also were on red alert through the night. We could not take Peteress down. So he was moved and covered with a poncho right above our hole. Then it began to rain. The Chinese were spotted with a probing patrol. Captain Allen started calling in artillery within about fifty yards from our position, walking it up to about twenty-five yards from our position. I don't believe any of the men worried about it. Someone else got wounded in the foot on that same hill, can't remember the name.

As far as I can remember we rested, cleaned weapons, drank booze, and wrote letters. At night some of us got together and did a little harmonizing.

I recall one time the general went past the lines we had been fighting on and got trapped up there. They sent 3d platoon and the rest of 2d up to rescue him.

He had to slide into the safety hatch under the tank so that he could get out of the gook-infested area.

At the end, we had to ride over in the Japanese or Korean ferryboat, which was packed to the hilt. I was really upset about the deactivation, thinking that all we did would have gone down the drain—and it almost did, if it wasn't for guys like Weathersbee, Queen, and many others who kept the fire lit.

Camp and in Pusan

When we got back from Korea lots of guys went on passes. Some of the guys bought these chrome-coated .45s or had some of them chromed up.

In joining the 187 RCT, I was a little apprehensive, because a lot of the 187th didn't like the idea of us bringing in so much rank. I recall when Trapnell raised hell with members and officers of the 187th. When he found out that some of the men and/or officers were discriminating and saying racist words toward the men of 2d Ranger Company, he said if someone called you a name you had his order to kick his ass and report it to him, and he would do the same. We were assigned to different platoons and companies within RCT. We spent lots of time in the field.

We were given passes to go into the G.I. Station in Pusan. I had a run-in with one of the guys from the other Ranger Co. The city was under a curfew and we had to meet a truck at a certain time, I think 1200 hours, to report back to the compound. We had some confrontation.

Some of the other activity was constant weapons inspection. The old man used to be a son-of-a-bitch about this and some other thing. William Tucker used to be my foxhole buddy, then Posey when he was BAR man.

The most memorable action was the first jump at Munsan-ni Hill 581. Our four-man team was on a O.P. (Listening Post) when the gooks ran patrol about one hundred yards below our position. We had orders: if attacked, destroy the radio and make it out.

Many of the men in this company should have been given some awards. I always thought that the Old Man wasn't too up on getting medals for his men. (Maybe only certain people.) I could name some of the men who should have been so honored.

After returning to the States I went to Fort Benning. Then I was sent to the 11th Abn 188 Regt. I was in this company under Sergeant Ames Anias, who was the 1st soldier of the company. Back at Bragg, Amos had been my platoon sergeant before I went to the Rangers.

I was not a career soldier. I had made sergeant and was going to Jumpmaster School. But because I had short time they did not want to give me another stripe unless I re-upped.

I have had no regrets at all about being a Ranger, a paratrooper, or being in the military. My only regret at not staying in is that I could see no farther than my nose.

This resumé is only a minute amount of information that I have to offer, of course there is much more.

I often thought about what would happen to us in a historical sense. If it was not for men like you (Weathersbee, Queen, Posey, Dias, and many others), we probably would go unnoticed or be forgotten. I recall at the 1987 Reunion when this white colonel told some of his men that there was no all-black Rangers company. A New York guy called him down, embarrassing him for making an idiotic statement like that.

I could not really say who was the ideal Ranger, but there were some who stood out just a notch above the other men. Sergeant Freeman, for example, who wouldn't tell his men to do something he wouldn't do. We had so many—I can't name them because I would not be just in doing so.

There were times we went into the attack with the 17th Regiment and 7th Division, securing the position, then turning it over to the 31st or 32d. And they would lose it within a couple of weeks. The 2d Ranger Company was called on every time. We would go into a limited engagement (ten days, two weeks). One time I thought they were really trying to kill us off by sending us to each regiment that was going into the attack.

Recollections of David "Tank" Clarke, 1st Plt. BAR, 1st Squad, Lt. Bernard Pryor, Plt. Leader, James Freeman, Plt. Sgt., and Herman Jackson, Squad Leader

We were still at Fort Benning, almost at the end of our Ranger training cycle, when the word was out that the North Koreans were whipped, they were on the run, and the action in Korea was just about over. All of the men would be home for Christmas. The UN army was at the Manchurian border, and it was just a matter of time before the police action was over.

Many of us were disappointed that we wouldn't get a chance to get into the action. After all, we had just ended a rather rigorous training period. We really wanted a chance to get into the fight. Then it happened: the Chinese entered the war and the UN army was in full retreat.

The word was out that we had a chance to get into action. On the train to the west coast we read about all of the mess that was going on, through *Time* magazine and *Newsweek*. I can remember seeing a cover story in *Newsweek* of an infantry column moving out in a blinding snow, heading south. At the time we didn't realize the extent of the chaos that must have existed at the front lines in North Korea with the retreating UN army.

After almost two weeks at sea the small troop carrier USS *Retreating* came into harbor in Japan, late December 1950. We were billeted in a small camp named Zama, where we were re-equipped for our assignment into action, winter equipment, etc.

I was rather curious as to what we were getting into. At the time I know that the men of 2d Ranger Company had no idea what we were getting into. Most of us were rather carefree and happy as we looked for women and drink. After all, we had just gotten off the boat after nearly two weeks on the water. We made the best of almost three whole days of liberty and a rather carefree existence. For some of the men it would be the last days of fun they would ever have.

For a couple of days we zeroed in our weapons and made sure everything was in order. Then we got the word that we were on our way to Korea. On December 29, in the evening, we went to an airfield for the flight to Korea, with full combat gear. I remember we were given "Mae West" flotation gear and parachutes for any emergency exit in case of aircraft failure. The chutes were manually operated with a ripcord, which none of us was really even familiar with. Even though we had made many parachute jumps, all of them were by static line.

It was dark when we took off in what I believe were 119s or C-47s. We arrived at an airstrip in Taegu. Early morning we were picked up by truck convoy and moved north to join the 7th Infantry Division on the central front.

Most of us still didn't know what the hell was going on. We pitched our newly-issued squad tents and were introduced to the 7th ID as the 2d Ranger Company Airborne. Here we were, an all-black company of paratroopers going into a combat situation with an all-white infantry division.

I can recall that one day we got a few cans of beer. I didn't know it at the time, but I was reminded that it was New Year's Eve. "Big deal," I responded.

Then we got the word that we were going north to meet the enemy. Then the fun began.

The one thing that most of the men will remember is the convoy going north and all of the refugee columns moving south crowding the road, getting in our way so that our vehicles could hardly move.

I was a BAR man assigned to ride in the C.O.'s jeep with Lieutenant Allen, along with Lt. Pryor, my Platoon Leader. Later in the day we passed a burned-out tank, our first taste of battle casualties. Then we arrived at a small village where the 32d Regiment had set up an aid station. It was our job to protect the aid station from Communist guerilla activity. We took advantage of the mud and straw huts in a small village for protection from the bitter cold, especially at night.

During the day we would go out to patrol; nights were spent on outpost and roadblocks, fighting the weather as well as the enemy. There was always constant activity, as the North Koreans watched us by day as we dug in for the night, or were put on outpost. When the sun went down they would come in and harass us.

This went on for a few days. Then we got the word that we were going into an attack situation. We were finally going after the enemy. We didn't know it at the time but 2d Ranger was going into a slaughterhouse. Our company was about to be cut almost in half in the next two days of fighting. We were about to get a taste of real combat.

On a cold January morning we loaded up for battle, almost double load; it was difficult to re-supply in the mountainous terrain. I had my BAR and helped carry ammo for the 60mm mortar.

We walked for a few miles on a railroad track that made it difficult to walk, then made our way into the hills for the night, no fires at night. We ate cold C-rations, then bedded down in the snow. We were cold and too tired to try to chop through the frozen ground. The next day we woke, freezing cold, and headed out to meet the enemy.

As we moved down into a valley, slipping and sliding all the way, we approached a small hamlet past dead cattle and a few dead civilians. Apparently, they just got in the way of the conflict. As we made our way up a ravine or valley we came upon some young civilian males. We didn't know if they were guerillas or whose side they were on. The word was out that if they were not in the army or in uniform they must be either guerillas or deserters. One of the officers from Baker (or "B") Company ordered them shot as guerillas. They were lined up against a stone wall and gunned down. We later regretted doing this. We didn't know it at the time, but the enemy was watching this execution.

When we continued up the valley, small arms fire broke out. We immediately took cover wherever we could find it. In my case it was behind a rather large boulder with some men from my squad. I still couldn't see the enemy, but I could sure hear the gunfire. Along with about six other men in my group, we began returning fire.

Sergeant Freeman, First Platoon Sergeant, began yelling at us to "put some fire on the hills." I was blazing away with the BAR. Then we got the mortar set up as best we could without the base plate and dumped all of the rounds we had on the surrounding hills toward the enemy. It was then that Lawrence "Poochie" Williams was hit in the head, killing him instantly. He almost dropped on top of me. I heard squad leader Herman Jackson yell, "Sergeant Freeman, Poochie got hit in the head!" but there was nothing we could do for him. I can remember how he hated to wear the steel helmet, and I often wonder if it might have saved his life.

Then another man near me, St. Thomas, was hit in the foot. His feet were frozen, and he was not really convinced he had been hit by a bullet. He removed his shoe-pac and asked me if it was really a bullet hole. I told him it was indeed. That was the last time I saw him alive. I was sure he got out safely, but he was killed a short time later. St. Thomas was one of my good stateside buddies. I found out later through Sergeant Herman Jackson that he had volunteered to go on this operation. He could have stayed behind because he was, after all, a cook, and not an assigned rifleman. That was when he got it.

We began to disperse or spread out. It was getting a bit hot behind that boulder. I had rather wisely removed the bi-pod from my weapon during this firefight. I knew how the enemy would always go after the automatic weapon, and this made me a somewhat less conspicuous target.

After I had used up most of my magazines in the return fire, I thought I had better save one for myself. I had used up all except one magazine, and I had lost contact with my assistant ammo bearers. One of them was Isaiah Woodard. Men were still being hit all around me. Then some guys from "B" Company came down the valley yelling "everybody out!" and the retreat was on. We still couldn't figure what was going on, so we began to withdraw.

On the way out I passed J. T. Holley. He had been hit in the back and said he couldn't move and asked me to help him to cover. That is when Boatwright was wounded; he had been hit twice. He came along and we helped him

[Holley] to a shelter beneath a ledge. If we had known what the situation was I know that we could have dragged him out. This still haunts me. I thought we were going to regroup and maybe counterattack, but I was wrong and we lost a few men that I knew were only wounded. The North Koreans moved in and executed them the same way we had shot their men down. After all, this was war.

I can also recall on the way out "Dude" Walker was giving us covering fire, saying, "Come on out, I got you covered." He was firing away with an M-1 rifle.

Up the ridge as we attempted to regroup and gather some of our walking wounded, Lieutenant Pryor staggered up. He had been hit in the head and blood was streaming down his face. We tried to get him on a litter but he refused. After a few moments he finally collapsed and some South Koreans carried him off to the aid station. In a couple of weeks he was back, only to be injured again. The next time I saw him we were back in Taegu, March 1951.

After we broke contact with the enemy we began to dig in for defense, as we knew that they would counterattack. I still didn't have any ammo for my BAR, so I began to empty M-1 clips to fill my magazines. We dug in for the night. The fighting went on into the night as the enemy counterattacked, but B Company held them off with machine gun fire and small arms.

The next day we moved up past a lot of dead Communists and a few dead from B Company; they had lost a lot of people. We dug in on a ridge to form a perimeter and set up for the night. As dusk began to settle elements of the 187 ABN RCT came up to relieve us. They wondered what all of the commotion was about, and I remarked, "You should have been here yesterday."

Lieutenant Allen gathered what was left of his company and we set off down the mountain in pitch black darkness to the village and aid station a few miles away. I still wonder why we couldn't have waited until dawn to make this move.

The next day we headed north again to a town called Tanyang. We spent days going on patrol and nights on defense perimeter in the hills. The cold was still unforgiving, so we took on more casualties from frozen or frostbitten limbs. It was a toss-up—frostbite or bullets.

Soon we were on the move again to Chechon. More defense, more patrols, attack and withdraw. We still didn't have our own mess hall. Always hungry, always cold, we were a rather sorry lot at times, but somehow we survived.

Then we got the word that we were on the move again. I didn't know it at the time but we were headed south to join up with the 187th RCT to make preparations for an airborne assault sometime soon called "Operation Tomahawk." Our first and only combat jump.

This was sort of a blessing in disguise, as it gave us a break from front-line duty and a chance to get out of the elements. We had served almost two solid months of front-line duty, and we needed a rest. We also got much-needed replacements.

P.S. "Big Jim"—This is really all I have on the situation at "Majori-ri." I know that a lot of men have different versions of their personal experience as to what really happened in this firefight—our first taste of real battle. Some of this material I have shared with Herman Jackson, and together we brought some of the details into perspective, and we agree on all of the things that I put into this writing. He (Jackson) remembers more about Glover than I can recall. Even though he was in the squad, I lost track of him in the din of battle.

Recollections of Herman Jackson, 2d Ranger Company (Airborne), transcribed by William Weathersbee, April 17, 1997

Hello, Weathersbee, this is Jack, in sunny California. I will try to get these tapes off today. I made a couple I wasn't satisfied with. I had started from the beginning when we were in the Tanyang Pass. I wasn't satisfied with them; anyway, I will get them off to you as soon as I can.

First, I want to give you some information on my background with mortars. In 1942, the last part of '42, I was assigned to Company E, 369th Infantry Division. I was in the weapons platoon. In the weapons platoon, we had a section of light machine guns and a section of three (3) 60mm mortars. I was assigned to the mortars. So I had been working on 60mm mortars all that time, from 1942 up until I went to Ranger School. In the military, I was in the 81mm mortar platoon in the 555th Parachute Infantry Battalion. We had six 81mm mortars in a separate platoon. So you can see, I had much experience with 60s and 81mm mortars.

So, what I will talk about, I will give you information on what happened while fighting in Korea.

Years later, I was assigned to the 187th Airborne Regimental Combat Team, in Japan. Later we gyro-scoped with the 508th Airborne Regimental Combat Team, back to Fort Bragg, North Carolina. That same year, we transferred to Fort Campbell, Kentucky, to form the 101st Airborne Division.

While at Fort Campbell, Kentucky, I was working as an instructor at the Division jump school and received orders for Korea, to be assigned to the 24th Infantry Division, 34th Infantry Regiment. This was in 1956. I was a platoon sergeant in company M, 34th Infantry Regiment.

More about my experience with mortars. I won every award that could be won in the 24th Infantry Division. I even beat out the reconnaissance company. They are always pretty good. I beat every other unit in the 24th Infantry Division that had mortars. I topped them all. I was put in for the I.D. White Leadership Award. You had to go to Japan to receive this award. They had a parade for me. After the parade, I was invited to the NCO Club for a party, and we had a swell time. I decided to go to the village, but the village was off limits, we were caught and I didn't get the I.D. White Award for outstanding leadership.

In Korea I was assigned to Camp Casey. The Third Battalion was in a small camp. Casey was no more than five miles from where we parachuted into Munsan-ni. You can imagine, I had plenty of time to go to the drop zone area. The DZ was in our defensive position for the 34th Regiment. Hill 151 was the main objective for the 2d Ranger Company during Operation Tomahawk. I could drive from my camp to the old DZ in ten to fifteen minutes. Being familiar with that area, I had an opportunity to go there several times to visit the area.

Upon my return to the area, word got around there was a sergeant in the Mortar Platoon of the 34th Regiment who had parachuted in there during the war. A couple of reporters came in to see me, seeking information about the drop. We went to the DZ, I pointed out to them where we dropped, where we assembled, and where we began our attack on Hill 151. Before we got to Hill 151, I took them to an area—this was the first time I had been there since the drop—where we mounted our 60mm mortars, after we assembled, and supported one of our platoons in the attack.

If you look north from Hill 151, the portion of the hill we took would be near the rear of Hill 151. In other words, the 1st and 2d platoons of 2d Ranger Company took the top of Hill 151, the hill leading to Hill 151, we were fighting up there. We were actually attacking the rear of Hill 151 at the same time.

I took those reporters up there, telling the story about our jump, our attack, and taking that hill, etc. I stopped in the same area where we placed our mortars and fired them. As you know, on a 60mm mortar round, the case they come in has a metal top and bottom. The rest of the case is fabric. Anyway, we stopped where we originally fired our 60's. The tops and bottoms of these containers were metal; amazingly, they were still there in our original position. I picked up a few of those metal tops and stuck them in my pocket. I am letting you know that I went back to Korea in 1956, visited the Drop Zone, and was standing in the position where we fired our mortars.

Tanyang Pass

I want to talk about what we were really doing down in the Tanyang Pass. I cannot remember the exact date, but I believe it was the Division evacuation. It was the last evacuation in that chain, it was the last position going south. Anyway, when we first arrived there, we immediately sent out patrols. We started patrolling that area, the mountains around that area. I remember going out one day when we returned from off those mountains. I was assigned a position with half of my squad. I was a squad leader in the 1st platoon, the 3d squad, 2d Ranger Company (Airborne).

SFC Freeman was our platoon sergeant. Lieutenant Pryor was the platoon leader. I remember coming in, tired, from climbing those mountains. The 2d Ranger Company always made a point, if humanly possible, of working our way to the top to do our patrolling. If we were attacked, we would always be on the high ground. That was the motto in our company.

On this particular day we came in in the evening, the sun was going down, and my squad was given the mission to defend the railroad tunnel. The tunnel was directly above the 7th Division Medical Evacuation heading north to the town of Tanyang. The mission for my squad was to protect that area that night. With me was Carrell, my asst. squad leader; David "Tank" Clarke, my BAR man; Curtis Courts, radio telephone operator; and Richard Glover, a rifleman in the squad. This is what happened that night. We moved into position and remained until around nine o'clock. Quietly, we moved back and joined the other half of the squad. We still had the tunnel in sight. You could see through the tunnel from our position. It was like a big tube.

Our reason for moving, we knew the enemy had pinpointed our position and knew our exact location. And they did. This is what happened: I sat at the head of my squad with my legs crossed and my rifle in my lap for at least three hours. What we didn't know was that during this time the enemy was closing in on us. My reason for saying that: Glover shot one just a few feet from me, where we were located. What gave this enemy soldier, this guerrilla, the protection for him to crawl beside me was this bank, a ditch. I was at the head of the squad, just sitting there looking directly into the tunnel. Suddenly, one shot was fired, then another one. When that happened, Glover was in position where he could see this guerrilla. When he saw him, he shot him. What happened after that, Tank Clarke threw a white phosphorous grenade. Now, we were just a few feet from where the huts started in this village and that white phosphorous got into the top of those shacks. When that happened, everything started burning. He probably threw a WP grenade because if he had thrown a fragmentation grenade, it would have hit some of us in the ditch. When this happened, Glover and Courts leaped over the bank and joined the rest of the squad. Now we had four men on the other side of the bank, but I was still in the ditch. I leaped over the bank and joined my squad. On the other side of the bank, I counted my men: everyone was present. The noise we were hearing wasn't 2d Ranger Company. Ice was cracking, people running; as you know, snow was everywhere, it was very cold, I thought it was below zero.

Spreading my squad out about five to ten yards, we formed a line. When they were in the proper position, we heard running toward us, to our front and on our flanks. The enemy was everywhere. We opened up with everything we had. We sprayed the whole area. I had one fire team with me, and we really poured it on. I would say this was around three or four o'clock in the morning.

Jesse Anderson, "Big Tech," brought a half squad to the area to relieve me. After Anderson relieved my squad, I looked in the place where Glover shot this enemy soldier. You could see plainly where he had been dragged off. Blood was there; someone had dragged him away. We were just about in the village, so we searched it. As we searched, we found more blood. I interrogated an old Korean man and pointed to the blood. He knew what I meant. He made a motion, flapping his hands and arms to pretend he had killed a chicken. I knew it was a damn lie, especially with all that blood in the snow. Whatever the blood came from—and we knew where it came from—it wasn't from a chicken. They were hiding this guerrilla. I can assure you, Glover shot that guerrilla at least two times. Had it not been for Glover—as close as this guerrilla had gotten to us, if I had to stand, I could have touched this guerrilla in the center of his back. That's how close he had gotten to us. There were two enemy grenades just lying there in the snow when Anderson relieved my squad.

When we returned to the perimeter, they were hitting us that night. I remember Paulding and Small, on a mountain south of the aid station. Both had been wounded; SFC Baker was killed during that engagement. You can tell what date it was, I cannot recall the date of that engagement. [January 7, 1951.]

We pulled out from the 7th Division Medical Evacuation and went into the attack with the 1st Battalion, 32d Infantry Regiment. Second Company was behind Company B, 32d Infantry Regiment. What happened that evening, prior to going into the attack, was we moved up into the mountains and saw some Koreans to our left front. We fired on them, but didn't hit anyone. That morning we pulled out and continued the attack up the mountain. Second Company was following B Company, 32d Regiment.

We filed down this mountain, there was a village in front of us. When we passed that village, there was a huge rock or boulder. It was a big one. Just as I was leading the squad, the enemy opened fire on us. Rembert was a few yards away. He was hit in the chest. I think it killed him immediately. When Rembert got hit, the only cover we had, going up this hill, was this huge boulder that was there. We took cover behind it. The enemy was firing at us from the rear of the boulder. In other words, the boulder didn't give us any protection whatsoever. People were hit all around that damn rock. That huge rock, or whatever you want to call it, actually didn't give us protection at all.

I had a bullet rip me on the tip of my chin. Had it been an inch over, it would have taken my chin off. I spread my men out, firing up the hill. My automatic rifleman (BAR man that was with me) was Tank Clarke, and Lawrence Williams. I directed their fire on that doggone hill. Williams was closest to me and was hit. I would say someone was firing at us from our rear. The bullet that hit Williams entered the top of his head and came out in front of his eye. I looked at it, his brains started running out of the bullet hole. Glover who was to my left, was also hit. He got it in the neck. That's how close I was to him. In all probability, this may have killed him immediately. Then, he was hit again in the neck.

We received the word to pull out. When I started moving back, Legree Aikens, who was about twenty-five to thirty yards from my position, was wounded. I ran across this rice paddy, and I think every Chinaman or Korean was shooting at me. I jumped in this huge ditch and crawled up to the bank. Standing no more than ten feet from me was a Korean. He didn't see me. I leveled down on him and got off two rounds, but my carbine jammed. I always had trouble with that carbine. Anyway, he was shooting, as I looked at it, to his left. Just before I had gotten into position on that bank, a man in my squad (Robert St. Thomas) yelled, "Jack, where are you?" I yelled back, "Down here!

Come on down!" Before I could get a shot off on this Korean in front of me, when I crawled up to the bank, he was shooting to my left. I am sure he was shooting at St. Thomas. Prior to this, St. Thomas had been hit in the foot, so I told him to come down where I was. When I called back up, standing before me, not more than ten feet, I mean ten feet, was a Korean. No way in the world I could have missed him. That's when I got my two shots off with the carbine and it jammed on me. If I had been a little earlier, I would have knocked him down before. I believe he was the one who killed St. Thomas.

I pulled back to this little village. On the way, I saw this cap on the ground. It was an old tanker's cap, lying in this ditch. You know, the kind that had flaps on it. It was the one Dude Walker had been wearing. When I saw the cap, I said, damn, they have gotten the Dude. When I arrived at the village, the Dude was there. He told me, "Look Jack, we've got a couple of wounded men here. I don't want a living ass to leave until we get the wounded out." I picked up a rifle and a belt with some ammo on it, and threw the belt over my shoulder. I took up a position on the high ground, not more than twenty-five yards from this Korean shack where several guys were lying wounded. Dude Walker and I were the last two men out of that place that day. I would like everyone to know what the Dude said on this particular day. He said, "Nobody will leave until all of the wounded are out of here."

We pulled back to our position. That night the enemy reassembled and hit us again (counterattacked). I was back at the aid station. I was at the aid station or the division evac. . . . I wasn't up there that night. Second Ranger Company and B Company, 32d Regiment made up for what the enemy had done to us on that bloody day.

Shortly after that we were relieved from duty around the 7th Division Medical Evacuation. We moved to the town of Tanyang itself. We set up defensive positions on the mountains in and around Tanyang. We had a chance to get some hot food, some rest, and at the same time we were patrolling, just keeping an eye on things in the mountains.

This incident happened while we were in Tanyang. We moved into those huts. Not being familiar with the way Koreans lived, we moved into those huts with all our equipment. We had lots of ammo, .45 and .30 caliber ammo, including hand grenades. The way you heat Korean houses, a fire is built on the outside in something like a small fireplace. The smoke from this fire goes under the house and comes out from a chimney on the other side of the house; the heating is done by heating the floor. Very little fire is needed to warm the house, but we put too much fire in the fireplace, and under the floor. Our ammo was in musette bags. The floor got so doggone hot the ammo was cooking off in those bags, which woke us up. We were lucky those hand grenades didn't explode.

We remained around there (Tanyang) getting some rest, patrolling, keeping an eye on things. After that, we moved to Chechon. This is where we were training replacements. This is where 7th Division put them off on us. We didn't mind at all. We had a chance to pull some good men out of that group, they joined the 2d Ranger Company. I remember after we trained them for a few days, things got hot up on the front line. Some ROK soldiers broke and we were sent to plug a gap in the line up there.

I'd like to mention that I had been hospitalized for having hepatitis. I was returning to the 2d Ranger Company. Traveling on the train Lieutenant Anthony and I happened to run into each other. Lieutenant Anthony was on his way to 2d Ranger Company. We were thinking the company was located at Chechon. Arriving at Chechon, we found out that the company had moved to Taegu. Lieutenant Anthony and I caught a train for Taegu, where we joined the company. When we reached Taegu, we went to the area where the company had been, but they had moved to a marshalling area, adjacent to the 187th Airborne Regimental Combat Team. The company had been assigned to the 187th ARCT for a combat parachute jump. When we arrived, we didn't know where the parachute assault would be. But I knew that when the day came, we would have all the information about the drop.

Lieutenant Anthony and I joined up with the Rangers in the marshalling area, located in an apple orchard, adjacent to K-2 Airfield, Taegu, Korea, to prepare for the parachute assault. We had a chance to get passes to Taegu, do some shopping at the Post Exchange, have a few drinks and some fun. We knew the day was coming soon when we would be returning to the front lines. The day did come for our briefing for the parachute drop. In the meantime, we had gotten a couple of replacements. Some of our old friends who were in the 555th Parachute Infantry Battalion, the 3d Battalion, 505th Airborne Infantry Regiment at Fort Bragg, North Carolina, had been transferred to Korea to join the 187th Airborne Regimental Combat Team for this operation. It was a relief to see the guys from the old days, go into combat along with the 2d Ranger Company, being assigned to the 187th Airborne Regimental Combat Team.

When we were briefed for the airborne assault, I remember Weathersbee had made a sand table. We were briefed thoroughly on our mission. The initial drop was to be the town of Chechon. Anyway, we were briefed, we went to the airfield, packed our crew-served weapons, and made up a section that would handle 60mm mortars. I was placed in that section, because of my experience with mortars. Before joining the paratroopers, and during the time I was assigned to the 555th Parachute Infantry Battalion, I was in the 81mm mortar section. We packed our bundles, marked them with blue ribbon so that when we hit the ground, we knew how to find our bundles quickly.

The next morning we were scheduled to head back to the front lines. We loaded up on those planes. The planes 2d Ranger Company were jumping were C-46's. We called it the old ass kicker. It was always a good plane to jump from. The unit flying our company was a National Guard outfit. I clearly remember the crew chief on the plane I was in was black. We loaded up and took off. We headed north, flew out over the ocean, made a turn, and came inland over the city of Seoul, the capital of South Korea. Then we headed for the drop zone.

When we made our turn, we were given the red light. When you get the red light, paratroopers know you will be exiting the aircraft in approximately ten minutes. The next thing you will see will be the green light. When the green light comes on, it is time to un-ass, or get out of that aircraft. The stick I was in was the left stick. To determine the right stick from the left of the aircraft, you face the cockpit of the aircraft, the door on your right would be the right door, and the door on your left would be the left door. My stick was jumping the left door.

The red light came on, we knew it was about ten minutes before exiting the aircraft. We went through the usual procedure before jumping: stand up, hook up, and check equipment. We were ready to go. All hooked up, we watched the red light. I remember Lieutenant Cliette was the jumpmaster of this particular stick. I cannot remember the number two man in the stick behind Lieutenant Cliette to help with our door bundles. When the green light came on, a bundle was crossed in the door. As you know, the 555th, the black paratroopers, were famous for exiting an aircraft on time. I mean, getting out of there, un-assing the aircraft. Well, this bundle got crossed up in the door. When the bundle got crossed, the right stick had completely cleared the aircraft and we had not even started jumping. That creates a real problem: you are either going to land on a hill occupied by the enemy, or you will land way down the field somewhere. What I did, I completely unhooked my static line from the anchor line cable, and was moving over to re-hook and jump from the right door. When I crossed over, the left door stick finally began to move. When the stick started moving, I was completely unhooked. So I moved toward the door, re-hooked, but didn't have time to insert the safety pin in the static line fastener. I moved to the door and jumped out. Behind me was Adell Allen. He was the twelfth man in the stick. Anthony Andrade was behind Allen. I believe David Lesure was behind the third or fourth in the aircraft, in this portion of the stick.

So I moved toward the door, not even hooked up, and exited the aircraft. I had a fairly good body position. If you have a bad body position, especially in the C-46, you will feel it when the parachute opens. I could have had a good or bad position when that chute popped open, but I felt good about it. I'm descending, and I've got a couple bullet holes in my chute. I'm thinking, "people are shooting at us because we were late getting out of the aircraft."

I landed in either an apple or peach orchard—some kind of fruit tree orchard. My chute got tangled in the small trees. I landed beside a small shack and heard a couple of shots. They were firing at us, so I crawled into the shack and was able to get out of my harness while in the shack. After removing my parachute, I had to go down field to get our mortars. Along the way I picked up the men who jumped behind me: Adell Allen, Anthony Andrade, David Lesure, and I cannot remember the others who were in the stick. We started looking for the bundles marked with the blue ribbon and couldn't find them. We found two bundles with machine guns in them, though.

We headed to the assembly area with the two machine guns and the ammo that was dropped with the guns. When we reached the assembly area, the company had dropped their rounds of ammo. Every man in the 2d Ranger Company parachuted into combat with 60mm mortar rounds in their packs. That was unusual. But if you load every man down with a single mortar round, it is a good way of getting ammo into the Drop Zone. When we reached the assembly area, we put the machine guns down and found our mortars. Second Company had taken our mortars off the DZ. At the assembly area we still had the machine guns. We left the machine guns and picked up our mortars. The 2d Ranger Company had dropped all those mortar rounds in the assembly area, so we had plenty of mortar ammo. We loaded up.

I met Hargrove, I think he was platoon sergeant of third platoon. [Hargrove was a squad leader in 2d platoon.] They had knocked out a Russian 82mm mortar, dropped an incendiary grenade in the tube to destroy it, and kept the sight, which he handed to me. Anyway, the 1st and 2d platoons of the 2d Ranger Company were fighting their way to the top of Hill 151. We (the weapons platoon) fell in behind our reserve platoon, which I think was the 3d platoon. When we reached the first ridge, the moving command post (CP), Captain Allen and Lieutenant Anthony were there behind 3d platoon.

The 3d platoon crossed two rice paddies to get to the upgrade on Hill 151. Third platoon was hitting the rear of Hill 151, while the 1st and 2d platoons were fighting on top of Hill 151. Second Ranger Company was hitting the top and the rear of Hill 151 at the same time. This was good. The 3d platoon, I think it was the 3d platoon, where Van Dunk was killed out there.

When we reached this ridge, along where the moving CP was located, Captain Allen said, "Get those mortars in action to support the 3d platoon going across those fields!" We mounted our 60mm mortars quickly. The range was about four hundred yards. It couldn't have been more than four to five hundred yards. What I did, I had them strip all the powder off the mortar rounds, you know they carry six charges. I had them remove all the charges except one, and started firing. We were dropping our fire directly in front of the 3d platoon. It was pretty close to them. I am sure they thought when those rounds started coming in, that we didn't know what we were doing, and thought we would drop them right on their heads. But we were watching from our position on the hill, and could see every round hit the ground. We fired a round from each mortar. We walked that fire in front of 3d platoon, step by step up that mountain.

Actually, as I said before, the portion we were attacking was the rear of Hill 151. The 2d Ranger Company was fighting on the flank and rear of Hill 151 the same time. After we captured part of Hill 151, the mortars displaced forward to Hill 151. We went almost to the top of Hill 151. I saw Weathersbee with a bunch of prisoners. Prisoners were running all over trying to surrender. We were also getting a lot of sniper fire and whatnot. The 1st and 2d platoons pushed over Hill 151 and received a lot of rifle fire. We advanced forward to Hill 151 and supported the 3d platoon.

It was then that artillery fire started falling around us. Whatever size weapon they were firing, it was very large. They fired a barrage of five or six rounds, and then it stopped. The enemy had seen this big cloud of dust in the vicinity of Seoul. That cloud of dust was the movement of armor: tanks breaking through, coming to our Drop Zone, linking up with the paratroopers. Those were our tanks that were breaking through the enemy lines, giving us some support and relief. The enemy shifted their fire from us, the 2d Ranger Company, to the tanks.

We moved the mortars to the top of Hill 151 and dug in for the night. I had given up on the carbine long ago and started carrying an M-1 rifle. I was the only man in 2d Ranger Company who jumped with an engineer tool. I jumped into

Munsan-ni with a D-handle shovel. The shovel was cumbersome, but I knew when we hit the ground that shovel would be needed to prepare our mortar positions.

We remained on Hill 151 and received continuous artillery fire. We also were getting rifle fire. But Hill 151 fell to 2d Ranger Company in record time. The next day, the tanks had a perimeter formed around the DZ. The heavy drop came in on the day we parachuted in, dropping supplies from the air to the troops. The pack howitzers that were dropped to the 187th Airborne RCT were positioned adjacent to 2d Ranger Company; they really cut loose.

The next day everything had been secured in that area, so we moved toward the DZ, where we boarded tanks and headed south. We were close to the Imjin River. We got to a point where we had to cross the river. Before crossing we approached some people who had been assigned to the 555th Parachute Infantry Battalion. They had been assigned to Mortar Battery, 187th Airborne Regimental Combat Team. (The 555th Parachute Infantry Battalion was an all-black parachute unit.) I saw Charles Bagley, a good friend of mine. They were firing 4.2mm mortars. Second Company crossed the river and headed north. When we crossed the river the enemy started dropping artillery in that area, so we crossed under fire. On the other side was a railroad and a surface road. We headed north, where elements of the 187th were fighting just ahead of us. The reached a place called Tonguchon. (On my return to Korea, I was assigned to the 32d Infantry Regiment. This unit was part of the 7th Infantry Division, and its main area was Tonguchon.)

When we arrived in Tonguchon the 187th ARCT was fighting on our right, attacking a mountain range there. The 4th Ranger Company (Airborne) was attacking a hill, and we were the only unit in position to give them supporting fire from our mortars. Captain Allen gave the order to support 4th Company with mortar fire. I remember 4th Ranger Company's attack. On top of the high ground was a huge hole full of Chinese. We gave the Rangers support, and when they got to the top of the hill, it appeared as if every Chinese soldier in Korea threw grenades at them—and then ran as fast as they could.

I would like to mention the 4th Ranger Company objective during the Munsan-ni operation: this hill was in front of the 7th Infantry Division Medical Clearing Company—the same one we defended in Tanyang pass.

The 4th Ranger Company took that doggone hill, that mountain. I saw one Ranger going across that mountain by himself. Fourth Company took that hill. I want to mention the 64th Tank Battalion also. This was an all-black tank battalion. I remember the 64th from way back. It had been the 758th Heavy Tank Battalion at Fort Bragg, North Carolina (they were billeted next to us at Bragg). They maneuvered against us at Fort Campbell, Kentucky. That whole area we were fighting in later became Camp Hovey, 7th Infantry Division, after the war. The main gate was at Tonguchon, where we fired our mortars.

The 64th Tank Battalion came up and raked those mountains in that area with .50 caliber machine gun fire and knocked out gun positions with 90-mm gun fire. They raked and raked that hill. That evening, just before the sun went down, the tanks pulled back so they could get proper protection that night. When they withdrew, 2d Ranger Company threw a perimeter around the 64th Tank Battalion to keep the enemy from destroying the tanks.

Hill 581

We had been on Hill 581 once before. We had been up there, found some ammo and buried it on the hill. We didn't know that one day we would return and use the ammo we had found on Hill 581.

We had been patrolling this area, then they decided to give us a rest. They put up these showers, real showers, like we had never seen before in Korea. We had been on the line all this time, so this was our first real rest. When we pulled back, we had a lot of weapons in the supply truck that had to be cleaned. We started cleaning our weapons after we had showered and changed clothes. They had a pile of clothing on the ground, so you could pick out something decent to wear. The clothing we were wearing was torn, filthy and needed to be changed. We had been in the mountains so long we had literally shredded our clothes. It was a relief to get some clean clothing. The sun was out and I recall it was hot. On this particular day, we had put up a supply tent. Several Rangers were cleaning weapons. I remember Captain Allen came into the supply tent and spotted this Korean sitting down cleaning a weapon. He didn't know this person was a Korean—I am sure he didn't know. Anyway, this Korean was helping us clean weapons, which wasn't too strange. Just about every outfit over there had Koreans working in mess halls, or somewhere else doing something useful.

On this day the sun was bearing down and was really hot. What bugged Captain Allen was that person was sitting in supply tent on a really hot day cleaning weapons with a field jacket on and the hood over his head. The captain asked, "It's hot. How in the world can you sit there, as hot as it is, wearing a field jacket?" He reached over and pulled the hood down, and all this black hair fell down. He was shocked to see a woman with us! Anyway, he pitched a bitch. We had a big laugh about it later, but the company commander didn't think this was very funny and he kicked her out.

We finished cleaning weapons, remained in the area for a few days, then it was time to go back into the hills. Fighting was going on everywhere. On our way back to Hill 581, we climbed this mountain and saw some Koreans in the valley below us. We fired on them, but they were out of range and we didn't hit anything. We pushed toward Hill 581. Our pilots were bombing in the vicinity. We crossed this valley between us and Hill 581 and started up the hill. As soon as we reached the top, we were ordered to make contact with the enemy. We dropped our mortars, with security, and started down the forward slopes of Hill 581, leap-frogging platoons. After we had completed one leap, the 4th platoon went into position, then we ran into heavy rifle fire. We had met the enemy.

I remember Sutton was with me during this time. He climbed this doggone tree to pull down some limbs to get a clear vision of the enemy situation and was wounded. I was about five yards from him. I had just moved forwarded. I remember yelling, "Let's get these m_____ f_____s!" The next thing I remember, I was hit in the stomach, the right thigh, and in the right wrist. When I fell to the ground—it was just a matter of a minute or so—Doc Rabbit (William Thomas) came up. Rabbit said, "Damn Jack, you are hit pretty bad." He gave me a couple shots of morphine. I think he did not believe I was going to make it and wanted me to die in comfort, or whatever. He cut my cartridge belt off me. I had two pouches of hand grenades and I was carrying an M-1 rifle. Rabbit cut all of that stuff I was carrying off me. Some medics came up and started walking me down the hill to the aid station, where they placed me in an ambulance and drove me to division evacuation. From there, I was moved to a MASH unit.

I remember that Koreans and Chinese were being treated at the MASH unit when I was there. It seemed odd because they were the enemy, and I remember that thought stuck with me. They operated on me there and eventually moved me to another MASH, and from there to a hospital in Japan, where I remained for some time. They were getting me ready to return to 2d Ranger Company in Korea. We went before a board of medical officers to prove we were fit, and test-fired our weapons to show we could engage again in combat, and were ready to leave. Some sergeant told me and another soldier to hold back. I guess they determined we weren't fit to return to the front. We turned in our equipment and were told, "You're going home."

I would like to mention Munsan-ni, where we dropped. Years later, they put a community center in the middle of the DZ. In the community center they had a large PX and a chaplain center. They also had a recreation center in that area we dropped on in 1951.

When I was with the 24th Infantry Division, I was about five miles from our DZ. The orientation for all new arrivals in the 24th ID was to go to the DZ and look at the North Koreans across the DMZ. In order to get there, you had to pass Hill 151. To the right of 151 was a bridge, they called it Freedom Bridge. In the 7th ID area, where we were fighting, is Tonguchon. I spent one year in that area. The main gate is where we (2d Ranger Company) set up our mortars.

Recollections of James H. Fields,
2d Ranger Infantry Company (Airborne)

I was assigned to the 80th Airborne Anti-Aircraft Battalion, Division Artillery, 82d Airborne Division from November 1948 until October 1950. The 80th had moved from its old area to barracks in line with the 505th Third Battalion. It was sometime after the evening meal when someone came into the barracks saying there were some officers in the 505 area interviewing volunteers for a new outfit. When I arrived at the drill field, there was a white officer standing on a P.T. stand.

When we were assembled he started to speak. He said something like this: "We are forming the toughest, meanest outfit in the United States Army. I don't know if you will go in by submarine, parachute or what, but you will be fighting. The unit will be called Rangers. We want volunteers. The line forms to the right."

Well, I had to be in this outfit. I knew what Rangers had been in World War II. I had done research on Darby's Rangers some time before. The post library had information and pictures of the men in the Rangers battalion. I knew about British commandos. I had this idea that we would be engaged in this kind of warfare: missions carefully planned, split-second timing, hit-and-run. I entered the building for the interview. I gave the interviewing officer such a persuasive spiel that I could not be turned down. I was in.

If I remember correctly, we cleared the post in three days and were on our way to Fort Benning, Georgia. We arrived by troop train and were transported out to the Harmony Church area to some drab barracks made like none I had ever seen before.

I was assigned to the first platoon: Lawrence Estell, squad leader; James Freeman, Platoon Sergeant; Bernard Pryor, First Lieutenant. Most of the men I did not know, with the majority coming from the third battalion 505th A.I.R. We were originally designated 4th Company—the last of the four companies. About two weeks into training we were changed to 2d Ranger Company. I never knew what that was all about.

I am convinced that 2d Ranger Company pushed itself to the limits training day and night to reach top combat efficiency. I arrived at Fort Benning and never left the post until we got on the train for Camp Stoneman, California. Lieutenant Allen and First Sergeant West said there would be no passes and I took them at their word. There were no public telephone lines out to Harmony Church. There was a public phone up on main post at the colored NCO Club. I got up to the main post by bus and the fellow in charge of the club gave me such a hard time I did not think I was going to be able to make my call. However, I did. I was just a Private First Class. I had heard stories of some of the fellows' unauthorized excursions into town. I did not think it was worth it, given the racist, domineering attitude of the Columbus police.

We trained extremely hard, learning not only about our weapons but foreign weapons and maps. Sergeant Freeman and Lieutenant Pryor were two of the best I had ever seen in the field at night. They would take a map, get under a blanket, orient it, shoot an azimuth and bring us right to our objective. Had we had the time, all of us could have sharpened our skills to that point.

I always had this desire for ice water. We almost never had ice water. We would come in from training and there would be this young fellow selling ice cream. I don't know where he came from out there in Harmony Church, but there he would be. I told him that I did not want any ice cream, but when he sold out, which he did, I would buy his dry ice. I took the ice and put it in my canteen cup and set my canteen on top of the ice and in minutes I would have cold water. Everything for the "Dogface" was so damned inconvenient. The taste of ice water was a luxury.

There were no rounds available for us to train on the 57mm recoilless rifle. We had to use a system called sub-caliber. A carbine barrel was placed in a dummy, a recoilless round was placed in the recoilless rifle and fired at miniature targets. It worked. I remember we were speed marching out to the sub-caliber training area one day. I had on combat boots, the ones with the two buckles. Someone stepped on one of my heels and it came off. I tried to get out of column and find it. That was impossible. I marched on with one heel missing and trained all day. There were civilian truck drivers on the post, and to my surprise trucks pulled in to take us back to the company area. This did not happen often in our training. We formed up in ranks. But some men broke for the trucks before Lieutenant Allen gave the order to mount up, and he sent the trucks away. We had to walk back, me with one heel missing.

There was also water training. I saw the training film the night before, and it looked pretty straightforward. You cross two rifles and secure them, and take two shelter halves and make a raft. Place your equipment on the raft and push it in front of you as you swim. The next day I was on K.P. (Kitchen Police). I don't know what happened at Victory Pond. I got several conflicting accounts. The noon meal was prepared and waiting. I saw the company come into the area, but no one came to chow. I could see the company commander. He always looked angry, but this time more so than usual. The company encountered some difficulties in training—some that could have been tragic. Tragedy was averted, and they did eat the evening meal.

There was a problem getting aircraft in so that we could make training jumps. My last jump was at night. I had made one other night jump at Bragg. This was a simulated combat jump. We were jumping into enemy territory, blowing a bridge and escaping and evading an enemy force comprised of elements from the 325th Infantry. That was the night I lost my rifle grenade launcher and had a statement of charges against my pay. It's funny how some things stick in your mind. We had completed our mission and were on our way out. There was a jeep coming up the road and we got into the woods just a few yards and they could not see us, but someone fired a blank and they were on us for most of the night. We had to stay off the road and go cross-country.

There was never a dull moment during training. I had never seen a flame-thrower in operation before and I was impressed. The demonstrator set an old P. T. stand on fire. I never wanted to be on the business end of one of those.

We were being trained to live off the land, and in some cases prepare our own meals. When food came to mind, the worst Thanksgiving I have ever had was Thanksgiving 1950. We had moved from our old area to barracks across the road and some of our guys were cooking. Talk about on-the-job training.

Under the command of Lieutenant Allen and his staff of career officers and top-notch NCO's, we were molded into a cohesive fighting force in a very short time. There were news reports that the war would be over by Thanksgiving, but our training never let up. We were given one Ranger Tab. The morning we were to leave Benning, brand-new city buses were lined up on the parade field to take us to the train in Columbus. We got off the buses and were faced with the colored signs indicating where colored people were to be seated. We took the signs with us.

It took five days to get to Pittsburg, California. We were in Camp Stoneman for a couple of days. My shot records were somehow lost and I had to take them again. The ferry carried us to San Francisco. I remember being in what looked like a warehouse by the water. Red Cross workers gave us coffee and donuts. I had seen in World War II newsreels how soldiers walked up a gangplank to board the ship, but didn't get to do that. The ship had giant metal doors that slid back, so we just walked off the dock into the *Butner*.

It looked as though we were stacked one on top of the other to sleep. If you were the least bit claustrophobic, you were in trouble. Before I could find a place to settle, Lieutenant Pryor told me I was on guard duty and to report to the brig. The brig was in the very bow of the ship. A Marine Corps Sergeant, who was in transit just as we were, was placed in charge. Lieutenant Pryor did me a great favor by putting me on guard. I had plenty of room where I was, could shower whenever I wanted, had a badge that allowed me to go to the head of the chow line, and pulled guard all over the ship.

We stopped in Pearl Harbor and got shore leave, which surprised all of us. I saw downtown Honolulu and ate a good Chinese meal. I had to be back on the ship for guard duty that night. It was hotter than blue blazes on shore and we were dressed in our winter uniforms. I got a taxi ride back to the docks. The next morning before we pulled out, 2d Ranger Company fell out on deck for physical training. From my vantage point above the fantail I could see the men of 2d Ranger Company with their Mohawk haircuts doing calisthenics with the precision of a well-practiced dance team. We had a long two-week trip across the Pacific to Japan, and disembarked at Yokohama on December 24th. Went to Camp Zama by train.

While at Zama we drew pistols, knives, and cold-weather gear. We went to the post theater for orientation: cold weather survival, the enemy, and the terrain. We test-fired and battle-sighted our weapons. Aircraft became available after a few days and we were airlifted from Tachikawa Air Force Base to Taegu.

There, our gear was thrown from the aircraft to the tarmac. It was not quite dark, so we were able to find our individual equipment. I was on the last truck in the convoy, and not very far into our journey north the truck I was riding on broke down. The truck ahead of us faded into the distance. It was extremely cold and it was some time before they realized we were not behind them and came back for us. I remembered thinking, "Is this the way it is going to be?" Others had it as bad or worse. I remember running across some troops who had been called up from the reserves and who were on the ship with us. They moved north by rail on a train whose windows had been shot out, and it was unheated.

The hills were barren, the roads so narrow around the hills, with such sharp drop-offs that convoys could only move in one direction at a time. I remember arriving at what I was told had been a school. It was then being used as an aid station, and medics were there unprotected. We were to set up a protective perimeter around the aid station and make part of it our command post. There was room for one platoon to sleep inside. First Platoon got the privilege. Our minds were not set at ease when we saw the bullet holes in the ceiling above us and in the floors on which we would be sleeping.

Second Company patrolled the hills around the aid station by day, set up defense positions and controlled the approach road at night. I recall returning from patrol and coming up to the command post from the rice paddies to the front. Our machine guns were pointed out *toward* us.

There were train tracks immediately above the aid station command post. The bullet holes in the ceiling and floors had been fired into the building from a train. We could hear a train coming when it was some distance from the aid station, and you could hear the distinct sound of burp gun firing. There were men lined up for chow on the far side of the station. I could see men moving about, seeking cover from what they knew was coming. Lieutenant Queen was patrol leader, and he gave the command to lay in on the train. It did not have many cars. I got off eight into the first boxcar, firing up and over the heads of our men. Shortly after that the train was in a tunnel, our machine guns were turned around and you could see tracers hitting in the tunnel.

One day coming off patrol into the command post my platoon leader told us we were moving after chow. We moved out toward an area we had never been before: up into the hills. As we set up a defense line for the night, jets flew over our positions firing at what seemed to be men running in a valley to our front.

I tried to dig a foxhole, but the ground was frozen so hard that I could only make a small depression. My canteen was frozen solid. Some G.I.s on a hill across from us were firing a machine gun almost all night. The next morning we moved out and joined a line of troops that stretched as far as I could see. I always thought that our mission would be when and if we got there. We came up to some huts. The people there were guerrillas and were shot on the spot. When they fell to the ground they were sprayed with automatic weapons. I could hear sporadic gunfire as we moved forward. The regiment was strung out up through a gorge and I could not see anyone, but I knew they were taking a lot of fire.

The enemy was on high ground and the fire was raining down on us. I was assistant BAR man to Billie Tate. He and I were together and caught in the open with no cover. I was carrying the BAR and could not get it to fire more than one or two rounds at a time. I told Tate to give me my M-1 and for him to take his BAR. Tate got the BAR to work. My M-1 worked fine for a while, popping them off as fast as I could load it. But after a while it would not extract, eject, and feed; I had to work it like a bolt-action rifle. Took my glove off my right hand to get the round out fast. Tate was hit and moved back. Higginbotham came up by my side and started to lay down a base of fire. Bullets kicked up the snow to our front and flanks. Everybody was shooting. I looked back and saw Lieutenant Pryor was standing, with blood streaming down from under his helmet and two men trying to restrain him. They led him away.

Lieutenant Allen seemed to have been hit in the hip. They had placed a soldier from the other unit just behind Higg and myself on a litter. He was covered with a blanket, but was shivering from the cold and had a strange pale complexion. Someone around the bend that I could not see yelled, "Here they come!" and that fellow got up off that litter and took off. There was all of this firing and fury of battle, then all of a sudden there was this silence. I looked around, it was just Higg and me. We looked at each other and not a word was spoken, but we both took off at the same time the way we had come. Moving down this steep, eroded ditch for cover, I became entangled in commo wire that regiment was laying as we moved forward. When I reached a point in the ditch it was as if a weight had been lifted off of my shoulders. I knew I was no longer in danger. I picked up an abandoned BAR, which I gave to Sergeant Dude Walker. We got back so far there was a bird colonel looking at a map. He looked up and just said, "Keep moving."

There were some Koreans with a huge stack of C-rations and they were handing them out. We had not eaten that morning and I was feeling the results. We did not get back to the aid station until that night, and we spent the night in tents.

The day after the Tanyang Pass action we moved down the road into a village. We burned everything we could get our hands on to keep warm. If I remember correctly, the floors were somehow heated from fires in the cooking area of the hut. My feet and right hand began to ache. The fingers on my right hand had started to turn purple. I knew that I was in trouble, but I did not know how much. Two officers came down from Division and interviewed Higginbotham and myself. We had been recommended for the Bronze Star. I was surprised at how many questions they asked, and the detail. Higg and I were interviewed separately. When the interview was over I went to the aid station, never thinking that I would not return. I left my rifle and other equipment in the hut. When I got to the aid station the medic took one look at my right hand and tagged me for evacuation.

After being tagged I waited for an ambulance. Soon we had a load and moved out just before dark to a field hospital, where we went to bed and stayed overnight. The following day we were transported to the railhead. To my surprise, there was my old Platoon Sergeant from the 80th. Sergeant Graham was a non-jumper. He had left Fort Bragg with an ambulance unit that was shipped to Korea in August. His unit was up north when the Chinese came into the war. He was telling me of the men he had seen out of 2d Ranger Company who had come through the hospital unit. One fellow he had seen was Donald West. West and I had been in Graham's platoon. He and I had served on various demonstration teams in the 80th. I never saw Sergeant West again.

The train took us to Pusan. In Pusan harbor there were two hospital ships, the *Consolation* and the *Repose*. I was placed on one, I don't remember which. I took a shower and I could not feel my feet. The last two fingers on my right hand were purple and hard to the touch. The next day I was lifted from the deck of one ship, set down on a platform, and lifted to the deck of the other. When the transfer of patients was finished we sailed for Yokohama. I think the hospital was 155th Army.

George Rankins was in the hospital and I saw Daniel Boatwright there. Rankins came down to the ward and told me he was going on convalescent leave, which he did, and then went back to Korea. The hospital was filling up with wounded. I could hear the ambulance come in at night and unload. They moved me to another ward and said a number of patients would be going to the Zone of Interior. A doctor came in, pointing to men, saying "ZI." He pointed to me and I was on my way to the U.S.A.

I was transported out to Kaneda Air Force Base with a bunch of other wounded G.I.s and placed on an aircraft rigged to handle litters. I was strapped up in my litter and looked down on the floor of the plane and saw a soldier in a body cast who looked familiar. He and I had been in the same basic training company in Fort Dix. I asked him what had happened. He said he was riding a motor scooter in Pusan and was hit by a truck. We took off from Kaneda in a driving snowstorm. We arrived at Midway Island, where it was warm and raining. Took off from Midway, and arrived at Hickam Air Force Base. Stayed at Tripler Army Hospital overnight. The next day we were placed on a civilian airliner with stewardesses and army nurses. We flew to Travis Air Force Base, to Scott Field, Illinois, stayed overnight, then flew to Kellogg Air Force Base, Battle Creek, Michigan. The home of Percy Jones Army Hospital—the Frostbite Center.

My treatment began there in earnest. It was intense and painful, and I lost the tips of two fingers. My feet were O.K. I saw on television where Rangers along with the 187th ARCT had made a combat jump at Munsan-ni. I knew that 2d Ranger Company was among those Rangers. The only real regret of my short-lived army career was that I missed the jump. If anything can go wrong for me, it will.

They were giving seven-day convalescent leaves, which were not counted against your furlough time. My hand was healing well, but I had some infection and I could not go on leave. Then, when I was all set to go, the program was discontinued. I settled for a three-day pass. We ate in a huge dining room, but we had to line up to be served. We were at the breakfast meal and I looked over at the chow line and there was Louis Adams. He and I were so glad to see each other that I guess they thought we were suffering from combat fatigue. We were both in the 1st Platoon and our birthdays are the same day. While in Korea we said we were really going to celebrate. But I was evacuated out before that date. We still exchange birthday greetings.

My mother spent five days of her vacation in Battle Creek visiting me in the hospital. Her being black, she could not get a hotel room in Battle Creek. The hospital was almost in the heart of downtown. One of her co-workers had some close friends there and suggested she contact them and try to get lodgings, which she did. We would have the noon and evening meal together and just sit around and talk. Some days they would have live shows featuring local talent in the theater. I have often thought about the fact that I could go fight and face death, but my mother could not get public accommodations. The people she stayed with were great. The lady of the house worked at the hospital. Percy Jones offered employment to Battle Creek. The hospital had been closed before the Korean War, but was in the process of being opened and staffed when I arrived.

My enlistment was up July 17, 1951, but I found myself possibly faced with another year in service (the Truman Year). I wanted to go back to Bragg, but that was not to be. In July 1951, I was released from the hospital and assigned to Company D, 367th Armored Infantry Battalion Reserve Command, 3d Armored Division, Fort Knox, Kentucky, as cadre. The basic training cycle was about three weeks from starting when I arrived and they were making up the company. I was one of the first to come into the company who had seen combat in Korea. I was constantly asked what it was like there.

These guys were called "homesteaders." I wore my jump wings proudly on my field cap and maintained the neat airborne appearance, with jump boots highly polished. I was made Platoon Sergeant of the 1st Platoon. I held that job until mid-cycle, when a sergeant rotated back. I was then his assistant. It was indeed satisfying to see raw recruits become soldiers. I had it in my mind that I was never going on bivouac again.

I tried to get transferred back to Fort Bragg. I wanted to get back to the 82d Airborne Division. I had a letter of acceptance to the 80th Airborne Anti-Aircraft Battalion, Division Artillery. I took a physical and training test. My letter of request for transfer, with all my documentation, went to 2d Army, but was rejected because I was on an involuntary extension. I never knew when I was going to be discharged. They first said you would have to do the year, then they started letting men out early.

A sergeant who was billeted in the company and I had talked on a number of occasions. He was assigned to Headquarters Reserve Command Training Committee. He needed an assistant and talked to his committee chief about me. They had made barracks available to the committee personnel and he moved to his new quarters. I had thrown the transfer out of my mind. We were preparing for bivouac. Orders came down that Friday that I was to report to my new assignment. On Monday, the company went to the field. I cannot remember that sergeant's name. He was a Sergeant First Class and had not been to Korea. For what he had done for me I tried to do an outstanding job. Our working relationship was cut short by his being sent to Korea. I took his job, but was only a corporal. I was in charge of making and maintaining lesson plans, classes on the function and disassembly of the Browning Automatic Rifle, and training aids. Sometimes myself and my assistant, who was a Private First Class who had rotated back from Germany, would run the BAR range.

The Committee Chief came out to the range and was surprised to see us running the show. He told us we were doing a great job. We asked him on the spot, if we were doing such a good job, what about promotions? He said his hands were tied because rank was frozen.

I could not get back to Fort Bragg. I could not get promoted. What the heck. One day out of the blue I was told to report to 3d Armored Division Headquarters to be processed for discharge. Nine months and sixteen days into my Truman Year, it was over.

Appendix 1

— *Ranger Whereabouts* —

2d Ranger Infantry Company (Airborne)
in Korea 1950–1951

A-1. ADAMS, EDWARD D. "Ed" was a member of the replacement platoon that was brought over by Lieutenant Anthony. He came from A Battery, 80th AAA Battalion. He earned the Bronze Star Award and resides in Indianapolis, IN. He was often seen by Jimmy Fields, but he has not come back to the herd.

A-2. ADAMS, LOUIS M. Louie was an original member. He settled in Milwaukee, WI. He worked in the public school system as an aide in some of the toughest schools. In 1995 the Buffalo Rangers, as guest of the Southern Milwaukee Chapter, 82d A/B Association, visited his school and made a Black Military History presentation. Louis has been a very active member in both RICA and the 82d A/B Association.

A-3. ADKINS, KIRK P. Kirk left the service after returning from the hospital to the 187th. His life-threatening wound on Hill 581 didn't stop him from returning to jump status. He married and settled in Pasadena, CA. He owns a building maintenance company. He attends most of the RICA and 555th Reunions. Kirk was an original member and came from Company K.

A-4. AIKENS, LEGREE. Legree was an original member and came from Company I. He remained in the service after his initial enlistment. He did twenty years of airborne service before retiring as a Master Sergeant. He married, had two kids, and settled in California. He still looks a youthful twenty and is an active skier. He married a second time but recently lost his wife to cancer. He has moved but is still working full-time in Tucson, AZ. He frequently attends the reunions.

A-5. ALLEN, ADELL L. Adell was an original member from Company M, where he was a 81mm First Class Mortar Gunner. He dropped out of sight after rotating to the 187th in Japan.

A-6. ALLEN, DONALD S. An original member from Company K. He returned to Washington, D.C., and married. He worked for the Washington Metro Transportation System until his retirement. He now resides in Temple Hills, MD.

A-7. ALLEN, JAMES N. James was a veteran trooper who had served overseas before coming to Company I and was an original member. We have lost contact with him.

A-8. ALLEN, WARREN E. The original Company commander who remained with the unit even after being wounded in January 1951. He remained in the service for twenty years and retired as a major, from the 18th A/B Corps at Fort Bragg. He and his wife Mary had a daughter. They went briefly into the electronics business in Washington, D.C. He died of a heart attack and is buried in Arlington National Cemetery. He was deceased before the formation of RICA and 555th Associations. Warren was inducted into the Ranger Hall of Fame in 1996.

A-9. ALSTON, MARION A. An original member from Company K; remained in the service for more than twenty years. Marion retired as Sergeant Major. He married Stina, and they have nine adult children (he is the Buffalo Ranger with the most children). The youngest son, Roger, who grew up attending reunions, is now attending college and has enlisted in the National Guard. Marion worked for an insurance company as an actuary until his retirement. He resides in Browns Mill, NJ, near Fort Dix.

A-10. ANDERSON, JESSIE. "Babe" was an original member from Company K. Babe was a WWII veteran. He remained in the service for twenty years and retired as a Master Sergeant. He first lived in Aurora, CO, and worked in the US Postal System until his second retirement. He and wife now live in Fayetteville, NC, near Fort Bragg. He is not too active in RICA or the 555th PIA.

A-11. ANDRADE, ANTHONY. Andrade was one of the original members who came from Company M, 81mm mortars. He was awarded the Bronze Star for Valor for the use of his mortar on Hill 581. Andrade remained in the service and retired as a Sergeant First Class. He did some time as cadre in a basic training unit at Fort Knox, KY. He was living in Montgomery, AL, with his daughter when he died. Big Jim Queen and his wife Phyllis visited him while on the way to the 555th PIA reunion in Oakland, CA, in 1982.

A-12. ANDRES, TEEDIES P. An original member from Company M. He left the service after his enlistment and moved to Maine, where he married. He became a professional artist and painter. He moved to Florida in about 1990 for retirement. He was not active in RICA and is now deceased.

A-13. ANTHONY, ANTONIO. "Red Horse" was the replacement platoon leader with the first replacements in late February 1951. He arrived in time for the Munsan-ni Jump. Red Horse came from Company I and commanded the Weapons Platoon. He took a reduction to Master Sergeant before retiring during the Vietnam Era. He was the only member of the unit to receive three Combat Infantry Badges and is listed in the Infantry School Hall of Honor at Fort Benning. He married Rene and retired in Montgomery, AL. Red Horse was a loud and very active BING player at the Fort Campbell Officers' Club. As a civilian he worked for a shipping company. He was not active in RICA or the 555th PIA. "Red Horse" died of a brain tumor in the late 1980s.

B-1. BAKER, ISAAC E. An original member, he started as 4th Platoon Sergeant during early training. He came to Company I because he couldn't make a rank in the 558th Ambulance Company. Baker was the first Ranger KIA. His legendary prediction of death to Master Sergeant Bates is recorded here. The Baltimore Chapter of the 555th PIA is named after him.

B-2. BARTON, RICHARD E. Richard was a veteran trooper, having served overseas in WWII. He was an original member and a driver in Headquarters Company, 3d Battalion. Contact with Richard was lost after rotation to CONUS.

BEDLEY, BELL, BEVERLY. Missing.

B-3. BIVENS, GEORGE. A member of the Replacement Platoon, coming from the 80th AAA. George left the service and settled in Baltimore, MD. He has attended several reunions but has health problems.

B-4. BOATWRIGHT, DANIEL. An original member from Company K. He went to OCS after rotating and remained in the service for more than twenty years before retiring as a Lieutenant Colonel. He is still a bachelor and lives as a "Country Gentleman Farmer" near Fort Jackson, SC, in the city of Kupuete, GA. He attends all reunions and is a generous activity supporter.

B-5. BRISCOE, RICHARD. Richard was an original member from the 80th AAA. He left the service after his enlistment and returned to Washington, D.C. He worked for a supermarket company as a 16-wheeler driver before retiring.

BROWN. Missing.

B-6. BRUCE, JOSEPH L., JR. Joseph was an original member. He had just enlisted in April 1950 and was a novice jumper but proved to be a good trooper. Contact with him was lost after rotation.

B-7. BUFORD, TASHAKA (DAVID). Buford joined the unit after going AWOL from 3d Battalion, 9th ID. Buford left the service after his enlistment. He wanted to become a writer but he had some problems adjusting to civilian life. He later became a Muslim. He married and moved to Chicago, IL, before dropping out of sight in the early 1990s.

B-8. BURSE, THOMAS M. Thomas was an original member. He left the unit before inactivation and no contact has been made since.

B-9. BUSH, HOMER. Homer was a member of the Replacement Platoon. He remained in the service for twenty years and retired as a Master Sergeant. He was the only member of the Company recalled to active duty during the Gulf War. He became postmaster in a suburb of Charleston, WV, where he now resides. Homer has been a very active participant of the RICA and 555th Association.

C-1. CAMPOS, VICTOR. Victor was a member of the Replacement Platoon and came from B Battery, 80th AAA Battalion. Victor was a member of the Puerto Rican clan that came from the east side of New York City, like Jose Escalera. He was in

Company F, 187th ARCT, after 2d Ranger Company was inactivated. Victor had voluntarily changed sides from a possible M-1 to M-2 side. He dropped out of sight soon after rotating to the States.

C-2. CARROLL, JAMES E. Carroll left the unit before inactivation and transferred to the 187th ARCT. We have not been able to re-establish contact with him.

C-3. CLARKE, DAVID A. "Tank" Clarke was an original member and the only Buffalo to come from the 758th Tank Battalion. Tank left the service after rotating and settled in Milwaukee, WI. He married Geraldine and they had two children, including a son who is now a detective in the Milwaukee Police Department. Tank worked in the U.S. Post Office before retiring. Tank and Louis Adams are from the same town and both are frequent participants in RICA and 555th activities.

C-4. CLEVELAND, CLINTON W. "Crying" Clinton was an original member from Company K. He remained in the service for twenty years and received a commission. He was forced to take a reduction to Master Sergeant, but moved up to First Lieutenant on the retirement list. He resides in Detroit, MI.

C-5. CLIETTE, ALBERT. Al came from Company L and was the only leader of the 3d Platoon. Al was awarded the Bronze Star for valor on Hill 581. He rotated back to the 82d A/B, was promoted to Captain later, but had to take a reduction to Master Sergeant. He remained in the service for thirty years and retired from Special Forces at Fort Bragg. He married Altamae Ford and they had two children. Al retired as a Sergeant Major (E-9) with a hip pocket promotion to Lieutenant Colonel. After his years of military service, he had a second career with the State of North Carolina. He resides in Fayetteville, NC. Al has been a supporter of the RICA and 555th PIA.

C-6. COLEMAN, EUGENE C. Eugene was an original member. He left the unit before inactivation and his whereabouts have never been determined.

C-7. COLEMAN, WILLIE L. Willie has been in the VA Hospital at Hampton, VA, for a long period and has not been able to participate in unit activities. Willie was an original member who came from the 80th AAA.

C-8. COLLINS, NORMAN H. Norman was an original member who came from the 80th AAA Battalion and had served overseas during WWII. Norman was a popular squad leader who only had a year left on his enlistment when he volunteered. Norman received a Silver Star. He is believed to have died in the VA Hospital in Erie, PA, but no family members could be located to confirm this information.

C-9. COURTS, CURTIS E. Curtis was an original member who came from Company M. He was awarded the Silver Star for action on Hill 581. He settled in Chicago, IL, and has been very ill for a long time. Previously, he was very active in the Chicago Chapter of the 555th PIA.

D-1. DANIELS, SHERMAN. Sherman was an original member from Company M. Sherman remained in the service and retired as a Staff Sergeant. His last residence was in San Francisco, CA.

D-2. DAVIS, JAMES R., JR. James Davis was an original member. He left the unit before inactivation and rotation to the 187th ARCT. There has not been any contact with him since Korea.

D-3. DAVIS, RICHARD E. Richard was an original member. He rotated after inactivation to the 187th ARCT but no contact has been made since that time.

D-4. DIAS, HERCULANO G. "Herc" was an original member who came from A Battery, 80th AAA Battalion. Herc left the service after he rotated. He married Linda and they had three children. Herc worked for the New York Telephone Company until his retirement. He has been a tireless 2d Ranger Company representative in RICA for many years. He has also been active in the 555th. Herc voluntarily undertook the task of trying to contact the families of those Buffalo Rangers killed in action. He resides in West New York, NJ, where he is Chapter Adjutant in New Jersey Chapter 49 of the Disabled American Veterans Association.

E-1. ESCALERA, JOSE A. "Kookie" was the Puerto Rican Ranger from New York who was an original member from Company M. Kookie transferred to the 3d Battalion because he was subjected to racial taunts in his first assignment in the 82d A/B. He was not used to the very cold weather, and often commented, "I'm frozen," when in Korea. He was sent back for a second tour with the 65th Infantry Regiment, from Puerto Rico's National Guard. Kookie was seriously wounded and retired medically. He returned to live in Puerto Rico where he began to lose his English language ability. Captain Joseph L. Stephenson, his CO in Company M, visited him when Stephenson sent his son, Steve, to college in Puerto Rico.

E-2. ESTELL, LAWRENCE L. Larry was an original member from the Pioneer and Ammunition (P&A) Platoon (under the command of Lieutenant Rudolph Kelker), Headquarters Company, 3d Battalion. Larry was wounded in the Tanyang fight and didn't return to the unit. He was hospitalized at Fort Benning, GA, where Colonel Van Houten frequently visited him and kept him abreast of the Buffalo Rangers' action. Larry became one of the first black instructors in Jump School. He later became a craftsman and has made many of the trophies for awards given to Rangers and Triple Nicklers. He lost part of his leg in Vietnam. He resides in Columbus, GA, and worked several years for Ranger Joe, the main store for military equipment and memorabilia, just outside the gate to Fort Benning. Larry frequently represents 2d Ranger Company and the 555th PIA in the Fort Benning Post activities that involve the Ranger and Airborne Departments.

F-1. FELDER, DONALD L., SR. Don was an original member who came from Company I. He was the youngest and an inexperienced trooper who had just completed jump school in August. He volunteered despite the warning from one of his company officers. Donald was profoundly affected by his combat service and expressed very serious feelings about man's inhumanity in war. After completing his service he went to college and became an electrical engineer. He married Maryanne and they had three children. Donald and Maryanne, with their grandson Drew, are frequent attendees at the RICA and 555th reunions. Donald has retired from his own private company and resides in North Philadelphia, PA.

F-2. FEREBEE, ROBERT. Ferebee was a member of the Replacement Platoon. He came from B Battery, 80th AAA Battalion. He left the service after his first enlistment and married Ella. They reside in East Patchogue, NY.

F-3. FIELDS, JAMES H. Jimmy was an original member who came from the 80th AAA. Jimmy was wounded and evacuated back to the States. He was awarded the Bronze Star and Purple Heart for the action at Tanyang. He also became a part of the training cadre at Fort Knox, KY. Jimmy almost reenlisted. He married Sallie. They have a son and reside in Indianapolis, IN, his hometown. He worked as a tool and die maker for General Motors before retirement. Jimmy and Sallie frequently attend RICA and 555th reunions. Jimmy is a great supporter of both organizations.

F-4. FLETCHER, HENRY. "Fletch" was an original member who came from the P&A Platoon of Headquarters Company 3d Battalion. He left the service after his initial enlistment and resides in Okalahoma City, OK. He worked in the Post Office at Tinker Air Force Base until his retirement. He married Anita Mae and has attended several RICA reunions.

F-5. FORD, JOHN E., Jr. John was an original member who came from Headquarters Company, 3d Battalion. He was on duty as a senior rigger with the 82d A/B Division Parachute Maintenance Company. John was an outstanding trooper, and when he made First Sergeant (E-8) in Vietnam, Major General Throckmorton, CG, came down to the unit to give him his stripes. In between times he was assigned to the St. Louis Depot as an inspector and procurer of parachute equipment. John married a newspaper reporter from St. Louis. They had a son who entered the banking business. John died in 1988 while on an inspection tour of a parachute manufacturing facility on an Indian reservation in Wyoming.

F-6. FREEMAN, JAMES E. Jim completed more than twenty years of service. He reached the rank of Captain before reverting to Master Sergeant. Jim was married to Mary before joining the Rangers and was living on post at Fort Bragg. He received a battlefield commission and rotated to the 503d Airborne Infantry Regiment, 11th A/B at Fort Campbell, KY. (The 503d Regimental Commander only very reluctantly accepted racial integration of officers, and almost every black officer had service-connected problems while in the regiment from 1952 to 1956.) Jim and Mary had five children. Jim did not go to Germany with the 11th A/B. He took an early retirement, during the Vietnam War, when they kept the homesteaders who had friends in high places at Fort Dix and began to send combat vets back for a second tour. Jim has taken part in several RICA and 555th events. He and his wife reside in Burlington, NJ.

F-7. FULTON, ROBERT A. Robert was an original member. Robert had less than a year's service on his first hitch when he volunteered for the Rangers. He left the unit before inactivation and no further contact has been made with him.

G-1. GARLAND, LESTER L. Lester was an original member who came from Company K. He was Captain Allen's jeep driver. After he rotated Lester re-upped in the 101st A/B and became First Sergeant of Replacement Company. He became the best-dressed trooper in the division, with his special form-fitting uniforms. Lester married Patricia and they had twins (a boy and a girl). Lester and his son were killed in an automobile accident near Eldorado, KS, in April 1952.

G-2. GATLINGTON, OLIVER. "Gat" is our Native American Ranger on the other side of the river. He received his Ranger training secretly and was deployed to Korea in clandestine activities. He gave HALO skydiving training to McBert Higginbotham, in the Special Forces, where he hooked up with the Buffalo Soldiers. Oliver spent almost twenty years in Special Forces and retired when he was sent back for a fourth tour in Vietnam while some homesteaders remained stateside. Oliver resides in Fayetteville, NC.

G-3. GERMAIN, GERARD S. Gerard was an original member who came from B Battery, 80th AAA Battalion. Gerard is from Jamaica, Long Island, NY. He and Joe Wells are from the same hometown, attended the same schools and were members of the same marching bands and Boy Scout troop, attended the same church and both served as altar boys after confirmation; but they didn't know each other until they joined the Rangers! Gerard remained in the Army for eight years. He married Nellie (deceased), had one son, and started a window-cleaning business. He started parachuting again in April 1985 and didn't stop until the age of 66. Gerard is a very close buddy of Herc, and they almost always attend RICA and 555th reunions. Gerard is an active supporter of both associations and now resides in Elizabeth, NJ.

G-4. GIBSON, CULVER. Culver is not listed as one of the original members, but he seems to have been with the unit very early. Culver was awarded the Bronze Star for Valor in the battle for Hill 581 in May 1951. He was another one of the Sergeant BAR Gunners because he could carry two basic loads and was very aggressive with the weapon. Culver rotated to the 187th when the unit was inactivated but he has not been in contact since that time.

G-5. GLOVER, RICHARD H. Glover was an original member of the Company. Richard was stocky and became a BAR Gunner. He was killed in the firefight on 14 January 1951, at Majori-ri Village, just west of Tanyang Pass. Surviving family members could not be located.

G-6. GORDON, ANDREW C. Andrew was one of the original members coming from Company K. After he left the service he went to Washington, D.C., where he and Roland "Monk" Hodges married sisters. Andrew pursued a career in the D.C. Metro transit system in which he became a coordinator, and he still resides in the city.

G-7. GORDON, MORGAN S. Not much is known about Morgan except that he was one of the original members. It is believed that he came from Company L. In late January 1951 he accidentally shot himself in the hand with his .45 pistol while 2d Ranger

Company was in Chechon-ni. None of the Rangers of 2d Ranger Company recall seeing him after that event. His last known address was in Pecos, TX.

G-8. GRASTY, ISAAC, JR. Isaac was one of the black-leg replacements who was placed on special duty with the Company for additional training. Isaac was drafted from Washington, D.C. He recognized Big Jim Queen during training and was "volunteered" for Ranger and Airborne training. General Ferenbaugh allowed ten of the more than three hundred men to be transferred in because of the lack of adequate replacements. Isaac worked in the D.C. public school system as a building supervisor/engineer before retiring. He married Juanita and they had two children; one son entered the U.S. Air Force and became a Major and a C-141 pilot. Isaac still resides in D.C. and was active in RICA and the 555th Associations.

G-9. GRAY, WALTER E. "Iron Head" was an original member from Company I. He was short and stocky in stature. Iron Head didn't rotate to the 187th with the men. We have not been able to locate him since.

G-10. GREEN, HERMAN J. Herman was an original. He was on his first enlistment and was another young soldier with less than a year under his belt when he volunteered for the Rangers. There has not been any contact with him since we joined the 187th ARCT. Herman was an ideal Ranger; he came in as a private in September 1950 and went to the 187th as a Buck Sergeant.

G-11. GUDE, JAMES H. James was one of the original members coming from the 80th AAA. James was living in Cleveland, OH, when contact was lost with him about ten years ago.

H-1. HALL, CARL D. Carl was a member of the Replacement Platoon and came over with Lieutenant Anthony. Carl came from the 80th AAA Battalion. After rotation Carl re-upped for the 82d at Bragg. He stayed in the service for seven years before becoming a policeman in North Carolina's Fayetteville Police Department. Later he moved over to the Sheriff's Department of Cumberland County, NC, where he worked until his death on December 26, 1988. Carl married and had one son who served in the Army.

H-2. HARDY, JAMES. Hardy was a member of the replacement platoon from Medical Company 505th. He went back to Japan for a second tour and married Yoshiko, who died in 1983. Jim has been very active in RICA and has been an American Legion Post Commander. He resides in Phoenix, AZ.

H-3. HARGROVE, WILLIAM. "Nite Ears" was an original member, believed to have come from the Machine Gun Platoon, Company M. He was on his second hitch, having already served eleven months overseas before coming to the 3d Battalion. He is best remembered for his contribution to the firefight at Tanyang Pass, where he was awarded the Bronze Star. He was a Sergeant when he volunteered but made Sergeant First Class by the time of inactivation. Hargrove was always the smallest person in his squad. He came to the 187th ARCT and became an acting Platoon Sergeant, but no contact has been made with him since that time.

H-4. HAWKINS, WILLIE C. Willie was an original member who came from the 80th AAA Battalion. Hawkins was one of a half-dozen troopers on a six-year hitch. He had enlisted in July 1950 immediately after the Korean War started, but he was Corporal in less than six months and volunteered for the Rangers. Willie came from the northwest part of the country. He made Sergeant before inactivation. There has not been any contact with him since 2d Ranger Company was inactivated and the Rangers joined the 187th ARCT.

H-5. HIGGINBOTHAM, McBERT. "McBert/Higg" was an original member from Headquarters Battery, 80th AAA Battalion. Higg was known by Big Jim Queen for more than fifty years, starting when they were both recruits at Fort McClellan, AL, in 1944. Higg served an early tour in Germany with the 777th Honor Guard, under Lieutenant Minton Francis (West Point, 1944). He participated in the Berlin Airlift and was widely known for his boxing skills ("The Brown Bomber"). He married Betty Jeanne Morgan, and entered training at Fort Benning. McBert was one of the first to be awarded the Bronze Star for bravery in the firefight at Majori-ri Village. He was Big Jim's First Sergeant in Headquarters Company, 3d Battalion, 511th AIR, 11th A/B Division, in Augsburg, Germany (1956-57). McBert was the first black EM to serve in the 10th Special Forces Group (1960) in Bad Tolz, Germany (1962-64). Although he repeatedly volunteered for tours in Vietnam, his requests were repeatedly denied, on the basis that "he was needed on Post." Higg retired from Special Forces as a Sergeant Major in June 1967 and he was immediately accepted by the Department of State (AID Program) as the Hospital Administration Officer for II Corps in Vietnam from 1967 to 1972. After retiring from the Department of State he returned to Fayetteville, where he earned a bachelor's degree in Business Administration from Fayetteville State University in 1977 and accepted a position as one of the University's administrative officers for the Fort Benning campus (1977-1984). Whenever RICA or the 555th gathered in the Fayetteville area, he and Betty always hosted the Buffalo Rangers in their home. Higg passed on to that Great Heavenly DZ in 1994.

H-6. HODGE, ROLAND. "Monk" was one of the original members who came from Company K. After being with the 2d Ranger Company he enlisted in the Air Force and served a tour in France. He and Andrew Gordon married sisters and settled in Washington, D.C. Monk drove a truck for a commercial photo company. He only lived about five blocks from Big Jim, and frequently walked past the house after retiring. He died suddenly in 1994, and his death was not known until his wife wrote to Herc about four months later.

H-7. HOLLEY, J.T. Holley was one of the original members. He was a WWII draftee who had already served fifteen months overseas and was one of those who had found a home in the Army. He was on a six-year hitch. Holley was killed in the firefight at Majori-ri Village on 14 January 1951. George Rankins recently reported that Holley's widow still lives in New York City.

H-8. HOWARD, BENNIE. Howard was an original member who came from Company I. He was short in stature and of quiet demeanor. He frequently worked in the kitchen with "Pop" Jones. Howard didn't go to the 187th ARCT after inactivation. He lived in Macon, GA, near Fort Benning and worked as a barber until a couple of months before his death.

J-1. JACKSON, GEORGE, JR. Jackson was the original personnel clerk and came over from the 80th AAA Battalion. He worked mostly at the Division Rear, but he had to come up and spend some time on the line to earn his CIB. The Company never had any records or pay problems, outside of the fact that he couldn't keep up with us on the Morning Report. He is believed to be a barber in Bedford, VA, at the foot of the Blue Ridge Mountains.

J-2. JACKSON, GEORGE. This George Jackson also came from 80th AAA. He came on separate orders as a replacement. Because he was black and Airborne, he was assigned to 2d Ranger Company. He fit in and served very well. When he returned to the States he re-enlisted in the Special Category Army Reassigned with the Air Force (SCARWAF). George attended the Ordnance Technical and Nuclear Weapons, Explosive Ordnance Demolition (EOD), and several aircraft repair and maintenance courses. George learned to fly choppers by repairing them. In 1957 he was appointed as a Warrant Officer. He served in Germany three times and flew downed aircraft recovery missions in Viet Nam. George retired from duty at Walter Reed Army Medical Center Flight Detachment as a W-4 in September 1969. George married, but his wife died in 1996. He is an avid golfer and resides in Silver Spring, MD, near Washington, D.C. He is a great participant in RICA and the 555th PIA.

J-3. JACKSON, HERMAN C. "Ole Cat Eyes" was an original member who came from Company M. Herman was one of the most experienced troopers in the unit. He was seriously wounded on Hill 581, and recently had his wounds re-evaluated and his VA disability increased. He did a second tour in Korea just after the truce, where he was the 81mm Mortar Platoon Sergeant for Captain Harry "Smiling" Jack, who was the former XO of Company M. Jack went over to Thailand and got married. His recollections of the Munsan-ni Jump and the battle on Hill 581 are very vivid. Cat Eyes is the only member of the Buffalo Rangers who has returned to the Munsan-ni jump area. He relates that there is a large U.S. Army garrison with a big PX located there now. He currently resides in Los Angeles, CA, and has become very active in the RICA and 555th reunions.

J-4. JACKSON, WINSTON. Winston was another leg replacement from Washington, D.C., who volunteered out of the 7th Division's black replacements. He served in combat with the 3d Platoon. He attended a company-level jump school in Korea in July 1951. He made three jumps in one day to qualify. When he went to the 187th he was lucky enough to find a home in the S-4 shop under Captain "Moon" Mullins. He often rides Paul Lyles about the special orders that he had to submit for Lyles' extra-large-size combat boots. Winston returned to civilian life and opened a barber shop in Washington, D.C. He recently began to participate in local 555th and RICA activities.

J-5. JENKINS, GLENN JR. Glenn was a member of the replacement platoon that Lieutenant Anthony trained and brought over in late February. Glenn was from the motor pool of the 80th AAA Battalion. He was slightly older than most of the men, and since he was a former mechanic and the Buffalo Rangers had acquired (via moonlight requisitions) an assortment of vehicles, he was assigned as the Motor Corporal. He rotated to the 187th after inactivation and was assigned to Service Company. There has not been any contact with him since that time.

J-6. JENNINGS, EUGENE. Eugene was an original member. He entered the service at the tail end of WWII and served ten months overseas. Eugene left before the unit was inactivated. There has not been any contact with him since Korea.

J-7. JOHNS, JOHN A. Johns was an original member who came from the 80th AAA Battalion. He was a WWII veteran on an indefinite enlistment (only Sergeant First Class Watkins, 3d Platoon Sergeant, was also in that category). Johns had served 26 months overseas before volunteering for the Rangers. He went to the 187th's artillery unit at Camp Woods when the unit was inactivated. There has not been any contact with him since Korea.

J-8. JOHNSON, BRUCE A. Bruce was an original member coming from Company K. After leaving the service Bruce went on to become New York City Mayor Edward Koch's personal bodyguard. At the same time he coached pre-Olympic-level divers. Bruce was one of the best swimmers in the unit, and frequently swam under Higg (McBert), who was one of the best swimming fakers. Bruce is still in excellent physical condition and always carries the Company Guidon on the reunion runs. Bruce is a very close buddy of Herc and a rabid RICA and 555th supporter. Bruce has been the main financial supporter of the placement of memorial bricks on the Ranger Memorial Walkway at Fort Benning, for the Buffalo Rangers KIA whose families we have not been able to contact. Bruce is married to Jackie and resides in Brentwood, NY.

J-9. JOHNSON, EARL. Earl was an original member who came from Headquarters Company, 3d Battalion where he was the NCOIC of the Enlisted Men's Club in the 3d Battalion area (Spring Lake). Earl was very light-skinned, so fair that he could have passed for white. Earl went back to CONUS before inactivation. There has not been any contact with him since Korea.

J-10. JOHNSON, EMMETT L. Emmett was an original member. He had just re-enlisted in September 1950 before volunteering for the Rangers. Emmett remained in the service and was killed in Vietnam (circumstances are not known).

J-11. JOHNSON, HAROLD A. Harold is another lifer and original member coming from Company L. Harold was one of a few who didn't enlist in the Army immediately after graduating from high school. He had been on the Camp Campbell, Benning, and Florida maneuvers with the 3d Battalion. Harold remained in the service and became a flying Warrant Officer. He attended engineering electronics school for

Raytheon Electronics in Lexington, MA, worked as a technical advisor for Raytheon during the Gulf War in 1991, and in the Hawk Missile and Patriot Missile systems, so he was frequently overseas during world crises. Harold lived in El Paso, TX, with his wife Mary Jo, with whom he had a daughter. Harold suddenly died in June 1998.

J-12. JOHNSON, MILTON. An original member. He was killed in the firefight in Majori-ri on 14 January 1951. No surviving family members have been located.

J-13. JONES, JOHN A. An original member of the company, and its oldest, hence his nickname "Pop." He was the first man in the company awarded the Silver Star. There has been no contact with "Pop" since coming back from Korea.

K-1. KELLY, JOSEPH. Joseph was an original member who came from the 80th AAA Battalion. He was a veteran soldier from WWII who had served 25 months overseas. He was on his second three-year hitch when he volunteered for the Rangers. Joseph left before the Company was inactivated.

K-2. KING, FRANK JR. Frank was an original member. He had just enlisted for three years in April 1950. He survived Ranger training in good shape but was killed in the firefight at Majori-ri Village on 14 January 1951.

L-1. LAND, ELMORE. Elmore was a member of the replacement platoon trained and brought over by Lieutenant Anthony. He came from the 80th AAA Battalion. Elmore remained with the Company until inactivation and made Corporal before shipment to the 187th ARCT. There has not been any contact with him since then. He was living in Norfolk, VA, before he died in March 1993.

L-2. LANIER, WILLIAM M. An original member from the Communications Platoon, Headquarters Company, 3d Battalion. Lanier had been in the wire section when Big Jim was Commo Officer. He was a veteran of WWII on an indefinite enlistment. Lanier had served twelve months overseas before volunteering for the Rangers. He was assigned duties as a Commo Sergeant. He had part of his ear shot off in the firefight at Majori-ri. He went to the 187th ARCT after inactivation and was assigned to the Regimental Commo. There has been no contact with him since Korea.

L-3. LEARY, FRED L. Fred was a member of the replacement platoon brought over by Lieutenant Anthony. He came from the 80th AAA Battalion (things were pretty rough in that unit in about November of 1950, and a lot of men wanted to leave). Leary became part of the mortar section. Upon the unit's inactivation he went to the 187th and was assigned to the Anti-Aircraft Battery at Camp Woods, Japan. Nothing has been heard from him since that time.

L-4. LEE, HOSEY. Lee was one of the black-leg replacements that the Buffalo Rangers got out of the pipeline going to the 32d Infantry, 7th ID, in early April. These men were given airborne training and completed their three qualifying jumps in one day during July 1951. Lee went to the 187th ARCT upon inactivation, and no contact has been made since then. He was a Korean War draftee.

L-5. LEGGS, RALPH JR. Ralph was one of the black-leg replacements who we got from the 31st Infantry, 7th ID in April 1951. He was a regular, in contrast to the majority of the ten, who were draftees. Leggs became a BAR gunner and had made Corporal by the time of inactivation. No contact has been made with him since that time.

L-6. LESURE, DAVID. David was one of the original members who came from the 80th AAA. David lives in Cleveland, OH.

L-7. LEWIS, CHARLES O. Charles was an original member. He only had nine months left on his enlistment when he volunteered. Charles made Corporal before inactivation and transfer to the 187th ARCT. There has not been any contact with him since Japan.

L-8. LOFTON, MATTHEW JR. Matthew was an original member who came from the 80th AAA Battalion. He was on his first three-year hitch and only had eight months remaining on that enlistment. Matthew made Corporal before inactivation and assignment to the 187th ARCT. There has not been any contact with him since that time.

L-9. LOUNDES, JOHN A. Loundes was a member of Lieutenant Anthony's replacement platoon and came from the 80th Battalion. He remained in the 60mm mortars with Lieutenant Anthony. After the unit was inactivated he went to the Anti-Aircraft Battery of the 187th ARCT. There has not been any contact with him since that time.

L-10. LYLES, PAUL T. Paul was one of the black-leg replacements received from the 7th ID after the Munsan-ni jump. Paul is a native Washingtonian who attended the same school as Big Jim Queen. When Lyles recognized Jim during the training, he was volunteered as a Ranger. After three months of combat with the unit, he attended a Company-run jump school in July. He qualified after making three jumps in one day, near Chechon, Korea. When the Rangers were inactivated and joined the 187th ARCT, Paul became a radio operator for the CG. After his discharge Paul worked for the Marriott Hotels System and as an independent contractor before retiring. Paul's wife died several years ago and he remarried. He has three daughters, and his grandchildren are doing well in the music field. Paul is a supporter of RICA and 555th activities, and he frequently provides video coverage of association events.

Mc-1. McBRIDE, CLEAVEN. A member of the replacement platoon that Lieutenant Anthony trained, he came from the 80th AAA Battalion. He was on a three-year enlistment but had spent only three months overseas and was due for discharge in December 1951. Awarded the Bronze Star. He went to the 187th upon inactivation and no contact has been made with him since that time.

Mc-2. McLEAN, LISLIE J. Lislie was an original member who came from the 80th AAA Battalion. Lislie was a late draftee in WWII who enlisted for three years and served four months overseas. He left 2d Ranger Company before inactivation. There has not been any contact with him since Korea.

Mc-3. McPHERSON, WILLIAM J. William was a member of the Replacement Platoon and came from Company K. William is married and lives in New York City.

M-1. MASON, JACOB. Jacob was an original member who came from Company I. After his enlistment he moved to Alaska and lives in Anchorage.

M-2. MATHIS, WILLIAM K. Bill Mathis was the third black-leg replacement who was volunteered for the Rangers after he recognized Big Jim Queen during training. Bill was a college track star before being drafted. The area in which he lived in Washington has been demolished, and he and his family have not been located. The rumor is that he lives somewhere in New Jersey.

M-3. MITCHELL, GEORGE H. George was an original member. He was a veteran from WWII who was on a three-year hitch and due to get out in November 1951. He is not listed on the boat manifest of the *USS General H.W. Butner*, but is on the shipment orders to the 187th ARCT for inactivation on 29 July 1951. There has not been any contact with him since that time.

M-4. MOLSON, GEORGE H. Molson was an original member. His three-year enlistment was up in September 1951 when he volunteered. He left the unit before inactivation. No contact with him has been made since that time.

M-5. MONTE, JAMES L. Monte was an original member who came from the 80th AAA. Monte came back to the 505th AIR before taking a discharge. After being a civilian for eight months, he re-enlisted for the 11th A/B, but wound up in the field artillery. He served in the artillery in Vietnam. After 22 years of service he retired as a Master Sergeant (E-8) and went to work in the Post Office. Monte retired a second time and resides in Columbus, GA. Monte lost his wife, Mary, several years ago. Monte and Larry Estell are sidekicks, and both attend and represent RICA and 555th activities at Fort Benning.

M-6. MOORE, KENNETH R. Kenneth was an original member and came from Company M. Kenneth was born of Canadian parents and had dual citizenship until age 21. He chose to enlist for the American Airborne forces in Port Huron, MI. Kenneth lives in Goldsboro, NC, near Fort Bragg.

M-7. MORRIS, UTHEL. Morris was a member of the replacement platoon brought over by Lieutenant Anthony from the 80th AAA Battalion. Uthel was a voluntary enlistee from California in WWII. He was still a Private, although he had served 23 months overseas. He made Corporal before inactivation and shipment to the 187th ARCT. Uthel remained in the service and made Master Sergeant. Last contact with him was in the early 1980s, when Big Jim Queen found Uthel was working for an undertaker in San Francisco.

M-8. MORRIS, CREW B. Crew was a member of the last training cycle and didn't get to serve with the unit. He is active in many of the RICA and 555th activities. He resides in Chicago, IL.

M-9. MORSE, CALVIN. Calvin came in with the Replacement Platoon from the 80th AAA. After leaving the service Calvin entered the Georgia State Police Department. He patrolled Interstate 95 for drugs. Calvin is married to Earsene and resides in Richland, GA, about 25 miles southeast of Fort Benning. Calvin is active in the RICA and 555th activities around Benning.

M-10. MURPHY, JACK. Jack was an original member, coming from Big Jim Queen's 75mm Recoilless Rifle Platoon in Company M. Jack was on a three-year hitch due to end in December 1950 when he volunteered for the Rangers. Jack was a big, strong, country boy who was like a li'l brother to Jim. He would do anything that was asked and was developing into an outstanding leader. Jack volunteered for a second tour in Korea and made Master Sergeant before he was killed in action there. His aunt and her husband, a retired Marine, have attended the RICA reunions in Fayetteville.

M-11. MURRAY, JAMES Murray was an original member. He had the unusual serial number of RA 45 041 010, which indicated that he was a very late draftee in WWII who had decided to enlist for three years. He had already served thirteen months overseas when he volunteered. Murray made Corporal before inactivation and transferred to 187th ARCT. There has been no contact with him since that time.

N-1. NEXION, SAMUEL. Nexion was an original member. Nexion was on a three-year hitch and due for discharge in February 1951, so he was another one who got a "Truman Year" (one year's involuntary extension) on his enlistment after he got to Korea. Nexion left before inactivation and rotation to the 187th ARCT.

N-2. NUNLEY, JOHN E. John was a member of Lieutenant Anthony's Replacement Platoon and came from A Battery, 80th AAA Battalion. John left the service after his enlistment and went to work in the Post Office. He lives in Okmulgee, OK. John has participated in several RICA and 555th reunions.

O-1. OAKLEY, JAMES. Oakley was an original member of the unit and came from Company K. He was performing duty in the Officer's BOQ and Club when he volunteered. Oakley became one of the best BAR gunners in the unit. He and Joe Oliver were like brothers. Oakley drowned when crossing a river in Korea. Oakley was loaded down with ammunition and was swept off his feet and carried downstream by the swift currents. The Rangers were unable to recover his body on that day. Contact has been made with his brother, who aided in the placement of a memorial brick at Fort Benning.

O-2. OLIVER, JOE. Joe was an original member and came from Company L. He and Oakley were sidekicks. Joe entered the ministry after leaving the service. He settled in Texarkana, TX. Joe passed in 1997.

P-1. PARKS, NATHAN. Nathan is now deceased, but his famous Sunday Apple Cobbler (made with salt) will never be forgotten. Nathan was the unit's only and original Mess Sergeant, who came from the Officer's Mess, 3d Battalion. Nathan was a golfing partner of Rigger John Ford. He was a hustler and go-getter who kept the unit kitchen operating in all conditions. He was the first Life Member in RICA and the 555th. He married Jettie, who accompanied him to all reunions. They resided in Phoenix City, AL. Nathan passed on to the great DZ in 1995.

P-2. PAULDING, CRAIG. "Little Man" was one of the youngest original members, coming from Company K. He and Herc are tied for the record of being most hospitalized from combat. Craig re-upped and went to Germany with the 11th A/B. After leaving the service he became an American Legion Post Commander and avid pinochle card player. "Little Man" is a great supporter of RICA and 555th events. He lives in Bessemer, AL.

P-3. PAYNE, SAMUEL JR. "Shorty" Payne was an original member who came from Company I, 2d Platoon. Shorty had attended Morgan State University in Baltimore, MD, before enlisting. Shorty was the shortest member of the unit, but he didn't cut any slack on any missions. He and Big Jim teamed up to become human mine detectors for the Buffalo Rangers. Payne is married to Vinita and they have five adult children (doing the Lord's work) and five grandchildren. They live in Baltimore. Shorty worked for Bethlehem Steel for 38 years before retiring. He is active in most of the RICA and 555th activities along the East Coast. Shorty says, "War is Hell!"

P-4. PETERESS, JAMES JR. Peteress was an original member who came from the 80th AAA Battalion. He was another one of the Rangers on a six-year hitch and had just enlisted in January 1950. He became one of the best and most fearless BAR gunners in the Company. He was always pushing forward to get a better firing position. Peteress was one of the last KIAs. Big Jim awarded him his third Purple Heart just before his last battle.

P-5. PLATER, JAMES M. Plater was an original member who came from the 80th AAA Battalion as a Private First Class but had made Sergeant by the time of inactivation, eight months later, as a fire team leader. He went to the 674th Artillery Battalion of the 187th ARCT at Camp Woods, Japan. Plater later moved back to Philadelphia, PA, where he died in November 1997.

P-6. POPE, JAMES J. Pope was a member of Lieutenant Anthony's replacement platoon who came from the 80th AAA Battalion. He was a draftee and veteran of WWII who had already served ten months overseas. He, too, was on a six-year hitch. Upon inactivation he went to the 187th ARCT, but no contact has been made with him since that time.

P-7. POSEY, EDWARD L. Ed was an original member who came from Company I. In June 1951, up near the Kansas Line, although wounded by grenade fragments while leading his squad against enemy fortifications, he led an advance on the enemy stronghold that routed the enemy from its position. He served a second tour of duty in Korea during which he was assigned to Company L, 31st Infantry Regiment, 7th Infantry Division, on Pork Chop Hill. In addition to his combat tours in Korea he served in the Dominican Republic and Vietnam. After 21 years of distinguished military service he worked his way up from a position as a correctional officer to Assistant Warden of Leavenworth Prison. Since his retirement from the U.S. Department of Justice he has performed special missions for the State Department in several different countries. In 2002 he was inducted into the Ranger Hall of Fame for his dedication to duty and distinguished military career. The 555th PIA Chapter in Baton Rouge, LA, is named for him. He is married to Mary Ann and has a daughter, Denise. They live in Fayetteville, NC.

P-8. PRYOR, BERNARD B. Bernie, the original First Platoon leader, was from Company K. Bernie received the Silver Star Award and the Purple Heart for the fircfight at Majori-ri on 14 January 1951. Bernie was famous for his Cadillac cars and paramour escapades. He was First Sergeant in an Engineer Unit in the CBI Theater during WWII and he attended OCS afterwards. Bernie rotated to the 188th AIR, 11th A/B Division at Fort Campbell, KY. He was one of the few black captains retained in the 11th A/B when the division was reorganized at ROTAD in Germany. After retirement from the service as a Major he attended Pepperdine University to obtain a Ph.D. in Political Science. Bernie married Irma while in Germany and they had two daughters. The family settled in Topeka, KS, near Fort Riley. Bernie taught at and became Dean of Students of Baltimore City College before he died in 1988.

Q-1. QUEEN, JAMES C. "Big Jim" (also called "Mother" because he took care of so many from the Company) was the original and only XO. He came from Company M, as the Recoilless Rifle Platoon Leader. Jim received the Silver Star for bravery in the battle for Hill 581 in May 1951. Jim remained in the service until he was medically retired while in the 7th Special Forces Group at Fort Bragg. He just missed being cut back to Master Sergeant in the RIF of 1957. After the 11th A/B was inactivated in Germany, he was sent to the 32d Signal Battalion, VII Corps, as a motor officer. He is married to Phyllis, with whom he had seven children, fifteen grandchildren, and six great-grandchildren. They reside in Washington, D.C., and both are retired from the D.C. public school system. In 1994 Big Jim became the first black Ranger inducted into the Ranger Hall of Fame.

R-1. RANKINS, GEORGE. George was an original member who came from Company I. George received the Silver Star for action in the Battle for Hill 581 in May 1951. George served two tours in Korea. He remained in the service for more than twenty years and retired at Fort Lewis, WA, as a First Sergeant. He started a new career in the Urban League of Portland, OR, where he began a mini-crusade to obtain jobs for African Americans in new areas as ironworkers, operating engineers, electricians, and within the airline industry. Later he dabbled in TV before going on to break "color barriers" in commercial film, collegiate football officiating, and national horseracing officiating. George married Dianne and has a daughter who is a Captain in Army Intelligence. In spite of his busy traveling schedule George is still very active in RICA or 555th activities. He currently resides in Lincoln City, OR.

R-2. REESE, EARNEST. Ernie was a member of the Replacement Platoon. He married while stationed in Germany and settled in Hanau, Germany. It is believed but not confirmed that he did not come back stateside before his death in 1996.

R-3. REMBERT, HERMAN L. Rembert was an original member. He was a member of the 1st Platoon when he was KIA in the firefight at Majori-ri Village on 14 January 1951. Rembert was on a three-year hitch, having just enlisted in April 1950.

R-4. RHODES, WILLIAM. "Thin Man" was an original member and came from the 80th AAA. In the firefight at Majori-ri on 14 January 1951 he was cut off. He was hidden by an old Korean family and recovered by a patrol the next day. He was a very close sidekick of Herc. Whenever you saw one at a reunion, the other was very close by. Thin Man married Michelle and settled in Bridgeport, CT. He died in 1996. Thin Man seldom talked about his ordeal of being cut off, but he was a delight to be with.

R-5. RHONE, RAY, SR. Ray was an original member and came from Company M. After leaving the service he worked in the Post Office until his retirement. He married Marcia and had a family, and they live in Chicago, IL. Ray attends and frequently supports the RICA and 555th activities.

R-6. RIDELL, WILLIAM H. L., JR. Ridell was one of the few black-leg replacements that General Ferenbaugh allowed to volunteer to join us after training. Ridell was a Korean War draftee. Ridell served in combat with the unit for three months before he went to a Company-level jump school. He made three qualifying jumps in one day from a C-119 aircraft at the Chechon airfield. Ridell went to the 187th ARCT upon inactivation, but no contact has been made with him since.

R-7. ROBERTSON, SMEAD H. "Cowboy" earned that nickname from his interview by a *Stars & Stripes* reporter after the Tanyang firefight. Smead was an original member who came from Company M, where he was the Company clerk. He remained as 2d Ranger Company clerk until he was promoted to Sergeant and moved to the 3d Platoon as a squad leader. Smead was married and moved to Los Angeles, CA. Smead is famous for telephoning at very odd hours. He attended the 555th meeting in L.A. with Herman "Cat Eyes" Jackson.

R-8. RUSSO, JOE. Joe is our Associate Ranger from the 15th AAA Battalion, 7th ID, who was sent over to provide medical coverage during the late spring of 1951. Joe went on to become a paratrooper. He is married and is a member of the North New Jersey Chapter, 101st A/B Division. The Buffalo Rangers conducted an initiation ceremony for Joe at the 101st's meeting in the winter of 1995. Joe provided some art for this book, and members of the original 2d Ranger Company were proud and honored to welcome him into the Buffalo herd.

S-1. ST. MARTIN, JUDE P. "Jude P." was an original member who came from Company I. He was on the tail end of his first three-year hitch and due for discharge in January 1951, so he ended up with the 'Truman Year" (involuntary extension). Jude P. left the unit before inactivation. He returned to his hometown of New Orleans and worked in the Post Office until retirement.

S-2. ST. THOMAS, ROBERT. St. Thomas was a original member who came from the 80th AAA Battalion. He was a veteran of WWII who had served sixteen months overseas when he volunteered. St. Thomas, a rifleman, was killed in the firefight at

Majori-ri Village on 14 January 1951. No surviving family members have been located. A memorial service was held for him at the cemetery in Bloomfield, NJ.

S-3. SCOTT, CHARLES D. Scotty was an original member who came from the 80th AAA Battalion. Scotty trained as a rifleman in the 1st Platoon. He was on a three-year hitch when he was killed in the firefight at Majori-ri Village on 14 January 1951. No surviving family members could be located.

S-4. SIMMS, WILLIAM. Simms was an original member who came from the 80th AAA Battalion. He was on the tail end of a three-year enlistment when he volunteered. Simms left the unit before inactivation. Herc saw Simms in the 1952 to 1954 period, at Birdland, a night club in New York City; he had re-enlisted in the Air Force. He has not been seen since that time.

S-5. SMALL, WHEELER S., JR. Wheeler was an original member who came from Company K with Joe Wells, who enlisted at the famous Whitehall Station, in New York City. After rotation he returned to the 3d Battalion before shipping off to the 4th ID in Germany. He was discharged in November 1954, then almost re-enlisted, before his mother said, "*My only child is not going back!*" Wheeler always liked to dress up sharply, so he went into the men's clothing business. He was promoted and managed a store from 1962 to 1983, where he learned all aspects of selling, fitting, tailoring, pressing, and buying. Wheeler later worked in the Post Office and married Tina. Both are very ardent supporters of RICA and the 555th. They now reside in Enfield, NC. Wheeler has recently been appointed as Assistant National Treasurer of the 555th.

S-6. SMITH, ROBERT L. "Smitty" was a member of the 32d Infantry, 7th ID, when he sought to transfer into the unit. He had boosted his age and enlisted at 14. He retired after more than 24 years of service. Smitty served three tours in Korea and two in Vietnam. After his first rotation from the 7th ID, he served briefly in the 511th AIR at Fort Campbell, KY. On his second tour with the 7th ID he was an advisor to the Ethiopian Battalion, attached to the division. He has served as an ROTC instructor and in the Army Exhibit Unit, where he modeled the current, new, Army Green uniform. Smitty married Ann and they settled in Florida. He went into the real estate business and was a principal coordinator in the establishment of Medal of Honor Park in Sebring, FL. Smitty and Ann retired a second time to Gilbert, SC, near Columbia.

S-7. SMITH, SCHERRELL. Scherrell was an original member who came from 80th AAA Battalion. He was on a three-year hitch and had served eight months overseas before volunteering. He made Corporal before inactivation. There has not been any contact with him since rotation to the 187th ARCT in Japan.

S-8. SQUIRES, HOWARD. Squires was an original member who came from 80th AAA Battalion. He was on a three-year hitch and due for discharge in December 1951. Squires was one of the physically big Buffalo soldiers, and he could easily handle his BAR. He was one of those soldiers you like to have around when "the going gets tough." He could carry two basic loads of ammunition. He went to the 187th ARCT upon inactivation and was last reported to be living in Pittsburgh, PA.

S-9. STROTHERS, STEWART. "Doc" Strothers was one of two enlisted reservists (ERs) called up to active duty who joined us in the marshalling area, prior to the Munsan-ni jump. Doc was a leg replacement and non-Ranger type. He had been a pre-med/dental student from the black enclave in Pittsburgh, PA. He was quiet and reserved but fit right in. He completed a weeklong jump school in the marshalling area by making three jumps; his fourth jump was into combat! Doc received the Bronze Star for his actions in June 1951. He remained with the unit, then went to the 187th Medical Platoon. We have heard rumors that he finished dental school and was practicing in Pittsburgh, PA, but we have been unable to contact him.

S-10: SUTTON, RALPH. A member of the replacement Platoon that arrived in Korea during March 1951, Sutton was killed in action on Hill 581 on May 20, 1951.

T-1. TATE, BILLIE. Billie was an original member who came from the 80th AAA Battalion. Billie returned to school after leaving the service. He became an elementary school teacher in Orlando, FL. Billie's famous picture was saved for him by Herc. He married Rosa and has become a golfer, according to George Jackson from Silver Spring, MD, who is the only RICA member who has met him on the tee.

T-2. TAYLOR, JAMES. A member of the Replacement Platoon that came over with Lieutenant Anthony. He came from the 80th AAA Battalion. He went to the 187th ARCT upon inactivation. After service in the Rangers Taylor re-enlisted in the Navy. He served several years as a Gunner's Mate before joining the SEALS, one of the first blacks to enter this elite group. He later married Juanita; they had two daughters, and settled in Chester, PA. James reported that he was awarded the Navy Cross for secret missions along the Vietnam-Cambodia border. James worked in the VA security service. Big Jim Queen visited him before his death and was the guest speaker at a 1996 dinner-dance held in Taylor's honor by the Philadelphia Chapter of the 555th PIA. However, James was too ill to attend, and he made his last mission in late 1996.

T-3. THOMAS, GEORGE. George was an original member who came from Company I. George's status was unique because he had a Korean War draftee serial number of "57" but he was a regular Army enlistee for three years, having enlisted in November 1949. George Thomas left the unit at inactivation, and no contact has been made with him since that time.

T-4. THOMAS, WILLIAM E. "Doc Rabbit" was the original Company senior medic. He came from the 3d Battalion Medical Platoon under Lieutenant John Cannon; before that he was a member of the 558th Ambulance Company in the Spring Lake area, where he had served with Sergeant First Class Baker. Rabbit was fearless in his care of the wounded and was awarded a Bronze Star for bravery. After the first firefight he began to carry a carbine for protection. When he rotated to the States he went to Fort Sam Houston, TX. Later, at an 82d A/B event, his First Sergeant said that Rabbit got married but had later died in an auto accident. Rabbit died before the RICA or 555th Associations were formed. There has not been any contact with his surviving family members.

T-5. TUCKER, ORRIE. The original and only Support Sergeant of the unit. He had been Supply Sergeant for Company K, 3d Battalion. Orrie was one of the few married Rangers. To date, he hasn't revealed what happened to the Class 6 rations (booze) the officers left in the Company field desk in Japan. Orrie became an auditor and resides in Framingham, MA. He and his wife Catherine have one son and were active in RICA and 555th events until he recently experienced some serious illness.

T-6. TUCKER, WILLIAM. An original member from Company L. After rotation Bill went to the 11th A/B at Fort Campbell, KY. He left the service after eight years and took two full-time jobs, at the Post Office and Wonder Bread Bakery Company. Bill married Norma and they had two sons and three daughters. In the 1980s, he became active in RICA. Tucker was wounded on his birthday (21 May 1951) in the firefight on Hill 581. His closest buddies were Marion Alston, Donald Felder, Herc Dias, Gerard Germain, and Jim Freeman. He lived in Lawnside, NJ, (historically, a predominantly black township) until he died suddenly in 1994 after his second retirement from the Post Office. Tucker was a full supporter of RICA and the 555th PIA.

V-1. VAILS, ROBERT A. He was a replacement who came through the replacement pipeline by himself without attending Ranger training. It appears he was shipped to the unit because he was a black paratrooper. Bob came from Company I, 3d Battalion and joined the Buffalo Rangers from Company F, 187th, while the units were in the marshaling area at the apple orchard, just north of the Taegu Airfield. (This was an unsolicited transfer from the 187th ARCT, which may support the rumor of that unit's preference for non-minority replacements before General Trapnell assumed command in Japan.) He remained on active duty longer than any other member of the Company. His last tour was with the Recruiting Command in New York City, where he often ran into William "The Ghost" Washington. He was perhaps the last person to run into "The Ghost" before he disappeared for good. Bob received his Ranger Tab at his retirement ceremonies at Fort Hamilton, NY, because of the work by Ranger Bill Weathersbee, through the Ranger Command at Fort Benning. He married Dorothy late in life and they reside in Jamaica, NY. He became an active member in RICA and 555th.

V-2. VALREY, CLEVELAND. Valrey was an original member who came from Company L. He was one of four of the 2d Airborne Rangers inducted into the U.S. Army Ranger Hall of Fame in 2005 for heroic actions in combat. Valrey graduated as an Army aviator in 1958 at Fort Rucker, AL., served two tours of combat duty in Vietnam in 1964 and 1968, and was inducted into the Army Aviation Hall of Fame in 2001. There has only been very limited contact with him since he rotated from the 187th ARCT. He still lives in Oakland, CA

V-3. VAN DUNK, WILLIAM. Arrived from the Replacement Platoon. An American Indian from the Ramapo tribe of New York, he served as a medic with 2nd platoon and was killed in action on Hill 151 at Munsan-Ni on March 23, 1951.

V-4. VICTOR, JULIUS. "Po White Boy" was an original Company member and came from Headquarters Company, 3d Battalion, where he was the driver for Major

Tenza, Battalion XO. It is said that he remained on jump status for over twenty years. Julius returned to Japan and married a Japanese woman. He has a taxicab concession at the Los Angeles, CA, airport. He lives with family in Huntington Beach, CA.

W-1. WADE, VIRGIL. Wade was a member of the group of black-leg replacements designated for the 7th ID. He was originally designated to be a driver in the 17th Infantry before he volunteered to join the Buffalo Rangers. He advanced rather rapidly and he was a Corporal and a qualified jumper by inactivation time, in just four months. Wade came to the 187th ARCT but no contact has been made with him since that time.

W-2. WALKER, JAMES T. "Dude" was the one and only 2d Platoon Sergeant. Dude came from Company K, and he was famous for his use of words (particularly those with the initials "MF") in an emergency, crisis, or just plain conversation. Dude took a discharge and went to work as a tool and die maker for an instrument maker. He married Ninetta and it is known that they had one daughter. They lived in San Jose, CA. Dude came to the RICA and 555th events. Dude passed on to that Great DZ in November 1991.

W-3. WASHINGTON, WILLIAM. "The Ghost" was an original member who came from the 80th AAA Battalion. The Ghost was a streetwise young man from New York City who became a very versatile soldier. He could weave a story around almost anything, if given the right opportunity and circumstances. But he promoted himself illegally one too many times, and was caught in the 187th ARCT, Counterfire Platoon. He was put in the Big-8 stockade in Japan. Ranger Vails later saw "The Ghost" in New York City, but all contact has been lost with him since that time.

W-4. WATKINS, ROBERT O. Watkins was the original third platoon sergeant who came from Company L. He was a veteran of WWII and was on an indefinite enlistment. He had served 25 months overseas before volunteering. Watkins was slightly older than most of the men. He was a steady hand and was our painter. He could slap a new marking on moonlight-requisitioned vehicles in a matter of minutes. Watkins designed a multi-colored parachute wings insignia for the Buffalo Rangers' steel pots (helmets). Watkins was promoted to Master Sergeant before inactivation and went to the 187th ARCT. Buffalo Winston Jackson reported that he saw him in Washington, D.C., after the Korean War. He had opened a sign painting shop and did the sign work on Jackson's barbershop window. However, no contact has been made with Watkins since the formation of RICA and the 555th PIA.

W-5. WEATHERSBEE, WILLIAM. "The Greaser" was an original member who came from the S-2 Section, Headquarters Company, 3d Battalion. The Greaser was a lifer who remained in the Army for twenty years and retired as Sergeant First Class. Weathersbee returned to Japan for a second tour with the 509th ARCT, which had replaced the 187th. He served in the Special Operations Command at MacDill Air Field, Tampa, FL (his hometown), before leaving the service. He was the Buffalo Ranger who discovered that 2d Ranger Company had been left off the list of 7th ID units receiving the Korean Presidential Unit Citation. His intervention prompted Major General Singlaub to present this award to Jim Queen on behalf of the Company in Colorado Springs at the 1984 RICA reunion. Weathersbee worked in the Post Office until his second retirement. He is married to Alberta and they have five children, including three sons who have served in the Army. The Greaser has been the Company Coordinator since 1993 and is responsible for the newsletter, the administration of award requests, and transcriptions for and editing of the manuscript for this book.

W-6. WEBB, BURKE. Burke was an original member who came from the 80th AAA Battalion. He was a veteran of WWII who was also on a six-year hitch. Burke had served thirteen months overseas before volunteering. Burke was also a BAR gunner of short stature. He left the unit before inactivation and no contact has been made with him since that time.

W-7. WELLS, JOSEPH, SR. Joe was one of the original members who came from Company K with his buddy, Wheeler Small. Joe was awarded the Bronze Star for Valor in the Battle for Hill 581 in May 1951. After leaving the service he began a career in law enforcement in the tough New York City Police Department. Joe returned to his home community and maintained his ties to the Catholic Church. He married Mildred and they became faithful attendees at RICA and 555th events. Joe moved to Southern Pines, NC, before he passed on to the Great DZ in June 1994.

W-8. WEST, DONALD. Donald was an original member who came from Company L. He had moved up rapidly and was a Buck Sergeant on a three-year hitch when he volunteered. Donald left before inactivation and has not been contacted since Korea.

W-9. WEST, LAWRENCE D. "Top Kick" was the original and only First Sergeant in the Company. He came from Company M, where he had the same position. Top was a steadying influence in the Company and often cautioned the men about going off "half-cocked" on some rumor or prejudicial remark made by a white officer. The details of Top's action in clearing out the assembly area of enemy on the Munsan-ni drop were not fully realized until the information for this book was being compiled. It was rumored the Top had a post-Korean War stress-related condition and was hospitalized by the VA before his death. He will never die in the hearts of the Buffalos.

W-10. WEST, RAMON. Ramon was a member of the Replacement Platoon trained and brought to Korea during the first week in March 1951. He volunteered from the 80th AAA Battalion. He soon made Corporal before inactivation. He has not been seen nor contacted since being in the 187th ARCT, but was known to have once lived in Elizabeth, NJ.

W-11. WHITE, LEROY. "Eyes" was an original member who came from the 80th AAA Battalion. Initially Leroy was perhaps the only Ranger with a camera. Eyes was a veteran of WWII who was on a six-year hitch. He had already served 24 months overseas before volunteering and was slightly older than the average Corporal. He made Sergeant and Assistant Squad Leader before inactivation. You always had to make sure that he had his glasses before going out on patrol. He went to the 187th ARCT but has not been heard from since Japan. His hometown was New York City.

W-12. WHITMORE, JOSEPH. Whitmore was a member of the Ranger Replacement Platoon who came from the 80th AAA Battalion. He enlisted in the service in March 1950 for three years. Upon inactivation he went to the artillery at Camp Woods. There has not been any contact with him since that time.

W-13. WILBURN, VINCENT. "Vince"/"Willie" was the original and only 2d Platoon Leader. He came from Company I. Willie enlisted in the 9th (Horse) Cavalry, Jefferson Barracks, MO, just before WWII. He became Company Clerk of Troop B, 9th Cavalry, at Fort Clark, TX. He went to the North African Theater when the unit was converted to the 127th QM Truck Battalion (Mobile) and was promoted to Sergeant Major. Willie's unit hauled supplies from the Port of Naples, Italy, for the 5th Army. It left Naples and sailed to Okinawa's Yellow Beach—3, when the atomic bomb was dropped on Japan. He left the Army briefly from December 1945 to April 1947, but the spirit of adventure led him back. Willie attended OCS at Fort Riley after WWII. On 7 September 1947 he married Dorothy, sister to Miles Davis, the great trumpet player. They had a son, Vincent Wilburn, Jr., who is nicknamed "Li'l Buffalo" (reflecting his daddy's military service). Willie rotated to the 188th AIR, 11th A/B, at Fort Campbell, KY. He went on to serve in Germany with the 5th ID, 11th ABN Division in 1956. Willie was RIF'd from the officer ranks back down to enlisted status by the Eisenhower Era Policy to reduce the Army's size. He went on to a successful ten-year career as a Recruiting Sergeant in Chicago. Big Jim Queen visited him as he went about with Peter Dickerson, formerly 366th Infantry and 3d Battalion, rounding up enlistment prospects. After retirement, Willie went on to a successful career in the Chicago municipal government. Dorothy passed in May 1997. Willie spends his winters in Arizona and summers in Chicago, with frequent visits to his son in Monterey, CA.

W-14. WILLIAMS, ADKINS W. Williams was an original member who came from the 80th Battalion. He was on a three-year hitch and due for discharge in June 1952 when he volunteered. He was promoted to Corporal before inactivation and went to the 187th ARCT. There has not been any contact with him since that time.

W-15. WILLIAMS, LAWRENCE J. "Poochie" was an original member who came from Company M. He enlisted in 1949 for three years. Williams was a member of the Third Platoon. He was slightly wounded while on patrol around Tanyang in early January 1951. He was killed in the firefight at Majori-ri Village on 14 January 1951.

W-16. WILLIAMSON, OTIS. Wounded in action on June 11, 1951. There has been no contact with Otis after Korea.

W-17. WILSON, HENRY. An original member who came from Company L. After his enlistment was over he married Ruth and then settled in Flint, MI.

W-18. WILSON, WILLIAM R. William was a member of Lieutenant Anthony's Replacement Platoon. He came from the 80th AAA Battalion. After William's second enlistment was up he maintained his close ties with the Army as a civilian working in the

Transportation Section of CONARC (the Continental Army Training Command, which is where the Army's military doctrine is developed; the current name is TRADOC, meaning U.S. Army Training and Doctrine Command) at Fort Monroe, VA. William is married and has a son who did an enlistment as a medic. William has attended several RICA and 555th events on the east coast.

W-18. WOODARD, ISAIAH. Isaiah was an original member. He was on a three-year hitch. Isaiah went to the 187th ARCT when the unit was inactivated. Nothing has been heard from him since that time.

Appendix 2

2d Ranger Infantry Company (Airborne)
Unit Roster During the Korean War

Note: This appendix contains the names of soldiers who were part of 2d Ranger Company (not attachments). The roster appears in its original form, including misspellings of Ranger names. For some soldiers, such as Isaac Grasty who spent the entire war with his first name misspelled as *Issac*, the misspelling of a name was simply an unfortunate and annoying fact of military life.

Commendations, Awards, Citations

Killed in Action: 12

Isaac Baker
Richard Glover
J.T. Holley
Milton Johnson
Frank King
James Peteress
Herman L. Rembert
Charles D. Scott
Robert St. Thomas
Ralph W. Sutton
William Van Dunk
Lawrence Williams

Silver Stars: 9

Warren E. Allen
Norman Collins
Curtis Courts

James Freeman
John A. Jones
James Peteress
Edward Posey
James C. Queen
George Rankins

Bronze Stars: 11

Edward D. Adams
Anthony Andrade
Albert Cliette
James H. Fields
Culver Gibson
William Hargrove
McBert Higginbotham
Cleaven McBride
Stewart W. Strothers
William E. Thomas
Joseph Wells

Purple Hearts: 103

Louis Adams
Kirk P. Adkins
Legree Aikens (2)
James Allen
Warren E. Allen
Jesse Anderson
Teedie Andres
Eugene Arnold
Isaac Baker
Daniel Boatwright (3)
Thomas M. Burse
Homer Bush
George Bynum
Clinton Cleveland (2)

Albert Cliette (2)
Eugene Coleman
Willie L. Coleman
Norman Collins
Curtis Courts
Sherman Daniels
James R. Davis
Herculano Dias
Lawrence Estell
Donald Felder
James H. Fields
John E. Ford
James Freeman
Gerard Germain
Richard Glover
John W. Gould
Isaac Grasty
Walter Gray
James Hardy
James Harvey
William Harris
Willie Hawkins (2)
McBert Higginbotham
J.T. Holley
Herman Jackson
Winston Jackson
Glenn Jenkins
Eugene Jennings
Bruce Johnson
Emmett Johnson
Harold Johnson
Milton Johnson
Frank King
William Lanier
Ralph Leggs
David Lesure (2)
Charles Lewis (2)

Jack Murphy
James Murray
John Nunley
Joe Oliver
Craig Paulding (2)
Samuel L. Payne (2)
James Peteress (3)
Edward Posey (3)
Bernard B. Pryor
James C. Queen
Herman Rembert
Smead H. Robertson
Charles D. Scott
Wheeler Small
Jude St. Martin (2)
Robert St. Thomas
Stewart W. Strothers
Ralph W. Sutton
Billie Tate
William E. Thomas (2)
William Tucker
Cleveland Valrey
William Van Dunk
Julius Victor (2)
James T. Walker
William F. Washington
Burke Webb
Donald West
Joseph Whitmore
Lawrence Williams
Otis Williamson
Henry Wilson (3)
William Wilson

Appendix 3

Glossary of Terms and Abbreviations

.30 cal: Size of a rifle or carbine bullet

.40mm: Size of an anti-aircraft shell

.45 cal: Size of a Colt automatic bullet

.50 cal: Size of a vehicle-mounted heavy machine gun bullet

75/105/155 mm: Size of artillery shells (from light to heavy)

368/369: Undesirable discharge given to soldier with discipline problems and/or poor performance

A/A: Anti-Aircraft

AAA: Anti-Aircraft Artillery

A/A Bn: Anti-Aircraft Battalion

ABN, A/B: Airborne

A/C: Aircraft

AFB: Air Force Base

AFFE: Armed Forces Far East

AFOD: Air Force Officer of the Day

Aggie: Native Korean child

AIR: Airborne Infantry Regiment

A&P: Ammunition and Pioneer

APO: Army Post Office

ARCT: Airborne Regimental Combat Team

Armd: Armored

Arr(d): Arrive(d)

Art/arty: Artillery

ASAP: As Soon As Possible

Asgmt/asgn(d): Assignment/assign(ed)

Assembly area: Prominent terrain feature where a unit assembles

ASTP: Army Specialized Training Program

ASU: Army Special Unit

Atch(d): Attach(ed)

Atck(d): Attack(ed)

ATT: Army Training Test; used in unit evaluations

Auth(d): Authority/authorized

AWOL: Absent Without Official Leave

BAR: Browning Automatic Rifle

B-Bag: Duffle bag that stores extra clothing

Battery: Company-sized artillery unit

Bayonet: Code name for 7th Infantry Division in Korea

BG: Brigadier General

Big Eight: Military prison in Japan

Bn: Battalion

Bn CP: Battalion Command Post

Bootsie Mae: Black soldier's foreign girlfriend

BS(V): Bronze Star Awarded for Valor

BTO: Big-Time Operator

Btry: Artillery Battery

Buffalo: Nickname for black soldiers (originally those fighting Indians in the American West)

Burp gun: Chinese sub-machine gun

BX: Base Exchange (store)

C-46: Early, two-propeller-driven paratrooper transport aircraft

C-47: Same as C-46, but with one door

C-54: Four-propeller-driven cargo or troop transport aircraft

C-119: Two-propeller-driven heavy cargo transport aircraft

C-123: Similar to C-119, but could land on an unimproved airstrip

Cal: Caliber (size of bullet fired from a weapon)

Capt: Captain

Carbine: Short-barreled rifle

Cathouse: House of ill-repute

CAV: Cavalry

CBI: China-Burma-India theater of operations

CC: Canadian Club (whiskey)

CCC: Civilian Conservation Corps

CCF: Chinese Communist Forces

CG: Commanding General

CIA: Central Intelligence Agency

CIB: Combat Infantryman's Badge

Class-6: Alcoholic Beverages

CMB: Combat Medical Badge

CO: Commanding Officer

Co: Company

Code-Talkers: Navajo Indian soldier radio operators

C of S: Chief of Staff

Col: Colonel

Colored or *: Morning Report designation for black personnel

Comdr: Commander

Commo: Communications

Conf: Confinement (jail)

CONUS: Continental United States on theater duty

COPL: Combat Outpost Line

CP: Command Post

Cpl: Corporal

C-rations: Individual food rations, good for one day

CSM: Command Sergeant Major

CSW: Crew-Served Wagons

DA: Department of the Army

DAC: Department of Army Civilians

DAR: Daughters of the American Revolution

DCNG: District of Columbia National Guard

DD: Dishonorable Discharge

Defilade: A defensive position against enfilading, or raking, fire

Deuce-and-a-half: 2-1/2 ton truck

Div: Division

DMZ: Demilitarized Zone

DOA: Dead on Arrival

DoD: Department of Defense

DOE: Date of Enlistment

DOR: Date of Rank

DOW: Died of Wounds

DR: Delinquency Report

DS: Detached Service

DSC: Distinguished Service Cross

Dtd: Dated

DUI: Driving under the Influence

Dy: Duty

DZ: Drop Zone

ED: Extra Duty

EDCMR: Effective Date of Change of Morning Report

E&E: Escape and Evasion

Eff: Effective

EIB: Expert Infantryman Badge

Eightball: Soldier who consistently fails to meet requirements

EM: Enlisted Man

EMB: Expert Medical Badge

EOD: Explosive Ordnance Demolition

ER: Enlisted Reservist

ETA: Estimated Time of Arrival

ETO: European Theater of Operations

ETS: Expiration of Term of Service (end of enlistment term)

EUSAK: Eighth United States Army Korea

F-51 or P-51: Propeller-driven aircraft that provides close air support to ground units

FA: Field Artillery

FAB: Field Artillery Battalion

FAC: Forward Air Controller

Fat Boys School: Training program for overweight paratroopers

FDC: Fire Direction Center (group that coordinates unit fire support)

FEPC: Fair Employment Practices Committee

First Sergeant: Head soldier in a company

FO: Forward Observer

Fr: From

G-1: Personnel section of division or higher staff

G-2: Intelligence section of division or higher staff

G-3: Operations and training section of division or higher staff

G-4: Supply section of division or higher staff

Geneva Convention: International body of rules governing warfare

GHQ: General Headquarters

GI: Government Issue: A term used to describe a member of the military

GI Jane: A member of the WACs

GI party: Barracks cleaning before morning inspection

GO: General Order

Got hat: Left an area very rapidly

Gyroscoped: When a unit was transferred from overseas back to the States

HALO: High-Altitude, Low Opening; a type of parachute jumping

HC: Harmony Church (located at Fort Benning, GA)

Hei-hei: North Korean and Chinese term for black soldiers

H&I Fire: Harassment and Interdiction Fire

HMG: Heavy Machine Gun

Homesteaders: Those who arranged repeated tours stateside or in a safe area

Hosp: Hospital

HQ: Headquarters

ID: Identification/Infantry Division

IG: Inspector General

Ike Jacket: Olive drab jacket named for General Eisenhower

Inf: Infantry

Institutional memory: Equivalent of oral history or folklore

I&R: Intelligence and Reconnaissance

Jd: Joined

JLC: Japan (Joint) Logistical Command

JrROTC: Junior Reserve Officer Training Corps (for high school students)

Jump School: Paratrooper training school, located at Fort Benning, GA

K-2, K-4: Temporary designation for United States airfields in Korea

K9: Dog corps, sentry patrol

KANSAS Line: Line of advance of UN forces in April 1951, just north of the 38th parallel

KASLC: Korean Army Service and Labor Corps (civilian personnel)

KIA: Killed in Action

KMAG: Korean Military Advisory Group

KP: Kitchen Police: duty helping the cooks

KPA: Korean People's Army

L-4: Small, observational airplane

LCI: Landing Craft Infantry

LCP: Landing Craft Personnel

Ldr: Leader

Legs: Airborne term referring to non-airborne soldiers

LMG: Light Machine Gun

LOD: Line of Duty

LOGCOM: Logistical Command

LSM: Landing Ship Medium

LST: Landing Ship Tank

Lt: Lieutenant

LTC: Lieutenant Colonel

LTG: Lieutenant General

Ltr: Letter

LWA: Lightly Wounded in Action

LZ: Landing Zone

M-1: Rifle used by most soldiers in Korea

MASH: Mobile Army Surgical Hospital

MAT: Military Air Transport

MC: Master of Ceremonies

MD: Medical Doctor

MG: Major General

MIA: Missing in Action

MLR: Main Line of Resistance

MOH: Medal of Honor

Mohawk: Hairstyle with uncut center strip flanked by bald sides

MOS: Military Occupational Specialty

MP: Military Police

M/R: Morning Report

MSC: Medical Service Corps

MSG: Master Sergeant

MSR: Main Supply Route

NAACP: National Association for the Advancement of Colored People

NCO: Non-Commissioned Officer; all enlisted men other than privates

NCOIC: Non-Commissioned Officer in Charge

NG: National Guard

NKPA: North Korean People's Army

OC: Officer in Charge

OCS: Officer Candidate School

OD: Officer of the Day/Olive Drab

OG: Officer of the Guard

OP: Observation Post/Outpost

P&A: Pioneer and Ammunition platoon; also called A&P: dealt with mines, barbed wire and the like; also carried ammo and was responsible for headquarters security

Para/par: Paragraph

Paratroopers: Airborne Infantry soldiers; deployed via parachute jump

PCS: Permanent Change of Station

PFC: Private First Class

PH: Purple Heart

PIB: Parachute Infantry Battalion

PIO: Public Information Office

PIR: Parachute Infantry Regiment

Plat: Platoon

POE: Port of Embarkation

Police Action: War waged without Congressional declaration

POM: Preparation for Overseas Movement

POW: Prisoner of War

PRO: Public Relations Officer

PT: Physical Training

Pvt: Private

PX: Post Exchange (store)

QM: Quartermaster

Quit Slip: Formal application to leave ranger/parachute training program

RA: Regular Army

RADAR: Radio Detection and Ranging

RCT: Regimental Combat Team

Rct: Recruit

Red Legs: Artillerymen

Red Tails: Black fighter pilots of the 99th Pursuit Squadron

Regt: Regiment

Rel/reld: Relieved

Repl: Replacement

Repo Depo: Replacement Depot organization

Ret: Retired

RICA: Ranger Infantry Company Airborne

RIF: Reduction in Force

Rigger: Person who packs or rigs parachutes

ROK: Republic of Korea (South Korea)

R&R: Rest and Recreation/Relaxation/Recuperation

RTC: Recruit Training Center

RTD: Returned to Duty

Rtn(d): Return(ed)

RTO: Railroad Train Office

/s/: Signature

S-1: Personnel section of regimental or lower staff

S-2: Intelligence section of regimental or lower staff

S-3: Operations and training section of regimental or lower staff

S-4: Supply section of regimental or lower staff

SAM: Surface-to-Air Missiles

SCR-300: Signal Corps radio that infantry companies used to contact battalion

SEAL: Sea-Air-Land: U.S. Navy Special Forces branch member

Serial: Group of aircraft operating together

SFC: Sergeant First Class

Sgt: Sergeant

Shavetail: Nickname for a new Second Lieutenant

Shpmt: Shipment

Sk: Sick

Slim Jim: Nickname of Major General James Gavin, 82d Airborne Division

SO: Special Orders

SOL: Shit Out of Luck

SOP: Standard Operating Procedure

SOS: Services of Supply (also slang for creamed chipped beef)

Sqd: Squad

SS: Silver Star

S/Sgt: Staff Sergeant

Str: Company's strength (number of personnel) at a particular time

SWA: Seriously Wounded in Action

/t/: Typed

T-34: North Korean Army tank

T/A: Table of Allowance

TACP: Tactical Air Control Point

T/D: Table of Distribution

TD: Tank Destroyer

TDY: Temporary Duty

TF: Task Force

Tk: Tank

TO: Table of Organization

TO&E: Table of Organization and Equipment (list of personnel and equipment belonging to a unit)

TOT: Time on Target (a type of artillery barrage)

Triple Nickels: Nickname of the 555th Parachute Infantry Battalion

Tvl: Travel

TWX: Telegram

UCMJ: Uniform Code of Military Justice

UN: United Nations

Un-ass: To exit from an aircraft in a very rapid manner

UNC: United Nations Command

Unk: Unknown

UP: Under the provisions of . . .

USCT: United States Colored Troops

USMA: United States Military Academy

USNS: United States Naval Ship

USNTS: United States Naval Transport Ship

USO: United Services Organization

VFW: Veterans of Foreign Wars of the U.S.

VIP: Very Important Person

VOCG: Verbal Order of the Commanding General

WAC: Women's Army Corps

Wheels: VIPs

WIA: Wounded in Action

WOJG: Warrant Officer Junior Grade

WP: White Phosphorus

XO: Executive Officer

Appendix 4

Table of Army Ranks, Branches, and Awards

Officer Ranks:

O-10: General (GEN)4 stars

O-9: Lieutenant General (LG) 3 stars

O-8: Major General (MG) 2 stars

O-7: Brigadier General (BG) 1 star

O-6: Colonel (COL)"Bird Colonel"

O-5: Lieutenant Colonel (LCOL)

O-4: Major (MAJ)

O-3: Captain (CPT)

O-2: First Lieutenant (1LT)

O-1: Second Lieutenant (2LT) "Shavetail"

(Five warrant officer ranks fall in between)
Enlisted ranks (all qualify as NCOs except privates):

E-9: Sergeant Major (SgtMaj)

E-8: First Sergeant (1stSgt) "Top Kick"

E-8: Master Sergeant (MSgt)

E-7: Sergeant First Class (SFC)

E-6: Staff Sergeant (S/Sgt)

E-5: Sergeant (Sgt)

E-4: Corporal (Cpl, Corp)

E-4: Specialist (Spec)

E-3: Private First Class (PFC)

E-2: Private (Pvt)

E-1: Private"Buck"

Explanation of Army Constituent Units:
Unit Size Make-up Command

("A ____ has about ____ men divided into _____with a _____ in charge.")

Army: 50 to 60 thousand: multiple corps: GEN, LG

Corps: 30 to 50 thousand: 2 or more divisions: LG

Division: 10 to 20 thousand: 2 to 4 brigades: MG

Brigade: 3 to 5 thousand: 2 to 5 regiments: BG (or 3 to 6 battalions)

Regiment: 2 to 3 thousand: 2 or more battalions: COL (or 3 to 7 companies)

Battalion: 300 to 1500: 2 to 6 companies: LCOL

Company: 70 to 250: 3 to 5 platoons: CPT, MAJ

Platoon: 25 to 60: 2 to 4 squads: 1LT, 2LT

Squad: 8 to 14: NCO

List of Army Branches

Air Defense Artillery
Armor (tanks)
Aviation
Chemical
Engineers
Field Artillery
Infantry (includes Airborne)
Military Police
Intelligence
Signals
Adjutant General (lawyers)

Finance

Ordnance

Quartermaster (supplies)

Transportation

Medical

Nurses

Hierarchy of Army Awards

Award: Year established and re-established

Congressional Medal of Honor: 1862

Distinguished Service Cross: 1847, 1918

Distinguished Service Medal: 1918

Silver Star: 1918

Legion of Merit: 1942

Soldier's Medal: 1926

Bronze Star: 1944

Purple Heart: 1782, 1932

Commendation Medal: 1945

Appendix 5

Phonetic alphabet, used by the Army (1944 version)

A - ABLE	B - BAKER
C - CHARLIE	D- DOG
E - EASY	F - FOX
G - GEORGE	H - HOW
I - ITEM	J - JIG
K - KING	L -LOVE
M - MIKE	N - NAN
O - OBOE	P - PETER
Q - QUEEN	R - ROGER
S - SUGAR	T - TARE
U - UNCLE	V - VICTOR
W - WILLIAM	X - X-RAY
Y - YOKE	Z - ZEBRA

Appendix 6

Chronology of the 2d Ranger Infantry Company (Airborne)

9 December 1947: The 555th Parachute Infantry Company was inactivated and its colors folded. Its new designation was the 3d Battalion, 505th Parachute Infantry Regiment, 82d Airborne Division. This was the Army's first integration of a black unit into an all-white unit.

26 July 1948: President Harry S. Truman issued Executive Order 9981 dated 26 July 1948, which officially desegregated the U.S. military.

25 June 1950: North Korean Army crossed the 38th parallel and invaded South Korea; thus the Korean Conflict erupted. The 38th parallel separated North and South Korea.

29 September 19: 504th Ranger Infantry Company (Airborne) was designated at Ft. Benning, GA. 1st, 2d, 3d, and 4th Companies were assigned to the Ranger Training Center.

September-December 1950: Members of the 2d Rangers were recruited, assigned, trained, and prepared for deployment to Korea. [The change of designation of 4th Company to 2d Ranger Company occurred in November 1950 when the Department of the Army changed all units from Army Special Unit (ASU) to Table of Organization and Equipment (TO&E) units (part of the Regular Army).] Personnel were taken from the 3d Battalion (a parent unit), 505th Airborne Infantry Regiment, and the 80th Anti-aircraft Artillery Battalion of the 82d Airborne Division. The parent organization of this unit was Company A, 2d Ranger Battalion, which had been inactivated after World War II. Characterized as the "best of the elite" unit, the 2d Ranger Company was the first, last, and only all-black Ranger unit in the history of the United States Army. The Company's first commander was 1st Lieutenant Warren E. Allen of Los Angeles, CA.

28 October 1950: 2d Ranger Infantry Company (Airborne) was activated at Fort Benning, GA.

November 1950: The 2d Rangers were sent to the Ranger Training Center at Fort Benning, GA, for special, rigorous, advanced training.

3 December 1950: 2d Ranger Company departed Fort Benning, GA, by train for Camp Stoneman in CA, along with the 4th Rangers. At that time the 2d Ranger Company had 5 officers and 116 enlisted men, and the 4th Rangers had 4 officers and 118 enlisted men.

7 December 1950: 2d Rangers arrived at Port of Embarkation to ship out, nine years to the day after the Pearl Harbor attack.

9 December 1950: 2d Ranger Company left San Francisco, CA, for Korea aboard the *USS General H.W. Butner*, stopping at Pearl Harbor en route.

23 December 1950: 2d Ranger Infantry Company met African American women serving in the U.S. Women's Army Corps aboard the *USS General H.W. Butner* en route to Yokohoma Engineer Depot, Yokohoma, Japan.

24 December 1950: 2d Rangers arrived in Yokohama, Japan, on Christmas Eve. The Company entrained at pierside for movement to Camp Zama, Japan.

30 December 1950: The 2d Ranger Company was airlifted from Tachikawa Air Force Base, Japan, to Taegu Air Force Base, Korea. The unit was assigned to the Eighth United States Army and attached to the 7th Infantry Division.

31 December 1950: The 2d Ranger Company closed into the 7th Division area on New Year's Eve. 2d Ranger Company arrived in Korea at a critical time in the war: the United Nations faced staggering odds. The CCF Intervention had been in progress since 3 November.

5 January 1951: 2d Rangers arrived in Wonju via Tanyang with the mission of blocking enemy threats from the northeast. They traveled 103 miles from Yongchon to Changnim-ni via Andong.

7 January 1951: 2d Ranger Company's first combat action in Korea began outside Tanyang Pass. The 2d Ranger Company was assigned to protect an important rail line running through central Korea at Tanyang Pass. This rail line allowed essential supplies to travel to the UN units further north that were fighting to halt the Chinese Communist forces that were attempting to push the UN forces off the peninsula and bring South Korea under Communist domination. A large North Korean unit, while attempting to infiltrate Tanyang and disrupt the flow of supplies to the front, engaged the 2d Rangers. Although outnumbered, 2d Rangers inflicted heavy casualties on and repelled the North Koreans. 2d Ranger SFC Isaac Baker was killed and Rangers Webb Paulding and Wheeler Small were wounded.

14 January 1951: 2d Ranger Company entered the village of Majori-ri with the mission of taking possession of the village and then continuing the assault with another unit. They drove the enemy from the town, but the Chinese ambushed the other American forces in a mountain counterattack. Eight 2d Rangers were killed and ten were wounded. This was the last enemy action the 2d Rangers engaged in during the CCF intervention.

21 January 1951: 2d Rangers established headquarters in Tanyang. Their mission was to search out enemy guerrillas.

24 January 1950: The Chinese/North Korean advance into South Korea was ground to a halt by UN forces, and the CCF Intervention Campaign officially ended.

25 January 1950: The first UN Counteroffensive officially began. 2d and 4th Ranger Companies were given a pivotal role: to accompany the 187th ARCT in an air assault on the city of Munsan-ni. Designed to curtail enemy units' retreat from Seoul, Munsan-ni was the first combat jump a U.S. Ranger Company ever made. The 2d Rangers began preparation for their first combat jump.

29 January 1951: 2d Rangers were attached to the 17th RCT.

20 February 1951: 2d Ranger Company captured Chuchon, 8 miles to the northeast. Received recognition for their attack in the *International News Service* "banzai."

22 February 1951: 2d Rangers were attached to the 187th ARCT.

28 February 1951: 2d and 4th Rangers were en route to join the 187th Airborne RCT. Ground linkup was Task Force Growden, including the 6th Medium Tank Battalion, Infantry, and Artillery. Their mission was to attack from Seoul to Munsan-ni. The 2d and 4th Ranger Companies would be a part of the second serial to jump on Drop Zone (DZ) North, preceded by the 3d Battalion of the 187th.

23 March 1951: 2d Ranger Company participated in the First UN Counter-offensive via airborne assault, jumping from C-46 airplanes, with the 187th ARCT at Munsan-ni. The 2d Ranger Company became the first United States all-black unit to make a parachute jump behind enemy lines. The 2d Rangers achieved their objectives the day of the air assault, while suffering relatively light casualties. The 2d Rangers moved through enemy gunfire across high terrain, killed many Communists, and captured 20 prisoners. 2d Ranger Company then participated in the assault on Hill 151. Its mission was to seize the hill, a key terrain feature in the zone of the 2d Battalion, 187th ARCT. The attack was supported by F-51 fighters and 81 mm mortar fire by the Company's executive officer, then-LT James C. Queen. During this attack one Ranger was killed (PFC William Van Dunk) and two wounded (SFC Boatwright and Sgt Robertson). The unit was awarded the Bronze Arrowhead for the parachute assault at Munsan-ni and its service throughout this dangerous and historic action.

4 April 1951: 2d and 4th Rangers received new assignments. The 2d Rangers spent the remainder of the campaign undergoing a period of training and reinforcement in the vicinity of Hangyee. 2d Rangers were to become a training unit for black soldiers assigned to the 7th Infantry Division. Their mission was to provide two weeks of training to 52 replacements.

21 April 1951: The First UN Counteroffensive ended.

22 April 1951: The CCF Spring Offensive began. 2d Rangers participated in the response.

29 April 1951: 2d Rangers were ordered to move a few miles northwest to occupy and hold a hill outside of the village of Chaun-ni.

30 April 1951: 2d Rangers had 125 men assigned and 282 attached.

8 May 1951: Extra attached soldiers were released to the 17th, 31st, and 32d regiments; the needs of war were beginning to break the color barrier.

Late April–early May 1951: Various operations: 2d Rangers performed combat patrols with the 3d Regiment, 7th ROK Division; about 123 men of the 2d Rangers occupied an outpost on Hill 258; 2d Rangers defended high ground near Chinon-ni.

19-21 May 1951: 2d Rangers led assault on Hill 581, killing 50 Chinese and wounding 90 in about 2 hours. Seventeen members of the 2d Rangers were awarded the Purple Heart, and 7 were cited for bravery.

1 June 1951: 2d Ranger Company occupied a position in the KANSAS Line in the vicinity of the Hwachon Reservoir.

11 June 1951: 2d Ranger Company assaulted and occupied Hill 545 in the vicinity of Yonochanga. Last engagement in which the Rangers would participate before the conclusion of the CCF Spring Offensive.

8 July 1951: 2d Ranger Company confronted its last enemies in a combat engagement during the Korean War.

9 July–27 November 1951: The UN Summer–Fall Offensive in progress; 2d Ranger Company was held in reserve. Its personnel were gradually reassigned. 1st, 2d, 3d, 4th, 5th, and 8th Ranger Companies were to be inactivated by the commanding generals of the divisions to which the Rangers were attached.

1 August 1951: 2d Ranger Infantry Company (Airborne) unit was officially inactivated.

Notes

Chapter 1

1. From www.suasponte.com.

Chapter 2

2. *Journals of Major Robert Rogers* (New York: Corinth Books, 1961), p. 43.

Chapter 3

3. From www.trumanlibrary.org/photos/9981a.jpg. Page last accessed December 2008.

4. Historical information on Camp Stoneman is from the California State Military Department's California State Military Museum web page, which can be found at http://www.militarymuseum.org/CpStoneman.html (last accessed December 2008).

5. J. C. Watts, Jr., *Korean Nights: The 4th Ranger Infantry (Abn), 1950–1951* (St. Petersburg, FL: Southern Heritage Press, 1997), pp. 77, 79.

6. Mary Allen shared her personal letters from her husband, Lieutenant Warren Allen, with the authors.

7. Statistics from the Women in Military Service for America Memorial Foundation, Inc., Washington, D.C.

8. Interview of Lorraine West, by Constance A. Burns in Washington, D.C., June 2003.

9. Interview of Arline Haywood Wall, by Constance A. Burns at the Armed Forces Retirement Home, Washington, D.C., March 2002.

10. Interview of Lorraine West, op. cit.

11. Computations performed with online calculator based on the U.S. Department of Labor's *Handbook of Labor Statistics*, which can be found on the Internet at http://minneapolisfed.org/research/data/us/calc/, last accessed November 20, 2003.

Part II

Chapter 4

12. From www.intellnet.org/resources/korean_war_docs/rhee.htm. Page last accessed April 2004.

13. "How to Interview MacArthur," *Time*, June 11, 1951, p. 93.

14. Interview of General Edward M. Almond, January 16, 1953; Box 11; "The Integration of the Armed Forces, 1940–1965," Publications, Unpublished Manuscripts, and Supporting Records, 1943-77; Records of the Historical Services Division; Records of the Office of the Chief of Military History; Records of the Army Staff; Record Group 319; National Archives, College Park, Maryland.

15. "Command Report of the 32nd Infantry Regiment of the 7th Infantry Division for the Period of 1 to 31 January 1951."

16. Queen learned of Baker's prediction many years later, after his retirement from the Army, when he and Bates happened to have lunch together and were reminiscing.

17. "Command Report of the 32nd Infantry Regiment of the 7th Infantry Division for the Period of 1 to 31 January 1951."

18. Interview of Lorraine West, op. cit.

19. "Command Report of the 32nd Infantry Regiment of the 7th Infantry Division for the Period of 1 to 31 January 1951."

20. Letter of Appreciation from Major General Claude B. Ferenbaugh, USA Commander, Headquarters 7th Infantry Division, Office of the Commanding General APO 7 to Officers and Men of the 2d Ranger Infantry Company (Airborne) APO 7, SCS 200.6, 30 July 1951.

Chapter 5

21. John Lucas, *The Big Umbrella: The History of the Parachute from da Vinci to Apollo* (London: Elm Tree Books, 1973), p. 3.

22. Interview of General Edward M. Almond, op. cit.

23. Clay Blair, *The Forgotten War, America in Korea, 1950-53* (NY: Random House, 1987), p. 849.

24. *The Rakkasan*, "Presentation for the Korean Conflict (War) Memorial," Charlestown Navy Yard, MA, July 27, 1997, 187th ARCT News booklet, Fall 1997, p. 56.

25. Sketches A through D show the original drawings from the Munsan-ni after-action report that was submitted as soon as the 187th ARCT was relieved by the 3rd Infantry Division and returned to the Taegu Airfield (K-2) marshalling area.

26. Special Order 96, author.

27. John Terrell only remained with the unit for a short period before he was transferred to an anti-aircraft unit in Japan. Robert Vails remained and, through special intervention by SMG Weathersbee, in 1992 he was awarded the official Ranger Tab at his retirement ceremonies from the Reserve Recruiting Command in New York City.

28. Shelby L. Stanton, *Rangers at War* (New York: Orion Books, 1992), pp. 7-13.

29. Robert W. Black, *Rangers in Korea* (New York: Ballantine Books, 1989), pp. 175-8.

30. Blair, p. 921.

31. Ibid., pp. 389, 581-3, 784-9.

Chapter 6

32. Black, p. 165.

33. The lead platoon, from what Queen believed to be Company A, remained in position but didn't aid the morning counterattack by the Rangers. It was at this time that Queen called, "Fix Bayonets!"

Chapter 7

34. *Encyclopedia of the Korean War: A Political, Social and Military History*, Spencer C. Tucker, ed. (Santa Barbara, CA: ABC-CLIO, Inc., 2000), p. 708.

35. Russo completed a civilian jump school before joining the 101st. There are no remarks about him on the Morning Reports of June, but it was not unusual for activity not to be recorded, or recorded very late and with errors. He became a commercial artist and has made numerous drawings of his days with 2nd Company.

Chapter 8

36. Watts, p. 299.

37. The eleventh person listed appears to be Lieutenant Jack Bink, 4th Ranger Company, because Joe Watts, *Korean Nights*, p. 304, wrote: "Lt. Jack Bink, who evidently was not parachute qualified, goes off to the Chunchon, K-47, to learn."

38. Category III meant that you were guaranteed another three years of active duty when the Army was still in the action, or an officer reduction. Officers whose category was not renewed but desired to remain in the service could usually enlist (re-enlist) at the rank of master sergeant (E-7). At the time of the Korean War, former officers who were now enlisted men (E-7) were being recalled to active duty. First Lieutenant Vernon Baker, belated World War II Medal of Honor recipient, was one of those recalled; however, he was not allowed to volunteer for combat duty in Korea. In his book *Lasting Valor* (1997) he states this was because he had been awarded the Distinguished Service Cross while serving in the 92nd Infantry Division in Italy.

39. Black, p. 200.

40. Ibid., p. 203.

41. Ranger Bob Black discovered the error and the necessary paperwork was submitted. "Big Jim" Queen and a large contingent of Buffalo Rangers attended. The award was made by Major General John Singlaub, who had spoken about the ability of black paratroopers. General Singlaub served briefly as XO, 3d Battalion, 505th Infantry Regiment, 82d Airborne Division, Fort Bragg, NC, and as a G-3 Training Officer in the Ranger Training Command at Fort Benning, GA.

Chapter 9

42. Robert Irving Channon, ed., *The Cold Steel Third: 3rd Airborne Ranger Company, Korean War, 1950–1951* (Franklin, NC: Genealogy Publishing Service, 1993), p. 637.

Bibiliography

Books

Appleman, Roy E., LTC, AUS (Ret). *East Chosin: Entrapment and Breakout, 1950.* College Station, TX: Texas A&M University Press, 1991.

Baker, Vernon, with Ken Olsen. *Lasting Valor.* Columbus, MS: Genesis Press, 1997.

Biggs, Bradley, LTC, USA (Ret). *The Triple Nickels: America's First All-Black Paratroop Unit.* Hamden, CT: Archon Books, 1986.

Black, Robert, Col., AUS (Ret). *Rangers in Korea.* New York, NY: Ivy Books, Random House, Inc., 1989.

Bowers, W. T., et. al. *Black Soldier–White Army: The 24th Infantry Regiment in Korea.* Washington, DC: U.S. Army Center of Military History, U.S. Government Printing Office, 1990.

Bussey, Charles M., LTC, USA (Ret). *Firefight at Yechon: Courage and Racism in the Korean War.* New York, NY: Macmillian, Inc., 1991.

Center of Military History, Department of Army. *KOREA–1950.* Washington, DC: Superintendent of Documents, U.S. Government Printing Office, 1989.

Chang, Iris. *The Rape of Nanking: The Forgotten Holocaust of World War II.* New York, NY: Basic Books, 1997.

Channon, Robert, Col., USA (Ret). *The Cold Steel Third: 3rd Airborne Rangers-Korean War (1950-1951).* Franklin, NC: Genealogy Publishing Service, 1996.

Clay, Blair. *The Forgotten War: America in Korea 1950-1953.* New York, NY: Random House, Inc., 1987.

Darby, William O. and William H. Baumer. *We Lead the Way.* San Rafael, CA: Presidio Press, 1980.

Encyclopedia Americana, International Edition. Volume 25. New York, NY: Americana Corporation, 1970.

Flipper, Henry Ossian. *The Colored Cadet at West Point.* Salem, NH: Ayer Company Publishers, Inc., 1991.

Franklin, John Hope. *From Slavery to Freedom: A History of the American Negro.* New York, NY: Alfred A. Knopf, 1967.

Gibran, D. K., et. al. *The Exclusion of Black Soldiers from the Medal Of Honor in World War II.* Jefferson, NC: McFarland and Company, Inc., 1996.

Goff, Stanley, et. al. *Brothers: Black Soldiers in Nam.* Annapolis, MD: Presidio Press, 1982.

Janowitz, Morris. *The Professional Soldier: A Social and Political Portrait.* New York, NY: The Free Press of Glencoe, 1960.

Kate, William Lorans. *Black Indians: A Hidden Heritage.* New York, NY: Ethrac Publications, Inc., 1986.

Lackie, William H. *The Buffalo Soldiers: A Narrative of the Negro Cavalry in the West.* Norman, OK: University of Oklahoma Press, 1975.

Lee, Ulysses. *U.S. Army in World War II, Special Studies, The Employment of Negro Troops.* Center for Military History. Washington, DC: Superintendent of Documents, U.S. Government Printing Office, 1966.

Moskos, Charles C. and John Sibley Butler. *All That We Can Be.* New York, NY: Basic Books, 1996.

Motley, Mary Penick. *The Invisible Soldier: The Experience of Black Soldiers, World War II.* Detroit, MI: Wayne State University Press, 1975.

Myrdal, Gunnar. *An American Dilemma: The Negro Problem and Modern Democracy, Vol. 2.* Rutgers University, NJ: Transaction Publishers, 1996.

Nalty, Bernard C. *The Right to Fight: African-American Marines in World War II.* WW II Commemorative Series. Washington, DC: Marine Corps Historical Center, The Washington Navy Yard, 1981.

———— and Morris McGregor. *Blacks in the Military: Essential Documents.* Wilmington, DE: Scholarly Resources, Inc., 1981.

Office of the Assistant Secretary of Defense for Civilian Personnel Policy/Equal Opportunity. *Black Americans in Defense of Our Nation.* Washington, DC: Superintendent of Documents, U.S. Government Printing Office, 1990.

Putney, Martha S., Capt. AUS. *When the Nation Was in Need: Blacks in the Women's Army Corps During World War II.* Metuchen, NJ: The Scarecrow Press, Inc., 1992.

Stillwell, Paul, ed. *The Golden Thirteen: Recollections of the First Black Naval Officers.* Annapolis, MD: Naval Institute Press, 1993.

Twitchell, James B. *For Shame: The Loss of Common Decency in American Culture.* New York, NY: St. Martins Press, 1997.

Washington, Booker T. *Up From Slavery: An Autobiography.* Avenel, NJ: Gramercy Books, reprinted 1993.

Watts, Joe C. *Korean Nights: The 4th Ranger Infantry Company (Abn), 1950-1951.* St. Petersburg, FL: Southern Heritage Press, 1997.

Weaver, John D. *The Brownsville Raid.* College Station, TX: Texas A&M Press, 1992.

Webster's College Dictionary. New York, NY: Random House, Inc., 1996.

Index

Truman, President Harry S., ix, xiii, xv, 59, 91, 124, 211

Tucker, SFC Orrie, 29, 31, 106, 189

Tucker, Cpl. William, 28, 44, 57-58, 75-76, 105, 140, 189, 197

United Nations, xiii, 33-35

United States Military Units; *1st Cavalry Division,* 17, 26, 58, 117; *1st Marine Division,* 31, 58, 114; *1st Ranger Infantry Company (Airborne),* 9, 12, 53, 117, 126, 129, 211; *2nd Army,* 167; *2nd Infantry Division,* 9, 31, 53, 62, 88, 117; *2nd Ranger Infantry Company (Airborne),* ix-x, xv, 3, 5, 11-14, 16-17, 23-34, 50, 53-54, 57, 58, 84, 169, 172, 175-177, 211-213; inactivation, x; "found a home," xi; all-black unit, xv; Combat Infantry Badge, xv; Combat Medical Badge, xv; "Buffalo Soldiers," xvii; Fort Bragg, 3-10; training, ix, 3-10; departs for Korea, 10; trip to Korea, 19-21, 24-25; San Francisco, 22; Camp Zama, 27-29; arrives in Korea, 30-31, 33, 35; Tanyang Pass, 36, 38, 40-42, 148; Majori-Ri, 43, 47-48; Chechon, 49; Ferenbaugh's comments, 50; frostbite, 50; Munsan-ni, 59-64, 67-71, 73, 75, 77, 79-81, 85-86, 89, 119, 166; racial pressure, 87; desegregation, 89-91; Hill 581, 93-99, 102-107, 138-139, 157-159; Hill 246, 109; Hill 545, 110, 113-114; Combat Infantry Company Streamer, 120; Company Jump School, 121-123, 125; order to Inactivate, 125-126; Korean Presidential Unit Citation, 126; Presidential Unit Citation, 126; disbanded, 127, 129, 131; Camp Chickamauga, 131; personal memoirs, 135-138, 141-143, 146, 149, 151-153, 155, 160, 162-163, 165, 173, 178, 181,

186, 189-190; discrimination, 140; Operation Tomahawk, 147; Hill 151, 154-157; roster, 194; chronology, 211-215, Chuchon, 214; *3rd Armored Division,* 167-168; *3rd Infantry Division,* 3, 31, 82, 85, 88, 117, 138, 218n; *3rd Ranger Infantry Company (Airborne),* 54, 117, 129, 211; *3rd Station Hospital,* 109; *4th Evacuation Hospital,* 77; *4th Infantry Division,* 187; *4th Ranger Infantry Company (Airborne),* 3, 11-13, 16-17, 20-23, 28, 57-58, 62-63, 71, 77, 81, 84-85, 91, 117, 119, 126, 129, 156, 160, 211-214, 218n; *4th Replacement Depot,* 27; *5th Army,* 192; *5th Infantry Division,* 192; *4th Ranger Infantry Company (Airborne),* 54, 117, 126, 131; *6th Medium Tank Battalion,* 114, 214; *7th Infantry Division,* 16, 19, 31, 33, 35, 41, 50-51, 53, 56, 59, 84, 86, 90-91, 93, 103, 110, 115, 121, 123-124, 126, 141-142, 151-152, 156-157, 159, 178, 180-181, 184, 186-187, 190, 212, 214, 217n; *7th Infantry Division Medical Clearing Company,* 156; *7th Infantry Division Replacement Company,* 28, 86; *7th Marine Regiment,* 107; *7th Ranger Infantry Company (Airborne),* 54; *7th Replacement Company,* 109; *7th Signal Battalion,* 110; *7th Special Forces Group,* 185; *8th Army,* 31, 49-50, 53, 62, 86, 88-89, 91, 126, 129, 138, 212; *8th Army Replacement Battalion,* 90; *8th Army Reserve,* 119-120; *8th Cavalry Regiment,* 17; *8th Ranger Infantry Company (Airborne),* 54, 114, 117, 125-126; *9th Cavalry,* 192; *9th Infantry Division,* 171; *9th Infantry Regiment, 3rd Battalion,* 62, 88; *10th Cavalry Regiment,* xvii; *10th Special Forces Group,* 177; *11th Airborne Division,* x, 1, 130, 140, 177, 182, 184-185, 189, 192; *11th Regimental*

About the Author

Master Sergeant (Ret) Edward L. Posey joined the US Army in 1947. After serving with Company L, 3rd Battalion, 505th Airborne Infantry Regiment, he volunteered for airborne training with the Rangers in 1950 and served with distinction in the Korean War (where he was wounded). Sergeant Posey retired from the service in 1969. In 2002, he was inducted into the Ranger Hall of Fame for his dedication to duty and distinguished military career.